Music by Numbers

Music by Numbers

The Use and Abuse of Statistics in the Music Industries

EDITED BY

Richard Osborne and Dave Laing

intellect

Bristol, UK / Chicago, USA

First published in the UK in 2021 by
Intellect, The Mill, Parnall Road, Fishponds, Bristol, BS16 3JG, UK

First published in the USA in 2021 by
Intellect, The University of Chicago Press, 1427 E. 60th Street,
Chicago, IL 60637, USA

A catalogue record for this book is available from
the British Library.

Copy editor: MPS Technologies
Cover designer: Aleksandra Szumlas
Production manager: Aimée Bates
Typesetting: Newgen KnowledgeWorks

Hardback ISBN 978-1-78938-253-2
Paperback ISBN 978-1-78938-752-0
ePDF ISBN 978-1-78938-254-9
ePub ISBN 978-1-78938-255-6

This is a peer-reviewed publication.

Contents

Permissions

Chapter 2 by Richard Osborne is based on his article 'The Gold Disc: One Million Pop Fans Can't Be Wrong', first published in *Civilisations*, 13 (2014), pp. 159–78. Reused with permission. Chapter 3 by Richard Osborne is based on his article 'Success Ratios, New Music and Sound Recording Copyright', first published in *Popular Music*, 16/3 (2017), pp. 393–409, © Cambridge University Press. Reused with permission. Chapter 10 by Dave Laing was first published as 'What's it Worth? Calculating the Economic Value of Live Music' on the *Live Music Exchange Blog* on 11 June 2012 and is reprinted with the permission of Adam Behr, Matt Brennan and Martin Cloonan.

Introduction

Richard Osborne

Music resides in numbers. In his original proposal for this collection, Dave Laing noted how 'from the music of the spheres deduced by Pythagoras to the cataloguing of works by classical composers, music and mathematics have for centuries been intimately connected'. These mathematical reckonings form the very basis of music: its pitches; its harmonic structures; its rhythmic divisions. They also accrue to the work itself. 'Number' has been a term for a piece of music since the late nineteenth century at least ('number, n.' *OED* 1989). This practice is derived from listing, whether that be the ordering of songs in a Hawker's collection, the division of parts in an opera or oratorio, or the sequential matrix and catalogue numbers that have been applied to recordings. The items in a programme of live music became known as 'numbers', a term that became most fully institutionalized in the world of jazz. The *Publication of the American Dialect Society* noted in 1958 that the habit of referring to any tune as a 'number' was 'deeply engrained in the speech of the jazzman' ('number, n.' *OED* 1989). As with many aspects of jazz, this custom was carried over into rock music. The Doors' recording 'The Soft Parade' provides one example. As the song unfurls, Jim Morrison declares that he is 'proud to be a part of this number' (The Doors 1969).

But would he be proud to be part of a statistic? Here music's connection with numbers can be more disconcerting. The mathematical formulas that underpin the creation of music do not diminish its wonder, but statistical reckoning can bring it crashing down to earth. Most pointedly, 'the collection or arrangement of numerical facts or data' only comes to be applied to cultural forms in the process of their industrialization ('statistics, n.' *OED* 1989). Statistics are an economic by-product of the mass manufacture and technological mediation of art.

It has been possible to view this industrialization in a positive light. In his pioneering 1935 article, 'The work of art in the age of mechanical reproduction', Walter Benjamin suggested that the duplication of cultural products would lead to a 'tremendous shattering of tradition' and would emancipate works of art from their 'parasitical dependence on ritual' ([1935] 1999: 215, 218). This was on the basis that, 'in permitting the reproduction to meet the beholder or listener in his own particular situation, it [mechanical reproduction] reactivates the object reproduced' ([1935] 1999: 215). At his most optimistic, Benjamin claimed that '[q]uantity has been transmuted into quality. The greatly increased mass of participants has produced a change in the mode of participation' ([1935] 1999: 232).

More commonly, the prognosis has been gloomy. In his 1977 book *Noise*, Jacques Attali introduced an economic perspective that was absent from Benjamin's work. He regarded the mechanization of art as ushering in an era of isolated 'repetition' in which 'each spectator has a solitary relation with a material object' ([1977] 1985: 32). He did not view this as being liberating. Attali claimed instead that 'with all mass production, security takes precedence over freedom; one knows nothing will happen because the entire future is already laid out in advance' ([1977] 1985: 121). The overturning of ritual is not a good thing. The 'opportunity for spectators to meet and communicate' has been replaced with the 'mass production of all social relations' and 'individualized stockpiling [...] on a huge scale' ([1977] 1985: 32). The economic valuation of art is additionally transformed. The cost of each item 'bears no direct relation to the production price, to the quality, properly speaking'; all works are instead priced in an 'approximately equal' manner ([1977] 1985: 101). Put another way, there are '[h]igh fixed costs of production [...] and low to zero marginal costs of reproduction and distribution' (Garnham 2005: 19). As a result, it is the volume of sales that matters. Attali suggests that it is inevitable that a 'statistical evaluation' of quantity will take hold ([1977] 1985: 84).

Music is not alone in engaging with these numbers. Other industrialized artworlds have a statistical bent. In this respect, the music business has most in common with the book trade (which employs similar methods of duplicative publication) and with cinema (which has some parallel divisions of labour in its studio productions). It is also with these forms that it is most closely related in copyright law. Music publishing owes its original copyright protection to the fact that scores can be read like books; the ownership of copyright in sound recordings is treated similarly to films. Yet in all instances the music business appears to take the statistical imperative further than its creative neighbours. Its engagement with these numbers is more widespread, more public and more profound.

Take 'hit parades', for example. Attali viewed these popularity charts as a means by which the statistical evaluation of the cultural industries would be made manifest; it is because of the 'identically priced objects that are flooding our lives' that we are in need of a 'ranking scheme exterior to their production' ([1977] 1985: 107, 108). These charts have a disorientating effect on the dispersal of culture. Trade becomes concentrated on a limited number of titles, while the top few items in the charts receive more exposure and exponentially more sales than those listed below. Charts have helped to engender 'winner take all' markets (Frank and Cook 2010), as well as statistical initiatives to correct their pull.

As Attali notes, '[i]t is clear that the hit parade is not unique to music' ([1977] 1985: 108). The film industry was an early adopter of such charts: its box office returns have been tallied since the early twentieth century. This precedes charts for book sales, which have existed in the United States since the 1930s, and in Britain since 1974. It is within music, however, that popularity charts have had their greatest resonance. The earliest of them concerned sales of sheet music and can be traced back as far as the second half of the nineteenth century (Strachan and Leonard 2003: 536). Next came charts that detailed the most popular songs on radio and the most played jukebox hits, both of which were initiated in the United States in the 1930s (Strachan and Leonard 2003: 536). Charts for record sales were established in the United States by *Billboard* in 1940, and in Britain by the *New Musical Express* in 1952. As well as being central to the music business, these charts have shaped the actions of those who mediate songs and records. Radio formats, television programmes, music magazines and retail outlets have each been structured in accordance with the top 40 hit records. To counteract this blockbuster environment, attempts have been made to promote a broader representation of culture by regulatory and philanthropic means. Quotas have been imposed on broadcasters to ensure greater generic representation; funding has been provided to aid economically imperilled forms.

The mass reproduction of culture has another evaluative consequence: payments 'are proportional [to the] number of copies sold' (Attali [1977] 1985: 99). The move to royalty payment systems happened quickly for publishers and for the manufacturers of mechanical reproductions, while the creators of content usually lagged behind. For example, the Gutenberg Press was developed in the 1430s, but it would be the late nineteenth century before royalties became common for the writers of books (Caves 2000: 59). Sheet music was regularly produced on printing presses by the eighteenth century, but the majority of composers and songwriters did not receive royalties until the 1920s and 1930s (Towse 2015: 8). It was in the same inter-war period that actors began receiving royalties for films, despite the medium being developed in the 1890s (Ravid 2005: 46). Sound recording was invented in 1877, but royalties were not widespread for recording artists until the mid-twentieth century or for recording studio personnel until the 1960s (Martland 2013: 308; Rye 2017: 110). From the creators' point of view, the demand for this form of payment has represented a cause for justice. Rather than receiving set fees or patronage, many of them have desired to be paid in accordance with the successes of their works.

This move has nevertheless led to an increasingly bureaucratic environment where accounting is continuous and there are complex procedures to ensure that payments take place. Artists negotiate royalty percentages with the companies they are contracted to, as well as agreements about advances, recoupments, reductions and deductions. The companies negotiate deals with the sellers of the products, arriving at wholesale rates and recommended retail prices. There is a need to provide tallies of each item manufactured, distributed and sold. Moreover, under the 'capitalism of mass production' the 'statistical evaluation' of art comes to be applied more widely (Attali [1977] 1985: 84). The royalty system does not only adhere to the retail of duplicated goods; it is also utilized for public performance and broadcast rights. These rights have an insatiable appetite for data. They expand outwards: there are always more performances and broadcasts to monitor. They also expand inwards: there is a gravitational pull towards providing ever finer detail about the works that have been used and the interested parties involved. Collection societies are created in their honour – organizations that are devoted to the statistical administration of art. Attali believed that their task is ultimately Sisyphean in nature, suggesting that

> [i]t is conceivable that, at the end of the evolution currently under way, locating the labor of recording will have become so difficult, owing to the multiplicity of the forms it can take, that authors' compensation will no longer be possible except at a fixed rate, on a statistical and anonymous basis independent of the success of the work itself.
>
> ([1977] 1985: 100)

Royalty administration still continues, nonetheless, and the music business pursues it further than any of its culture industry partners. This is, in part, because of the large number of participants involved. Whereas a book commonly has a single author, there are multiple creators of a successful piece of music: writers, publishers, musicians, record companies and studio personnel all compete over royalty splits. Meanwhile, although a film will have an even broader array of participants, only a limited number of them will be on royalty-based payments. In addition, the deployment of both books and films is narrower than that of music. Book publishing is generally limited to the reproduction and adaptation of works. The film industry is more diverse. As well as its box office returns, there are television broadcasts and the retail of videos, DVDs and other audio-visual formats to recompense. This activity pales in comparison with the music industry, however. In fact, as John Williamson and Martin Cloonan have pointed out, there is not one industry, there are separate music 'industries' (2007). Until the mid-twentieth century, music publishing was the sector that was most economically prosperous. It was originally focused on the duplication of sheet music, but by this period was prioritizing other forms of revenue, including synchronization fees for matching images with sounds and the various rights that are administered by collection societies (the mechanical rights concerning the use of compositions in a variety of different reproductive formats; the performance rights for the use of music in different public settings; and the broadcast rights for the licensing of songs to radio and television). Music publishing was overtaken economically by the recorded music industry, the trade that is at the heart of Attali's analysis. It should nevertheless be noted that as recorded music forged ahead, it too was broadening its economic base to include public performance rights, broadcast rights and sync fees.[1]

The royalty-paying culture industries document their economic activities in two main ways. On the one hand, there is their accounting to their artists, where each use of a work and each division of rights is outlined in some detail. On the other hand, there are their public-facing statistical yearbooks. Here, they delineate the monies generated by each of their revenue streams, but they do not disclose the division of these spoils between the various parties involved. It is also usually only collection societies who provide accounts of their operating costs. As a result it is hard for artists to use this reporting data to measure the equitability of their pay.[2]

The publication of reports is another practice that is most extensive in the music industries. There are the figures collated by umbrella groups for the industries, such as UK Music's annual *Measuring Music* reports.[3] There are the national yearbooks of the recording industries and the *Global Music Report* produced by its International Federation of the Phonographic Industry (IFPI). There are the figures issued by each of the performing right societies, as well as the annual accounting of the International Confederation of Societies of Authors and Composers (CISAC). There are also the various documents produced by management forums, musicians' unions and other organizations for performers, songwriters and publishers, as well as the statistics that are compiled by the mediators of music. None of these are neutral and nor do they pretend to be. They are each accompanied by commentaries that announce the organizations' interests and campaigns.

Some of these campaigns take the forms of internal battles. The various sectors of the music industries have employed statistics against one another, as well as against their mediators, as they have fought competitively in the market to secure their interests. This practice goes back as far as the early twentieth century, when music publishers accused record companies of being pirates because they were not paying them royalties for their use of compositions. Each party used data to back up their claims. Similarly, in the mid-twentieth century, the recording industry campaigned against radio companies in order to gain broadcast royalties, again using numbers for their cause. These conflicts have continued into the current century. The recording industry has commanded a large share of the pie for streaming revenue; a share that is being challenged by the publishing industry as being numerically unfair.

In the meantime, a separate statistical tendency has witnessed the need to coalesce. The recorded and music publishing industries have realized that policy-makers will be more accommodating to their needs if they are expressed collectively. Those lobbied against prefer one 'big number' rather than a plethora of conflicting statistics. In coming together like this, these music industry sectors are reflecting wider trends. Ruth Towse has noted the growth of 'cultural accounting' over the past forty years (2001: 26). Starting at the highest level, there has been a move by global bodies, such as the United Nations Educational, Scientific and Cultural Organization (UNESCO), to identify the total economic worth of the cultural industries. Thereafter, this cause has been taken up at continental, national, regional and civic levels. A notable initiative was conducted by Britain's 'new Labour' government of 1997–2010. They rebranded the culture industries as the 'creative industries' and undertook mapping exercises to assess their contribution to UK gross domestic product. These exercises were undertaken, in part, because there was a drive for governmental departments to 'show measurable outputs' in order to gain 'investment' from the Treasury (Garnham 2005: 16). More broadly, the Labour party wished to document and support a transformed society, as well as a transformed socialism, which were shifting from heavy industry to a 'creative' economy (Garnham 2005: 16).

These government-led initiatives have been echoed by creative businesses, with music companies being particularly adept at adopting the 'facts for advocacy' approach (Towse 2001: 27). Thus, the Labour party's mantra that the creative industries are more economically important than heavy manufacturing industries (Newbigin n.d.) has been followed by suggestions that the music business is worth more than the steel industry (Cloonan 2007: 68) and that the recording industry invests more in research and development than the pharmaceutical sector (IFPI 2012: 9). Music industry journalist Chris Cooke has noted the circularity of this process, suggesting that the music companies calculate their value 'so that stat-loving politicians can then quote it back at them' (2019). Having attracted the interests of policy-makers via their economic vitality, the music industries then indicate the means by which they can be further nourished. For much of the twenty-first century the focus of the recording and music publishing industries has been on the need to 'ratchet up' copyright law (Sell 2010). Piracy has been a principal target. Its costs to the industries have been calculated, somewhat dubiously, on the basis of lost sales. Latterly, the copyright holding industries have also coalesced around the subject of 'safe harbours' and the 'value gap', arguing that service providers such as YouTube should be liable for content that has not been properly licensed. Lobbying is an ongoing project: the overall message is that more can be done. The music industries outline their monetary and cultural riches, but suggest that these can only be extended if the political economy is fine-tuned to their needs.

The decline of mass manufacture has happened both beyond and within the production of culture; hence, it is possible to contrast the triumphs of the creative economy with the falling away of heavy industry. When it comes to the music industries this transformation is manifesting itself in two ways. First, there has been the rise of third main pillar of the business: the live music industry. It has been suggested that this sector is now more economically important than either the recording or music publishing industries. Second, there has been the decline of physical sales of recordings and the turn towards digital formats such as downloads and streams. These developments bear out and challenge some of Attali's claims. Central to his analysis was the idea that music is prophetic. He argued that it heralds each 'new stage in the organization of capitalism' ([1977] 1985: 32). With the triumph of live music we nevertheless have a retreat to one of Attali's earlier musical stages: the era of 'representation', which was dominated by 'spectacle' ([1977] 1985: 31–32). We also witness the return of 'competitive capitalism, the primitive mode of capitalism' ([1977] 1985: 31–32). Despite some appearances, live music is not mass produced; its products are differentially priced and its spoils are determined by negotiation rather than 'statistical keys' ([1977] 1985: 84). As a result of this economic variety, the live music business has historically not been as pre-occupied with data as the royalty-paying industries have been. It also has different concerns. Rather than focusing on intellectual property and its abuses, the interests of venue owners and operators have instead been focused on achieving favourable licensing and planning regulations. From the perspective of policy-makers, these concerns are most redolent when live music is couched as a positive factor in the economic and cultural vibrancy of cities and towns. The growing importance of these issues and the increasing wealth of this sector have between them prompted a statistical turn. Recent years have seen a number of live music censuses, as well a trend for figures that attempt to calculate the overall value of the trade.

The digitalization of culture has further complicated Attali's analysis. The recording industry has been at the vanguard. It experienced the threat of peer-to-peer 'piracy' ahead of the other cultural industries and it is arguable that it has adapted to the online economy more quickly than other sectors. This would appear to bear out Attali's prescience: music is again acting as 'a herald of times to come' ([1977] 1985: 32). There are aspects of this digital embrace that are prosaic and conservative, however. Sound recordings only experienced file-sharing ahead of films, for example, because they occupy less code and therefore their digital files have been easier to compress. Moreover, while it looked for a time as though online piracy would break the hegemony of the major record companies, they were eventually able to use its statistical trail for their own ends. The data helped them to extend copyright's reach, both legislatively (in terms of gaining longer and stronger terms) and punitively (in enabling them to clampdown on the transgressions of individual consumers). And it is not only the threat from file-sharing that has been withstood; the record companies have also held their ground in the face of digital pioneers. Service providers such as Apple and Spotify now constitute major forces in the music world, but they have not become rights holders. This is in contrast to the film and broadcast industries, where companies like Netflix are not only offering new means of distributing audio-visual material, they are also creating content.

To reinforce its position, the recording industry has established legislation which ensures that its revenue for downloads and on-demand streams is treated in a similar manner to the revenue from mass reproduction: the 'making available' right exempts it from collection society administration.[4] As a result, it is the record companies who determine the remuneration rates for their artists. They also have responsibility for negotiating licences with service providers. Consequently, their control over copyright continues: the service providers want access to their full repertoire of works; to gain it they are willing to forgo the creation of content of their own. And so, while Attali argued that music's 'styles and economic organization are ahead of the rest of society because it explores, much faster than material reality can, the entire range of possibilities in a given code', this has not yet happened in the digital domain ([1977] 1985: 11). Most of the old major music companies remain incumbent. More generally, the industries' practice has been expanded rather than transformed. Downloading and streaming have stimulated the growth of a long tail of cultural creators (Anderson 2009), but the market remains skewed to the blockbuster hits of the larger corporations (Elberse 2014). Similarly, the rise of new economic systems, such as crowdfunding, has not witnessed a parallel decline of earlier remunerative methods. Royalties are predominant.

There has nevertheless been a revolution in musical statistics. Ironically, this is because Attali was mistaken in another of his prognoses. He believed that music was presaging the 'the disappearance of use-value in mass production and the final triumph of exchange-value' ([1977] 1985: 84). With the rise of on-demand streaming, we are witnessing the reverse. Streaming now generates greater revenue than mass-produced physical formats. It has also brought with it the return of use value. This use value is different in kind to most of its predecessors, however: exchange value has been collapsed into it.[5] Every play of a recording can now be documented. The result is challenging ontologically; popularity charts that were once focused on exchange are now having to incorporate use. It is also challenging in terms of the volume of data. Royalties are based on the number of times a recording is accessed rather than the number of times it is sold. This practice, combined with the openness of the digital environment, has meant that collection societies, music publishers and record companies are now attempting to capture trillions of lines of information about millions of songs and recordings. It has also led to speculation about how best to tackle this Sisyphean task. Technologies such as blockchain promise not only to capture all of the data about each of these recordings, but also to report and remunerate every usage the instant it occurs.

Audience analysis has been similarly transformed by the rise of on-demand streams. Purchase habits have long been monitored, and there have also been examinations of the uses that consumers have made of songs and recordings. These investigations have previously been restricted in nature, however. Prior to this century they were based on the narrow circulation of questionnaires, surveys and focus groups. Downloading upped the ante somewhat, but its returns look quaint in comparison to the information that is supplied by streaming. The listening habits of all consumers can now be documented. Furthermore, while this data is generally restricted to the capture of quantitative rather than qualitative use, it is nevertheless being employed in the service of listening activity. Audience engagement shapes and is shaped by the algorithmic conventions of streams.

Musical statistics have always been troubling. They have helped to construct the blockbuster markets of the music industries; they have been deployed in partisan debates about royalty payments; and they have been used in lobbying campaigns to sway governments and other policy-makers. Now they are being generated by audiences who they, in turn, attempt to generate. These practices lead to a supplementary issue: what if the figures are falsified? As the main reporters or commissioners of their own statistics, the music industries have the ability to distort, bury or utilize them in accordance with their own desires. This has led some people to doubt the veracity of their numbers, calling out the industries whenever a loose statistic or rough estimate can be discerned. These complaints are most pronounced in respect of the figures for piracy, and with some justification. Not only are piracy statistics some of the hardest to verify, they are also amongst the most consequential.

It is not just governments, legislators and consumers who are manipulated by statistics; the music industries conduct their own businesses in accordance with figures they have biased. They invest in artists on the basis of chart placements and sales figures that they have massaged themselves. They believe their own hype. It is tempting to see something hyperreal in this process. In line with Jean Baudrillard's theories, the music industries' activities are based on 'models of a real without origin or reality' (1994: 1). Yet it would be a mistake to go this far. Most industry statistics are based on some form of truth. As such, the role of researchers should not be to adopt the position of numerical deniers, rejecting figures out of hand as fictitious creations. More fruitful pursuits are to find out what has been framed, what has been obscured and what is of consequence.

About this book

The purpose of *Music by Numbers* is to explore the manifold uses and abuses of statistics within the music industries. Contributors have been invited to analyse, expose and even create their own numbers. The authors have a range of professional and disciplinary backgrounds. This book includes explorations of industry activity from academics versed in sociology, media studies, communication studies and popular music studies. Some of the contributors are industry insiders, offering their own perspectives on the professional deployment of statistics. Others are academic insiders, providing self-analyses of their involvement with data.

The book opens with a section on winners and losers, which is comprised of three inter-related chapters by Richard Osborne. In the opening chapter he addresses the manipulation of the UK singles chart, tracing the manner in which it has been hyped by record companies and how its rules have been changed to suit the recording industry's needs. The second chapter looks at the sales awards issued by this industry: gold, silver, platinum and diamond discs. Here Osborne examines the mutability of criteria and looks at how the awards conceal as much as they reveal. They are concerned solely with sales and usage, saying nothing of the relative profitability of recordings. Following on from this, profitability is the focus of the third chapter, which explores the consequences of the recording industry's axiom that only one in ten of its projects will achieve financial success. Most notably, this statistic has been used in defence of the record companies' ownership of sound recording copyright and the restrictive nature of their contracts.

Part two of the book looks at music policy. David Arditi's chapter assesses the annual revenue figures issued by IFPI. It is his argument that the organization has consciously precluded general access to its full reports, which in turn has meant they have withheld a narrative that counters the prevailing story presented by the recording industry in the first decade of the twenty-first century. The industry argued that digital piracy was the sole reason for the decline in their trade, whereas IFPI's analysis sometimes belies this fact. In addition, Arditi reveals that IFPI's data has been inconsistent. Their reports have featured different sources of revenue and they have altered their figures, falsifying a downward trend as a means of arguing for increased copyright protection. Where Arditi's work demonstrates the mutability of numbers, the succeeding chapter by Shain Shapiro investigates their strict imposition. He addresses popular music funding in Canada, where quotas have been implemented to ensure that broadcasters play a set amount of music by local artists and that funding is distributed in accordance with the national industries' needs. These figures can still be tactically manipulated, nonetheless. Shapiro demonstrates means by which record companies and artists have negotiated access to funding, and ways that radio companies have manipulated quotas to suit their own broadcast interests. He is focused on changes that transformed Canadian funding during the twenty-first century, witnessing a turn towards commercial rather than cultural support, and to newness defined by quantitative rather than qualitative means.

The third part of the book turns to the live music industry. In the first chapter of this section Adam Behr, Matt Brennan, Martin Cloonan and Emma Webster provide an account of their experiences producing a national live music census. They document the rewards and drawbacks of working with industry partners, as well as the difficulties and imperatives involved in accumulating data. There is a drive, from media and industry, to produce a 'big number' that totalizes value. The results of a census are, however, more diffused than this. Big numbers are also conjured in the next chapter, in which Dave Laing examines attempts to calculate the overall value of the live music industry. He looks at data compiled for Australia, France, Germany, Italy, the United Kingdom and the United States/Canada, and tabulates the different sources of revenue that have been employed in the countries' surveys. These figures have been used to compare the revenue of live music with the trade figures for recorded music, commonly as a means of establishing the ascendancy of the former over the latter. In the following chapter, Richard Osborne takes a closer look at such analyses, highlighting fundamental differences in the way the figures for live music and recorded music are compiled.

Part four addresses piracy. This section begins with Lucas Logan's examination of the police raid and criminal prosecution of OiNK.CD, which he regards as exemplary of the 'upward ratchet' of copyright law. It is his argument that this prosecution misrepresented the nature of this file-sharing site and misunderstood the activities of its users. In the following chapter, Lola Costa Gálvez explores the situation in Spain, which has responded to its status as a notoriously piratical country by criminalizing infringing activity. She looks at the questionable role of professional institutions as they influence the government with data and inculcate school children with propaganda. Costa Gálvez joins Logan and Arditi in querying the veracity of piracy statistics. In the following chapter, Vanessa Bastian and Dennis Collopy take a closer look at the compilation of these figures, detailing a report they were commissioned to write for the UK's Intellectual Property Office in 2013/2014. They were requested to examine methods used to measure the infringement of intellectual property rights. Unsurprisingly, they found weaknesses and biases. The authors did, however, also find some practices to commend.

In conclusion, the fifth part of the book takes us towards digital solutions. In his chapter tracing the receipt of one penny from Brazil, Michael Jones gives a first-hand account as a songwriter facing the bewildering environment of digital royalties and music publishing contracts. He delves into the reams of data with which publishers now 'dazzle' their songwriters and contemplates their misleading habit of referring to them as 'clients'. Jones contrasts the lack of industry employed by his publishers to promote his songs with the considerable effort they expend in tracking miniscule royalties. The next chapter, by Marcus O'Dair, examines one of the vaunted solutions to these issues. He addresses blockchain technology, which among other things has been proposed as a means of revolutionizing artist contracts and improving the efficiency of payments. O'Dair explores claims made for and against this technology, arguing that the financial speculation around it is misleading. He suggests that if we wish to properly gauge blockchain's worth we should conduct specific, small-scale studies and bear in mind its longer-term value. Undertaking his own measurements, O'Dair seeks to determine whether blockchain has the potential to be a 'disruptive technology' and concludes that it could well be transformative for the music industries.

In the final chapter, Craig Hamilton contextualizes and critiques his own Harkive Project. First established in 2013, Harkive invites participants to reflect about their experiences with music. This includes 'reflections on how recently emerged data-derived technologies now play a key role within that activity'. Hamilton raises crucial issues about the use of online data. He questions whether it can ever accurately profile the engagement of a consumer, but notes at the same time that consumers are being constructed by their profiles. He indicates the complicity of researchers as they undertake their own work in this field; they may well have intentions to operate critically and independently, but they are also accumulating information that can be utilized by governments and corporations. Hamilton nevertheless argues that the data generated by Internet technologies has the ability to expand the scope of humanities research. Ultimately, he recommends a 'reflexive, experimental and exploratory methodological approach' for engaging practically and critically with these technologies. He also provides a nuanced account of how statistics can be used and abused.

Dave Laing (1947–2019)

Music by Numbers is Dave Laing's idea. He coined the title and initiated the concept. Given his conviviality, it is fitting that I first heard him propose this book over drinks in a pub. He was in search of a young and energetic co-editor. Fitting neither characteristic, but interested in the topic and keen to collaborate with him,

I volunteered anyway. From January 2016 until late 2018 we worked together on the project, issuing the call for chapters, editing the contributions, establishing the structure of the book and securing a contract.

Dave died in January 2019. The effect on his colleagues has been profound and the tributes have been manifold, appearing on scholarly websites, in academic journals, trade magazines and national newspapers. Their diversity and emotional tenor are testament to Dave's widespread influence and appeal. He had a unique knowledge of popular music, he was exceptionally generous with this knowledge and he was phenomenally good company. I always made a beeline for him at conferences, relishing his incisive intellect and wit.

He was a father figure of popular music studies. His book *The Sound of Our Time* was published in 1969. It can be regarded as the first scholarly monograph about popular music written by an insider and fan. He was one of the founding editors of *Popular Music*, the first academic journal devoted to the subject. His 1985 book *One Chord Wonders* offered one of the original, and still one of the best, scholarly analyses of punk rock. Dave was also one of the most knowledgeable and perceptive writers about the music industries. He was the person to turn to whether you required historical information or if you wanted to assess contemporary transformations.

Dave achieved most of this outside of academia. He did not hold a university post until 1996. Before that he was a freelance author, journalist and lecturer. Between 1972 and 1984 he contributed to *Time Out, Sounds, Let It Rock,* the *Radio One History of Pop* and many more besides. In 1984 he assumed a post as Research and Press Officer for IFPI. From 1987 to 1996 he worked as an editor for the music industry journals *Music Week, Music Business International* and *Financial Times Music & Copyright*.

I first got to know him when he was one of the examiners for my Ph.D. He was rigorous, picking me up on what others might pass by (I was reprimanded for detailing the wrong year for Friedrich Kittler's *Gramophone, Film, Typewriter*, listing the date of the German language publication rather than the translation I had used). He also improved the work tremendously. The structural changes he recommended helped me turn the thesis into a book (Osborne 2012).

The process of working on *Music by Numbers* together was hugely rewarding. I am glad that the collection includes chapters by his friends and by people whose careers he guided. All of the contributors are admirers. Dave was due to write two chapters: one on the charts and one exploring calculations of the economic value of music. We both felt that the former topic must be covered in a book such as this. In his absence, I have tackled it myself. I would not dare to presume that my thoughts about the charts are the same as Dave's, however, or that I could address the topic with his level of experience and erudition. In place of the second of his proposed chapters, I have included a blog entry that Dave contributed to the *Live Music Exchange* (Laing 2012). It provides an example of the breadth of his knowledge, and the thoroughness and concision with which he completed each writing task.

To say that Dave will be missed is an understatement. He is irreplaceable. In the aftermath of his passing I found myself turning to Laurie Anderson's 'World Without End', which has one of the most devastating lyrics in all of popular music:

> When my father died we put him in the ground
> When my father died it was like a whole library had burned down
>
> (Anderson 1994)

Music by Numbers is dedicated to Dave's memory.

NOTES

1. Although the percentage splits for synchronization licences are contractually agreed, each licence is negotiated competitively in the market rather than being set by pre-agreed terms. Licensor and licensee arrive at a one-off fee rather than a repetitive rate that will devolve into royalties. A similar process takes place for the sound recording copyright element of sample clearance and for the broader licensing of recordings between audio companies. As such, the recording and music publishing industries have a number of revenue streams, some of which are repeatedly bargained over and some of which are determined on the basis of statistical formulae.
2. An exception was provided by the early yearbooks issued by the British Phonographic Industry (BPI). Between 1977 and 1990 they provided a 'cost breakdown' based on the retail price of physical formats. Some of the results were dubious. In 1977, for example, the BPI was suggesting that for every full-price (£3.25) album sold in the previous year, recording artists were making 42 pence per copy, while record companies were only making three-pence profit (Hunter 1977: 147). This would work out at pre-tax profits of less than one per cent of sales revenue for the record companies, but later reports suggested that their pre-tax profits in 1976 were thirteen per cent of sales revenue (Scaping 1986: 32). BPI came to acknowledge the variability of the figures: by 1979 they were providing the caveat that '[t]he costs associated with any new release are different in virtually every case' (Scaping 1979: 127). Moreover, given the inconsistency in artist royalty rates, which 'naturally vary' (Scaping 1979: 127), it is perhaps not surprising that the BPI eventually decided to withheld their information about costs.
3. These reports were issued from 2014 to 2018. In 2019, UK Music updated their methodology and gave their report a new name. It is now known as *Music by Numbers*, a title that was already familiar to the editors of this book.

4. The making available right was formulated as part of the World Intellectual Property Organization's *Performances and Phonograms Treaty* in 1996. It addresses digital formats that the public can access 'from a place and at a time individually chosen by them' (WIPO 1996: Art. 10, Art. 14). Not only does this definition echo Benjamin's description of mechanical reproduction 'permitting the reproduction to meet the beholder or listener in his own particular situation' ([1935] 1999: 215), the making available right also facilitates the continuation of previous economic practices. Although it can be enacted as sub-set of the distribution right, the communication to the public right is 'probably the preferred choice in most countries' (IFPI 2003: 2). The making available right does not have to operate as other communication to the public rights do, however. In many countries it is not subject to equitable remuneration rules, which would mean that recording artists receive a set percentage of revenue, administered by a collection society. Instead, the record companies have an exclusive right, which they can control as they wish.
5. Jukeboxes and radio broadcasting each offer something of a precedent. Jukebox profits are determined by the amount of times a song is played. This usage has not devolved to royalty payments, however: in America, jukeboxes were for a long time exempt from copyright royalties, while in the United Kingdom the copyright licensing of jukeboxes has been set by the size of the venue rather than the music played. It is, therefore, only the jukebox operators who receive payments by results. Broadcast royalties, in contrast, are frequently determined by usage. Nevertheless, this is not a usage that is made 'on demand' by consumers. The choice of listening is determined, in the first instance, by the broadcasting companies.

REFERENCES

Anderson, Chris (2009), *The Longer Long Tail*, London: Random House Business Books.

Anderson, Laurie (1994), 'World Without End', CD, Burbank: Warner Bros.

Attali, Jacques ([1977] 1985), *Noise: The Political Economy of Music* (trans. B. Massumi), Minneapolis and London: University of Minnesota Press.

Baudrillard, Jean (1994), *Simulacra and Simulation* (trans. S. F. Glaser), Ann Arbor: The University of Michigan Press.

Benjamin, Walter ([1935] 1999), 'The work of art in the age of mechanical reproduction', in H. Arendt (ed.), *Illuminations* (trans. H. Zorn), London: Pimlico, pp. 211–44.

Caves, Richard E. (2000), *Creative Industries: Contracts Between Art and Commerce*, Cambridge, MA and London, UK: Harvard.

Cloonan, Martin (2007), *Popular Music and the State in the UK: Culture, Trade or Industry?*, Aldershot: Ashgate.

Cooke, Chris (2019), 'Value of UK music industry tops £5.2 billion, says UK Music', 20 November, https://completemusicupdate.com/article/value-of-uk-music-industry-tops-5-2-billion-says-uk-music/. Accessed 22 November 2019.

The Doors (1969), 'The Soft Parade', LP, New York: Elektra.

Elberse, Anita (2014), *Blockbusters: Why Big Hits – And Big Risks – Are the Future of the Entertainment Business*, London: Faber & Faber.

Frank, Robert H. and Cook, Philip J. (2010), *The Winner-Take-All Society*, London: Virgin Books.

Garnham, Nicholas (2005), 'From cultural to creative industries: An analysis of the implications of the "Creative Industries" approach to arts and media policy making in the United Kingdom', *International Journal of Cultural Policy*, 11:1, pp. 15–29.

Hunter, Nigel (ed.) (1977), *BPI Yearbook 1977: A Review of the British Record and Tape Industry*, London: BPI.

International Federation of the Phonographic Industry (IFPI) (2012), 'Investing in music: How music companies discover, nurture and promote talent', http://www.ifpi.org/content/library/investing_in_music.pdf. Accessed 25 January 2013 [no longer available].

——— (2003), *The WIPO Treaties: 'Making Available' Right*, London: IFPI.

Kittler, Friedrich (1999), *Gramophone, Film, Typewriter* (trans. G. Winthrop-Young and M. Wutz), Stanford: Stanford University Press.

Laing, Dave (1969), *The Sound of Our Time*, London and Sydney: Sheed and Ward.

——— (1985), *One Chord Wonders,* Milton Keynes: Open University Press.

——— (2012), 'What's it worth? Calculating the economic value of live music', Live Music Exchange Blog, 11 June, http://livemusicexchange.org/blog/whats-it-worth-calculating-the-economic-value-of-live-music-dave-laing/. Accessed 26 January 2019.

Martland, Peter (2013), *Recording History: The British Record Industry 1988–1931*, Lanham: Scarecrow Press.

Newbigin, John (n.d.), *What Is the Creative Economy?*, British Council: Creative Economy, https://creativeeconomy.britishcouncil.org/guide/what-creative-economy/. Accessed 7 November 2019.

'number, n.' (1989), *Oxford English Dictionary*, 2nd ed., Oxford: Oxford University Press.

Osborne, Richard (2012), *Vinyl: A History of the Analogue Record*, Farnham: Ashgate.

Ravid, Abraham S. (2005), 'Film production in the digital age', in C. Moul (ed.), *A Concise Handbook of Movie Industry Economics*, Cambridge: Cambridge University Press, pp. 32–58.

Rye, Mark (2017), *Inside Looking Out: Rock and Roll Stories from Inside the British Music Business,* Surrey: RockHistory.

Scaping, Peter (ed.) (1979), *BPI Yearbook 1977: A Review of the British Record and Tape Industry*, London: BPI.

——— (1986), *BPI Yearbook 1986: A Statistical Description of the British Record Industry*, London: BPI.

Sell, Susan (2010), 'The global IP upward ratchet, anti-counterfeiting and piracy enforcement efforts: The state of play', *PIJIP Research Paper Series*, http://digitalcommons.wcl.american.edu/research/15/. Accessed 6 November 2019.

'statistics, n.' (1989), *Oxford English Dictionary*, 2nd ed., Oxford: Oxford University Press.

Strachan, Robert and Leonard, Marion (2003), 'Charts', in J. Shepherd, D. Horn, D. Laing, P. Oliver and P. Wicke (eds), *Continuum Encyclopedia of Popular Music of the World: Volume 1: Media, Industry and Society*, London and New York: Continuum, pp. 535–41.

Towse, Ruth (2001), *Creativity, Incentive and Reward: An Economic Analysis of Copyright and Culture in the Information Age*, Cheltenham, UK and Northampton, MA: Edward Elgar.

——— (2015), 'Copyright and business models in UK music publishing', working paper, Glasgow: University of Glasgow/CREATe.

Williamson, John and Cloonan, Martin (2007), 'Rethinking the music industry', *Popular Music*, 26:2, pp. 305–22.

World Intellectual Property Organization (WIPO) (1996), *Performances and Phonograms Treaty*, https://www.wipo.int/treaties/en/ip/wppt/. Accessed 22 November 2019.

PART I

WINNERS AND LOSERS

1

At the Sign of the Swingin' Symbol: The Manipulation of the UK Singles Chart

Richard Osborne

Entering the chart

What has been the purpose of the singles chart? Ostensibly it has reflected the popularity of music, but really it has driven it. To enter the Top 40 has been to access a new promotional world: there have been Top 40 broadcasters, Top 40 retailers and Top 40 music journals. As Martin Parker has stated, a good position in the singles chart will 'amplify success as well as quantifying and advertising it' (1991: 208). The chart is as an echo chamber that resounds loudest at the top.

But what is it advertising? Singles promote themselves, yet they are just as likely to be promoting something else. They have been used as loss leaders for albums and they have provided an effective means of introducing the public to nascent acts. Their currency is newness. To this end, the popularity of a single has to be marshalled. The record business has desired that they generate the right publicity for the right product at the right time. Hence, if the singles chart is not working in their interests they will exploit and manipulate the statistical variables in the way it is compiled.

These variables are the subject of this chapter. I will address who is responsible for compiling the singles chart, the breadth of the survey, the representation of the results, the frequency of the chart and how a 'single' is defined. I will do so through the lens of the singles chart in Britain, but by way of comparison I will also address charts in the United States. Britain has been chosen because it is a country where the singles chart has been particularly central to musical life. This has been attributed both to the national character and to the political economy of its media and music industries. In turn, this centrality has caused fears within these industries that the chart can be 'broken'. The concern moves in cycles. It can be prompted by anxiety that the chart has been manipulated too much; therefore, it no longer represents the public's taste and will not garner its attention. On other occasions, it will arise because the public's taste is considered boring and is not serving the interests of the industries; therefore, the chart needs to be manipulated to make it serviceable again. The effects of digital technologies have been felt keenly. The inclusion of data from downloads and streaming has transformed the construction and conceptualization of the chart. The great quandary for British music businesses is whether it has overturned its importance.

Who is doing the counting?

The UK singles chart and the US charts both have their roots in the entertainment press. The American charts were launched in trade papers such as *Variety* and *Billboard*, while the British chart arrived in journals aimed at the public. The *New Musical Express* (*NME*) issued the first chart based on singles sales in November 1952, followed by similar charts in *Record Mirror* (1954) and *Melody Maker* (1956). The impetus was financial and promotional. Percy Dickens created the *NME* chart in the hope it would provide record companies with a tool to advertise in his publication. He was successful too. The first number one was Al Martino's 'Here in My Heart'. Within weeks it was being advertised by Capitol Records as a chart topping single (Whalley 2012).

The British trade journal *Record Retailer* launched its own chart in 1960, which has subsequently been used for historical chart data. Nonetheless, there continued to be a number of rival charts in the United Kingdom until 1969, when the British Market Research Bureau (BMRB), funded by *Record Retailer*, initiated a unified singles chart. Thereafter, this chart has been compiled by a variety of research organizations, funded in various forms of partnership with *Music Week* (the successor to *Record Retailer*), the BBC, retailers associations and/or the British Phonographic Industry (BPI). BPI is the trade association for the UK recording industry. While it is possible for most British labels to become members, it has been viewed as being dominated by the multinational major companies (Cloonan 2007: 49). Since 2001, the chart has been the responsibility of The Official Charts Company, an organization that is funded by BPI and the Entertainment Retailers Association (ERA). The UK singles chart has never been independent of industry interests.

How wide is the survey?

The first American record charts were introduced in *Variety* in the late 1930s. They concerned jukebox popularity. Jukeboxes were useful for statistical purposes as they tabulated each time a record was played. A 'Top 40' was chosen because this was the standard number of discs in a machine (Brewster and Broughton 2006: 58). The earliest British record charts, in contrast, were concerned with sales and their statistical basis was less systematic. Although it was billed as the first 'authentic weekly survey of the best-selling "pop" records', the original *NME* chart was compiled loosely, arrived at by asking a mere 25 retailers what records had been selling (Anon. 1952: 8). The breadth of the surveys had expanded by the mid-1960s, by which time the *Melody Maker* was targeting 250 'chart return' shops to gain their data (Leslie 1965: 50). The rigour of these surveys remained questionable, however. Writing in this period, Peter Leslie noted:

> Although the integrity of those who compile the charts from the returned questionnaires (about 50 per cent only) is beyond question, the data on the questionnaires must be suspect: no figures of actual sales are given, only the order of customers' preference – and the compiler has no way whatever of telling if the person who filled in the form was accurate or not.
>
> (1965: 50–51)

It was not long before suppliers were falsifying data or having it falsified for them. The return shops remained limited in number: after it was taken over by BMRB, the survey still addressed only seven per cent of record retailers (Hunter 1971: 11). Their identity was an open secret and they were therefore an easy target, falling prey to record companies, managers and agents, whose practice of chart 'hyping' was widespread and has since been openly admitted. As an example, Dave Arden, the son of manager Don Arden, has detailed how his father would employ agents to work upon chart return stores, getting them to elevate the sales figures of his own charges and decrease the popularity of his rivals (Rye 2017: 32–33). The bribes offered to record retailers took a number of forms, including money, gifts and free stock. Another method of manipulation was for the record companies to buy their own records. They would pay consumers to visit chart return shops and purchase copies of their singles.

It has been claimed that it was only possible to hype a record into the lower reaches of the charts. Radio producer Phil Swaren has stated, 'I don't think that many records became massive hits because of manipulation. I do believe that if the public didn't like a record they wouldn't buy it, no matter what you did' Whalley 2012). A different point of view is that the manipulators deliberately limited their activity. According to Arden, '[t]he old man was very careful, he always knew there's only so far you can push something, and then it's got to have its own legs and then he also didn't want people thinking it was being hyped' (Rye 2017: 32). Furthermore, by reaching the lower rungs of the charts, key promotional benefits would already have been gained. As Swaren states, 'a record going in the charts at number 39 and the radio stations would suddenly take a bit more interest in it and therefore might begin to play it' (Whalley 2012).

By the early 1980s it was believed that the chart was 'clogged up with hyped records' (*World in Action* 1980). This situation resulted in investigations by the *Daily Mirror* and the television programme *World in Action*. BPI countered that there was 'no widespread hyping' (*World in Action* 1980). They also maintained there was nothing wrong with the fact that they were responsible for policing the chart and therefore the record companies in effect 'sat in judgement on themselves' (*World in Action* 1980). In 1987, the BMRB's successor, the Gallup Organization, widened the chart survey to approximately 500 stores and brought in barcode scanners to monitor record sales. Chart return shops nevertheless continued to be targeted.

Throughout this period, the incompleteness of the survey had considerable effects. Although many singles were hyped, the success of some genres was overlooked, as was the output of smaller record labels and specialist record shops (Stanley 2013: 596). Significant sales of reggae and Asian records took place in localized stores that did not provide chart returns. Consequently, the popularity of this music was not accurately reflected in the Top 40. There were also chart rules stating that sales needed to be registered across retailers from around the country (Cope 1999: 91). As a result, the regional hits of independent labels were hampered.

It was only in the 1990s, when a particular aspect of barcode technology came to the fore, that the hyping of chart return shops was reduced. The larger record chains introduced the practice of centralized buying, whereby their head offices would use barcode data from sales to order stock for an entire chain of shops. As a result, the effectiveness of targeting individual retailers was negated (Negus 1992: 129). In the twenty-first century, it has been eliminated completely. This is in part because the vast majority shops now provide chart data: the Official Chart Company claims to document the sales of '15,000-plus chart-reporting retailers, who together represent an estimated 99% of the singles market' (Official Charts 2019a). It is also because physical retail constitutes an insignificant element of singles 'sales'.

The Official Charts Company first incorporated download sales figures into its main singles chart in 2005, and has included information from streaming companies since 2014. In turn, these digital formats have come to dominate the charts. With their arrival, the practice of manipulating sales figures (or 'sales equivalent' figures, in the case of streaming) has lessened. It has not been eliminated entirely, though. There have been reports of people setting up false streaming accounts to register multiple plays for artists. Some of this activity is coming from 'superfans', who are attempting to raise the profile of their favourite artists (Montgomery 2018). Elsewhere, artists and record companies are employing 'streaming farms' to generate millions of plays for particular songs (Ingham 2018). These digital platforms have in addition raised new questions about the breadth of the survey. They have a worldwide span. Thus, it has been claimed that it is 'a genuine possibility that a global chart, pushed by the major record companies and adopted by these "gatekeepers", could become a bigger priority than local equivalent charts' (Lambot 2015: 9).

How are the figures represented?

Billboard has presented the main American singles chart as a 'Hot 100' since 1958. In Britain, the number of songs listed has varied and expanded with time. The original *NME* chart detailed twelve titles; the current Official Charts Company chart lists the hundred most popular singles. There has nevertheless been continuity and correspondence in the printed or online display of the figures. The published charts in both countries place the number one single at the top; the bottom placed song is at the bottom. Beyond this there is little to distinguish the representation of each individual title. The top singles might be given a bit more space than those below, but only to a marginal extent. In addition, the only numbers provided are the order of preference. The charts do not publicly document a record's sales figures.

This presentation masks considerable differences between the chart positions. The charts in Britain and America have various cut-off points, the most important of which is the split between the Top 40 singles and those below. Although this division is not marked in the charts themselves, it has traditionally been at this point that media companies' most significant promotional activity has kicked in. This number is also utilized by record companies, who recognize a Top 40 position as a marker for the success of a record, as well as a trigger for the resources they will commit to an act. There are further cut-off points within the Top 40. A new level of promotional activity will ensue if the single reaches number 30 or above. This process redoubles as the chart numbers ascend, reaching a climax with the number one record, which receives considerably more media and record company attention than any other chart position. There is something curious about this process. The companies influence the way the charts work, but then allow the charts to influence their own working practices.

The statistical dispersion is reflected in sales. In Britain, the number one record will regularly sell double the amount of the single below. The same is true of the top ten singles in relation to the singles from eleven to twenty, and of the top twenty when compared with singles in positions from 21 to 40 (Whalley 2012). The music industries have nevertheless chosen to mask the differences between these numbers, presenting the charts as a 'Top 40 democracy' (Weisbard 2014) and promoting a 'false equivalence' between its songs (Laing 1969: 28). This suits their dual purposes. On the one hand, they wish to use the charts as a marketing tool for new material, which will gain its most important fillip as long as it reaches the top 40. On the other hand, the charts are a means for ensuring that blockbuster releases achieve maximum returns.

The presentation of the numbers has further effects. Most countries have an array of singles charts, covering different sectors of their markets. Yet they differ in the attention that they give to each chart and in the way their charts relate to one another: charts are shaped by the political economies of national music industries and in turn help to shape them. Looking at America, for example, we can see how the country's scale and diversity is reflected in its charts. *Billboard*'s Hot 100 offers a broad overview of the popularity of recordings, but the trade journal also publishes significant minority charts, which are demographically and regionally based. Historically, the most notable have been the rhythm and blues chart (which has detailed the popularity of records among African-American audiences) and the country chart (which first tabulated this music's popularity in the southern states from which it hailed). These charts, along with others such as the Latin chart and the gospel chart, have commanded considerable attention. They have acted as barometers, taking the measure of discreet markets of American music. They have also been the source of 'cross-over' singles, records that have come to fruition in one sector but have then been promoted in other charts. An ideal has been to 'break' a hit in a minority chart and then work it towards the Hot 100. In fact, this is why the *Billboard* chart features 100 songs. According to Ernest A. Hakanen, 'it expanded many times in the 1950s to accommodate primarily the crossover market' (1998: 105).

The United Kingdom also has a number of singles charts, addressing different formats, genres, regions and business practices. The national singles chart is more dominant and immediate than its American equivalent, however. The niche charts have rarely operated as sources for it. Instead, for those with commercial ambition, the 'official' singles chart has been their target from the start. It has provided the major record labels with their main means of promoting new acts and new music. They have worked in sync with media companies and retailers to ensure this chart works quickly and effectively. Music journals such as *Melody Maker* (in the 1960s), *NME* (in the 1970s and 1990s) and *Smash Hits* (1978–2006) have let the Top 40 dictate their editorial decisions. The charts have similarly shaped (and been shaped by) the playlists of the BBC's national youth radio station, Radio

1(1967–present), and the selection policy of its most viewed music programme, *Top of the Pops* (1964–2006). High street record retailers have put the Top 40 countdown of the singles chart on prominent display. As well as providing a pull for UK record companies, this concentrated promotional activity has attracted interest from abroad. Writing in the early 1990s, Keith Negus documented how success in Britain was being 'used as a lever to negotiate the release of material in other territories' (1992: 11). The UK charts 'set the agenda for record companies and radio stations across Europe', while American labels sought 'British success as part of their global strategies rather than simply to gain more sales' (Negus 1992: 11).

It has been argued that the British are 'more interested in charts than any other nation' (Jones 2002: 3) and that the singles chart has 'a special appeal to the British sensibility' (Stanley 2013: 3). It is not for everyone, however. While there are record companies, artists and audiences who regard the chart as the apex of their musical world, there are others who have viewed the Top 40 as something to kick against. At times, this chart has been so pervasive that the market has bifurcated around it. Its most successful rival has tabulated independent singles. The independent chart first emerged in the polarized 1980s. Tellingly, it has not operated on a regional basis nor has it been used as a feeder for the main chart. It has instead monitored the means of production. If you are 'independent' of the major labels you are in; if you are signed or distributed by them, you are not. The usefulness of this chart has been debated. There are those within the independent scene who have purposefully sought escape from the Top 40; there are others who have not wanted to become ghettoized from the commercial centre of British musical life.

How frequent are the charts?

It has been a recurring feature of singles charts around the world that they are tabulated weekly. This accords with the rhythms of commercial life: retailers make singles available on a set day of the week; they reach peak points of sales according to daily shopping patterns. This policy is not without its effects. Martin Talbot, the chief executive of The Official Charts Company, has noted '[i]f the public don't like the record, it won't go to number one. If they like it, and the conditions are right. The sales come in over the right span [...] the planets have aligned' (Smeaton 2015). The key words here are 'over the right span'. The weekly charts are biased towards records that can achieve popularity in a limited time period. This favours the singles that are being promoted most heavily, as well as artists who have the most dedicated sets of fans. The weekly tally has had a further distorting effect.

A hit record will have to sell fewer copies to reach the top of the charts in the summer than it will in the Christmas period. Record companies organize their release schedules accordingly, promoting their newer artists in quieter periods and saving major releases for the weeks of blockbuster sales. These phenomena were most notable when the charts were concentrated upon physical product. As we shall see, the larger record companies had means of getting consumers to buy their chosen records at the most apposite time. Meanwhile, the task of creating a hit was harder for those with smaller budgets. As Parker has noted, a weekly chart 'discriminates against minority musics in an apparently democratic fashion' (1991: 208).

Previously, chart weeks were marked by space as well as by time. Recordings were released in different territories at different times and on different days. The charts are now more global. The span of the Internet has meant that recordings released in one territory but not in another are liable to be pirated. The industry's solution has been to launch 'New Music Fridays', a worldwide correspondence of release dates, which was first established in 2015.[1] This initiative was opposed by smaller and more localized record labels, who feared that it would lead to a homogenization of the world's charts. Martin Mills, chairman of the Beggars Group, predicted that the resultant 'lack of diversity will strangle innovation and music will become moribund and uninteresting, and consumer interest will erode. It will also dis-empower the artist, since the major labels will regain total control of access to market. It will create short-termism, and damage career longevity' (Cooke 2015).

The results have been mixed. On the one hand, international artists are now responsible for a higher proportion of chart hits. In 2016, they claimed 95 per cent of the top ten most streamed tracks in the United Kingdom (the remaining five per cent was due to 'This is What You Came For', a collaboration between the British artist Calvin Harris and the Barbadian singer Rihanna) (Ingham 2017a). On the other hand, the concept of 'international' has become broader. Mills's fears appear to have been sparked by Americanization, but some of the biggest selling singles are now by Latin artists.

Turning full circle, downloads and streams have not only affected the geography of the singles chart, they have also raised questions about time. Rather than collating data and reporting it on a weekly basis, it is now possible to have a continual update of sales and usage. As such, there have been suggestions that the charts should be more frequent. This has been realized in America, where *Rolling Stone* launched daily updated charts in 2019. In Britain, details can be gained about mid-week chart positions but the official chart remains weekly. This has been defended as being in the national interest. Talbot has stated, 'we have 60 years of heritage: there have been more than 1,200 Number 1 singles. If the chart was changing day-by-day, you could multiply that by 19. It dilutes how special it is for an artist to take the crown' (Anon. 2012: 14).

What counts as a 'single'?

Billboard's Hot 100 always reached beyond sales, as it incorporated radio play from the first. Aligned with America's commercial broadcasting system this meant radio stations were the major target of hyping activity. The trade journal married together sales figures and broadcast figures by weighting each component in the chart. Using the same technique, *Billboard* has found it relatively easy to incorporate streaming information into the Hot 100. They have included data from audio streaming services since 2012, and from YouTube since 2013. In that year *Billboard*'s average weighting was 35–45 per cent of the chart tally for physical and digital sales, 30–40 per cent for airplay information, and 20–30 per cent for streaming data (Trust 2013). In contrast, the UK charts have been focused solely on sales. As a result, the Official Charts Company has found the incorporation of streaming data problematic both technically and conceptually.

The attempts to reconcile streaming with chart criteria have garnered considerable attention, but this masks the fact that there has long been flexibility and manipulation regarding what constitutes a 'single'. In the earliest years of the UK charts, some compilers listed the two sides of a single separately, while others incorporated separate cover versions within a single chart entry. The first charts also documented hits rather than singles per se. In the 1950s and early 1960s, most of the records sold were singles, but some artists also achieved significant album sales. Frank Sinatra was the most notable, and in 1956 his *Songs for Swingin' Lovers* collection became a top ten hit in these 'combined' charts. The same feat was realized by some of the Beatles' early albums. As overall album sales increased, it gradually became established that there should be separate charts for singles and albums. In addition, the idea of a 'single' coalesced so that in chart terms they were equated with physical products by individual acts: the b-side formed part of the chart placing; the cover version did not.

This did not mean that chart rules were fixed for all time. They have been expanded to accommodate other singles formats. Twelve-inch singles were included in the chart in 1983, and cassette singles and CD singles by the end of the 1980s. A 'single' chart entry, therefore, has not been made up of a single product. Instead, various formats have been collated to establish the result. There have been differing rules about the extent to which these formats should resemble each other. For example, it was originally stipulated that a twelve-inch single should have the same tracks as its seven-inch equivalent. There has also been flexibility.

It later became acknowledged that, as long as the formats share a 'lead' track, it would be possible to have various b-sides and remixes across the different versions of a single. Restrictions have remained, nonetheless. The Official Chart Company rules for July 2019 stipulate that a seven-inch single can have no more than three different songs and must be under 25-minutes duration; a twelve-inch single or CD single is limited to four different songs and must be under 25 minutes; a 'remix' single can have any number of remixes of the lead title, but must be under 40-minutes duration (Official Charts 2019b).

Following the 1980s introduction of barcode data as the source for chart information, record companies used multi-formatting as a means to hype records into the Top 40. They would increase sales of a single by issuing it in as many versions as possible, having realized that some dedicated fans would purchase every iteration of a release. Multi-formatting was also used to sustain a single's chart success. One of the reasons why Frankie Goes to Hollywood's 'Two Tribes' remained at number one for nine weeks in 1984 was because new twelve-inch versions were regularly being issued. This practice was viewed as getting out of hand, with some singles being released in ten or more editions. Chart rules were subsequently introduced that reduced the number of eligible formats: record companies were restricted to five in 1991, then four a few years later, and then three physical formats in 1994.

Singles have also been defined by their cost. Chart compilers have established rules about the minimum dealer price of a record. The July 2019 guidelines have these at 40 pence for a download, 50 pence for a seven-inch single, £1.79 for a CD single and £1.99 for a twelve-inch single (Official Charts 2019b). There have also been criteria about minimum retail price. For example, the independent singles issued by Crass in the 1980s were ruled out of chart contention because they were deemed to be too cheap (Stanley 2013: 312). BPI later changed its tune about this policy, lifting any restrictions on retail price (apart from free product). This was in response to the major record companies' demands.

In the 1990s a new method of hyping was adopted. Singles would be priced cheaply in the first few weeks of release (often at half the recommended retail price and thus selling at a loss) and would sometimes include limited edition free gifts (records that include gifts of posters, cards and/or stickers remain eligible for the charts). Record companies would issue these singles to broadcasters for radio play well ahead of their release dates. These tactics prompted fans to purchase records as soon as they were issued, ideally with the effect of forcing them into the charts. With these means the recording industry was able to influence purchasing behaviour so that singles would enter at high chart positions, including at number one. This was not without consequences. Bob Stanley has noted how this 'looked very impressive in theory, but it just meant that people were losing interest in the chart because the charts weren't a consensus of what the country was listening to or what the country liked' (Whalley 2012).

This practice reached a climax in the year 2000, when the UK chart featured 43 separate number one singles, all of which entered at the top. This marketing practice, coupled with the onset of file-sharing, led to a decline in sales of singles. Across the whole of 2004, only 32 million singles were sold, the lowest annual figure. In 2005, the re-release of Elvis Presley's 'One Night' reached number one selling just 20,463 copies, whereas in the 1980s a number one single would regularly sell ten times that amount (McLean 2005). The policy had an effect on the television chart show *Top of the Pops*, which since the 1970s had been the music industry's most valuable asset for promoting singles sales. According to BBC producer Trevor Dann, '[t]he old dynamic of the chart, where records entered low and rose, peaked and then fell, changed completely. Every number one was a new record and that meant that *Top of the Pops* was not playing big hits, it was playing new releases' (Evans 2016: 259). Audiences for the show dwindled, leading to its cancellation in 2006.

This might be considered poor timing, as by this point the chart was incorporating downloads. The inclusion of this format boosted sales (189 million singles were sold in 2012, the highest annual figure) and was viewed as restoring the health of the Top 40. Downloads have rarely been sold to the public at discount prices and they do not include free gifts. Thus, as their contribution to the charts grew in importance, it made the record companies' pricing and promotional practices somewhat redundant. Consequently, the charts slowed down.

Compared with streaming, downloads were relatively easy to incorporate into the chart. Download singles are bought individually and their sales can be tabulated. In this sense they can be equated with physical singles. There were some hurdles to overcome before they could receive chart recognition, nevertheless. A lead track on a physical single is distinguished from a track on an album. It is given its own packaging, price and targeted promotion. It will also probably have limited availability: from the 1980s onwards it became standard practice that singles would be deleted shortly after they exited the charts (and sometimes before they did). In contrast, a downloading platform is full of 'single' songs, but there is little means to distinguish a song that is planned as a single from one that is an album track. There is also little to distinguish new songs from old songs. The Official Charts Company fought against this. When downloads were first incorporated in the chart there was a stipulation that for songs to qualify they must contemporaneously be issued as a physical single. However, as downloads came to dominate the Top 40 – by the first three months of 2006 they had come to represent 88.7 per cent of all single sales (Williams 2007: 12) – the idea of releasing physical singles became less desirable. In response, the industry allowed itself to drop this chart ruling.

In January 2007, all download tracks were made eligible for the charts. This meant that any song of any age could be a single. Old songs entered the Top 40, including Rage Against the Machine's 'Killing in the Name', which reached number one in 2009 on the back of an anti-*X Factor* crowd-funding campaign. In general, these developments were viewed positively. The music journalist Miranda Sawyer argued, 'the charts are good again; with the resurgence of the single and downloads now being counted, there are climbers and non-movers and novelty tracks' (2006). Reggie Yates, who was responsible for the chart countdown show on Radio 1 from 2007 until 2012, claimed that the charts had become 'important' once more (Whalley 2012).

Streaming, in contrast, has been regarded as diminishing the value of the chart. Reflecting some awareness of the problems to come, the chart compilers approached this format with notable reluctance. Spotify was launched in Britain in 2008, but audio streams were not incorporated into the charts until 2014. Talbot claimed that '[b]ecause of the nature and the status of the Official Singles Chart here in the UK, with its 60 years of history and its cultural heritage, it wasn't something we could rush into' (McGuinness 2014). The main numerical difficulty was how to equate a stream with a sale. A ratio of 100:1 was eventually adopted. This was justified on the grounds that a single download would generate the same royalties for rights holders as one hundred streams. The Official Charts Company was cognizant of the fact that different streaming tiers deliver different royalty rates, but chose 'a blended rate' averaging out the royalties for subscription and ad-funded services (Anon. 2014: 1).

The main theoretical problem was how to move from a chart based solely on exchange to one that includes a focus on use. The issue here was not that sales provide a more accurate reflection of taste than streams do (after all, streaming details the employment of a song, whereas buying a single does not guarantee it will be played). Conversely, it was not felt that quantifying sales should be abandoned as being inferior (it can be argued that the purchase of a single is indicative of a commitment to music, whereas streaming gives no indication of a listener's investment in a song). Instead, the public debate centred on the awkwardness of placing these two forms of quantification together. The record companies, meanwhile, had a different concern. What was most problematic for them was a shift in the chart's utility. They had valued the chart less as a measure of popularity than as a guide to consumerism. An exchange-based chart has been useful for them because it tabulates newness; ideally the engagement of a new consumer with a new product. In contrast, a usage chart is statistically biased towards re-use; it details the same consumers listening to the same old songs. It is therefore less effectual for the industry's promotional and marketing campaigns.

This became apparent as streaming became dominant in the chart. Because there is no weighting in the British system, it could quickly displace other formats. In early 2014, before streaming was incorporated, downloads were responsible for 99.5 per cent of chart activity (McGuinness 2014). Immediately afterwards, streaming activity made up half of the chart, and within a year it constituted the vast majority of 'sales'. It was a blockbuster release that highlighted how things had changed. In the summer of 2016, Drake's 'One Dance' remained at number one for fifteen weeks. Its longevity demonstrated wider trends: the Top 40 was slowing down and was featuring fewer new releases (Sutherland 2017b: 1). Although the chart had once been engineered to reduce the rate of change, people now complained that it was 'stagnating' and had become 'sluggish and dull' (Sutherland 2017a: 12; Jones 2016).

Playlists were held responsible. Identified by streaming companies as their distinguishing feature, they were accounting for 58 per cent of their listeners' activity by March 2017 (Mulligan 2016, 2017). According to critics, it has not been the general public that determines playlist consumption, but instead the streaming companies' 'editors' (Sutherland 2016a: 1). The resulting listening experience has been deemed to be 'passive' (Ingham 2017b). Moreover, the streaming companies have agreed that they are 'presenting' music to the public:

> Most people in the world are passive listeners. They don't actively seek new music. They do not read music blogs. They hardly listen to radio. They don't read music magazines. They don't share music and they like being spoon-fed. What they are listening to just so happens because they are listening to it.
>
> (Anonymous Spotify employee, quoted in Sun 2019: 157, 158)

Playlists have been blamed for 'the lack of new artist breakthroughs' and 'the stagnation of the chart', as well as 'UK music being superseded by America' (Sutherland 2016b: 12). Facing the need to speed up the Top 40, the first response of the Official Charts Company was to rebalance its ratios. In January 2017 it was decided that 150 streams would now equate to one sale.

Streaming growth remained exponential. Despite this new ratio, its overall contribution to the chart increased, accounting for 85 per cent of all calculations within six months (Sutherland 2017b: 1). Consequently, a further measure was introduced. In June 2017, it was stipulated that if a single had been in the charts for ten weeks, it would be made subject to 'accelerated decline'. Thereafter, if the single experienced three consecutive weeks of diminishing popularity, its stream to sale ratio would be increased to 300:1. Talbot stated, '[t]his is all about supporting new music. We're making sure the chart continues to be a place that reflects the consumption of new records in a fast-changing world' (Sutherland 2017b: 1).

At the same time, the Official Charts Company tackled a separate issue, which was highlighted by another blockbuster release. When Ed Sheeran's album *Divide* was released in March 2017, all sixteen of its tracks made the singles top twenty, nine of them in the top ten. Sheeran proved that new releases could still have an impact on the charts, but for some this only served to illustrate the extent to which the charts were 'broken' (Mulligan 2017). It was suggested that the Ed Sheeran phenomenon was the result of including streaming data, but it in fact had its roots in an earlier decision. Streaming was incorporated in the charts in the same manner as downloads: all songs were eligible, regardless of their age or whether they had been promoted as singles. This was no longer viewed as being fit for purpose. To ensure that individual performers would not clog up the charts, it was decided in June 2017 that in any given week only the three most popular 'singles' of any given artist would be allowed space in the Top 100. With this measure there was a return to the idea that a single was a bespoke object, albeit that singles were being determined by their popularity and not necessarily because they had been chosen by the industry.

Further tinkering ensued. An argument was put forth that subscription streams should be valued more highly than ad-supported streams. This was on two grounds. First, it was claimed that paying subscribers were somehow more attentive than those who listened to streaming services for free (Ingham 2017b). Second, it was argued that the industry gains more revenue from subscription services. Therefore, if streaming ratios were supposed to reflect royalty payments, the 'blended rate' should be replaced with separate calculations for different types of streams. In June 2018 it was decided that the rate for subscription services would be 100 streams to one sale, whereas for ad-supported it would be 600:1. The 'accelerated decline' figures were recalibrated accordingly: subscription services would be quantified at 200:1, while the ad-supported ratio would be 1200:1.

There are a number of curious aspects to these developments. One is the fact that they were so openly discussed. In the past there had been a desire that the compilation of the Top 40 appear 'natural' to consumers. There was little mention of statistical methodology and amendments to rules were considered a trade concern only. The incorporation of streaming into the charts made public the idea that they must operate in the interests of the national music industries. Following on from this, changes to methodology have become more frequent. As it has become accepted practice that the charts can be manipulated, this has liberated the compilers to make repeated changes to get the balance right. The third development is more reactionary. One of the oddities about the solutions to these digital problems is the extent to which they are rooted in the physical past. Where the acceptance of streaming data used to be broad and open, single tracks are now distinguished from album tracks. In addition, the industry cannot stop equating value with money. The problem of passive streaming has been blamed upon playlist culture, a practice that exists across both subscription and ad-supported tiers. However, this is not where the chart compilers have looked for a remedy. Instead, listening for free is regarded as being six times less important than paying for a service.[2]

This outlook has coloured one of the latest developments in the UK charts. Data from YouTube was first incorporated in July 2018. The reason given for its previous exclusion was that YouTube was not a member of ERA and therefore not eligible for the chart. There was also concern that YouTube data would not be the sort to keep the chart alive. This service is free to access; the motivations for viewing a video are not clear; it contains unlicensed material; its content is international rather than localized; and it is enormously popular. The final factor was the one that was most feared. Globally, YouTube provides the main means for consuming music; it has the ultimate capacity to transform local charts. This popularity also provides the reason why the Official Charts Company had to come to terms with YouTube data at some point: if it had failed to do so the chart could have been considered irrelevant. The acceptance is only partial, however. The Official Charts Company accepts data from 'official' video platforms (that is, licensed material from recognized record companies). User-generated content does not contribute to the chart. In addition, YouTube content is penalized in the same manner as other ad-supported audio streams. It is calibrated at one sixth of the value of subscription services. It will not be a surprise if this ratio is ratcheted up further if the distorting pull of YouTube begins to be felt.

Exiting the chart

The singles chart is not broken because it has never been fixed. It is mutable and at no point has it offered a straightforward presentation of the public's preference for recordings. Record companies have manipulated it. They have falsified sales and bent the rules. The chart has symbols that swing.[3] The public has manipulated the chart too. They may have fallen prey to the record companies' promotional strategies, buying into the popularity of records that have been hyped, lapping up multi-formats and rushing out to purchase cut-price singles on the day of release. But one of the reasons why they bought these records is because they wanted their favourite acts to be promoted. There was a desire to hear them on the radio, read about them in the music press and watch them on *Top of the Pops*. If they got them into the charts then this could happen.

This leads us to something that has been broken. The UK singles chart used to matter. This was not because it documented what had already happened with a single, but instead because it triggered what would come next. There was a link between a single's chart position and the level of attention it would go on to receive. There was a system of mediators who would know what to do with it. It is this relationship that has been severed. The Official Charts Company may well find a formula that will make the rhythm of streaming consumption match their desired rhythm for the chart. What they will find harder to restore is the dynamic spark that a Top 40 chart placing used to provide. Record retailers have long since given up displaying the singles chart; there is no music journal that is tied in to it; radio broadcasters are no longer attuned to a Top 40 ideal. Streaming companies such as Spotify and YouTube are in fact the main mediators of their own hits. This means that when a song receives a high chart placing there is little impact for the consumer. The song will already be on the streaming company's playlists and its video will already have been viewed. If the singles chart has lost its significance it is because it is now doing the job that it originally purported to do. It no longer drives the popularity of music; it merely reflects it.

NOTES

1. A similar initiative is 'on air/on sale', which was launched in the summer of 2015. Where tracks were previously broadcast ahead of their release date, they are now made available to download or stream at the same time they are issued to radio. While this initiative combats piracy, it clashes with British record companies' policy of using pre-release broadcasts to build pent-up demand. It has also been viewed as a contributory factor in the slowing down of the chart. In response a 'feeder' chart has been introduced in the United Kingdom. This 'trending chart' aims to identify 'those new artists showing most growth and greatest momentum' (Williamson 2016: 4).
2. Music business analyst Mark Mulligan has offered a twist on this development. He argues that the record companies' concentration upon playlists means that casual listeners are now more economically important than engaged listeners, leading to the production of music that is 'creatively bankrupt' (Mulligan 2019). In order to reorient the industry towards committed listeners and creative artists, Mulligan suggests that royalty rates should be reduced for playlist streams. The question that follows on from this is whether a parallel penalization of playlists could offer a statistical salve for the 'broken' charts.
3. A sign of the centrality of the singles charts to British life is the redolence of the theme music that has been employed for radio and television chart shows. Popular music fans of certain ages will be familiar with 'Yellow Pearl' by Phil Lynott or the CCS version of 'Whole Lotta Love'. 'At the Sign of the Swingin' Cymbals' by Brian Fahey and his Orchestra was

one of the earliest and most evocative themes. It sound-tracked the chart countdown for Alan Freeman's 'Pick of the Pops' on the BBC Light Programme from 1961 to 1966.

REFERENCES

Anon. (1952), 'Announcing the first Record Hit Parade', *New Musical Express*, 14 November, p. 8.

——— (2012), 'Taking care of No. 1', *Music Week: 60 Years of the Official Singles Chart*, 9 November, pp. 12–14.

——— (2014), 'Why 100 to 1? That streaming-to-download ratio investigated', *Music Week*, 27 June, p. 1.

Brewster, Bill and Broughton, Frank (2006), *Last Night a DJ Saved My Life: The History of the Disc Jockey*, updated ed., London: Headline Book Publishing.

'Chart Busters' (1980), Ray Fitzwalter and Allan Segal (dirs), *World in Action*, Season 16 Episode 30 (18 August, UK: ITV).

Cloonan, Martin (2007), *Popular Music and the State in the UK: Culture, Trade or Industry?*, Aldershot: Ashgate.

Cooke, Chris (2015), 'Beggars chief supports ERA in opposing Friday release day', *Complete Music Update*, 24 February, https://completemusicupdate.com/article/beggars-chief-supports-era-in-opposing-friday-global-release-day/. Accessed 23 January 2019.

Cope, Julian (1999), *Head On: Memories of the Liverpool Punk-Scene and the Story of the Teardrop Explodes (1976–82)*, London: Thorsons.

Evans, Jeff (2016), *The Story of Rock and Pop on British Television*, London: Omnibus Press, 2016.

Frith, Simon (1978), *The Sociology of Rock*, London: Constable.

Hakanen, Ernest A. (1998), 'Counting down to number one: The evolution of the meaning of popular music charts', *Popular Music*, 17:1, pp. 95–111.

Hunter, Nigel (1971), 'How the charts are compiled', *Record Retailer*, 17 July, p. 11.

Ingham, Tim (2017a), '3 Ominous problems the UK music business must overcome in 2017', *Music Business Worldwide*, 3 January, https://www.musicbusinessworldwide.com/3-ominous-problems-the-uk-music-business-must-overcome-in-2017/. Accessed 23 January 2019.

——— (2017b), 'Jimmy Iovine isn't always right – But this time, he's on the money', *Music Business Worldwide*, 14 March, https://www.musicbusinessworldwide.com/jimmy-iovine-isnt-always-right-but-this-time-hes-on-the-money/. Accessed 23 January 2019.

——— (2018), 'Spotify still pays artists out of one big "pot": Should the company change its policy?', *Music Business Worldwide*, 10 December, https://www.musicbusinessworldwide.com/spotify-still-pays-artists-out-of-one-big-pot-should-the-company-change-its-policy/. Accessed 2 April 2019.

Jones, Alan (2002), 'Charting history', *Music Week: Celebrating 50 Years of the Singles Chart*, 16 November, pp. 3, 5–6.

Jones, Rhian (2016), 'The UK singles chart is sluggish and dull. Is this the solution?', *Music Business Worldwide*, 11 September, https://www.musicbusinessworldwide.com/the-uk-singles-chart-is-sluggish-and-dull-is-this-the-solution/. Accessed 23 January 2019.

Laing, Dave (1969), *The Sound of Our Time*, London and Sydney: Sheed and Ward.

Lambot, Michael (2015), 'Viewpoint: "Global chart could become a bigger priority than local charts"', *Music Week*, 27 March, p. 29.

Leslie, Peter (1965), *Fab: The Anatomy of a Phenomenon*, London: MacGibbon and Kee.

McGuinness, Ross (2014), 'Will music streaming make an impact on the official singles chart', *Metro*, 25 June, https://metro.co.uk/2014/06/25/will-music-streaming-make-an-impact-on-the-official-singles-chart-4774409/. Accessed 23 January 2019.

McLean, Matilda (2005), 'What becomes of the single minded', *Telegraph*, 20 January, http://d2ybq9unw89ve4.cloudfront.net/culture/music/3635323/What-becomes-of-the-single-minded.html. Accessed 23 January 2019 [no longer available].

Montgomery, Blake (2018), 'Fans are spoofing Spotify with "fake plays", and that's a problem for music charts', *BuzzFeed.News,* 13 September, https://www.buzzfeednews.com/article/blakemontgomery/spotify-billboard-charts. Accessed 23 January 2019.

Mulligan, Mark (2016), 'After the album: How playlists are re-defining listening', *Music Industry Blog*, 26 April, https://musicindustryblog.wordpress.com/2016/04/26/after-the-album-how-playlists-are-re-defining-listening/. Accessed 23 January 2019.

——— (2017), 'How Ed Sheeran broke the charts', *Music Industry Blog*, 13 March, https://musicindustryblog.wordpress.com/2017/03/13/how-ed-sheeran-broke-the-charts/. Accessed 23 January 2019.

——— (2019), 'Playlist malfeasance will create a streaming crisis', *Music Industry Blog*, 9 May, https://musicindustryblog.wordpress.com/2019/05/09/playlist-malfeasance-will-create-a-streaming-crisis/. Accessed 21 May 2019.

Negus, Keith (1992), *Producing Pop: Culture and Conflict in the Music Industry*, London: Arnold.

Official Charts (2019a), 'How the official charts are compiled', https://www.officialcharts.com/getting-into-the-charts/how-the-charts-are-compiled/. Accessed 23 January 2019.

——— (2019b), 'Rules for chart eligibility singles', July, https://www.officialcharts.com/media/656892/official-uk-singles-chart-rules-july-2019.pdf. Accessed 24 October 2019.

Parker, Martin (1991), 'Reading the charts: Making sense with the hit parade', *Popular Music*, 10:2, pp. 205–17.

Rye, Mark (2017), *Inside Looking Out: Rock and Roll Stories from Inside the British Music Business*, Surrey: RockHistory.

Sawyer, Miranda (2006), 'What's in a format?', *Observer,* 19 March, https://www.theguardian.com/music/2006/mar/19/2. Accessed 23 January 2019.

Smeaton, Bob (2015), *How to Make a Number One Record*, UK: BBC.

Stanley, Bob (2013), *Yeah Yeah Yeah: The Story of Modern Pop*, London: Faber and Faber.

Sun, Hyojung (2019), *Digital Revolution Tamed: The Case of the Recording Industry*, Basingstoke: Palgrave Macmillan.

Sutherland, Mark (2016a), 'Could the charts run out of stream?', *Music Week,* 25 July, p. 1.

——— (2016b), 'The revolution will be analysed', *Music Week,* 28 November, pp. 10–12.

——— (2017a), '1 Direction', *Music Week,* 6 February, pp. 10–12.

——— (2017b), 'Chart breakers', *Music Week,* 26 June, p. 1.

Trust, Gary (2013), 'Ask Billboard: How does the Hot 100 work?', *Billboard,* 29 September, https://www.billboard.com/articles/columns/ask-billboard/5740625/ask-billboard-how-does-the-hot-100-work. Accessed 23 January 2019.

Weisbard, Eric (2014), *Top 40 Democracy: The Rival Mainstreams of American Music*, Chicago and London: University of Chicago Press.

Whalley, Ben (2012), *Pop Charts Britannia: 60 Years of the Top 10*, UK: BBC.

Williams, Paul (2007), 'Rampant digital revives charts at physical singles' expense', *Music Week*, 19 May, pp. 12–13.

Williamson, Coral (2016), 'On trend: New OCC Chart will highlight tomorrow's hits today', *Music Week,* 15 February, p. 4.

2

The Gold Disc: One Million Pop Fans Can't Be Wrong

Richard Osborne

One million is the magic number, or is it 500,000, or 100,000 or 400,000? The recording industry has a confusing relationship with statistics. Looked at from one perspective, sales figures are central to its operations. In this chapter I am going to explore the phenomenon of gold, silver, platinum and diamond discs; awards that are presented to artists and industry personnel when specified sales or 'equivalent sales' have been achieved. Although other cultural industries have their sales charts – the *New York Times* has been publishing its lists of best-selling books since 1931, and the box office returns of movies have been enumerated since *Birth of a Nation* in 1915 – the recording industry is alone in offering trophies based on the number of copies sold. These awards are more than markers of success; they provide a symbol of the recording industry's preferred business model. This is an industry in which the recording is central and sales numbers are fetishized.

Yet the recording industry is also vague when it comes to calculating its returns. The sales charts for books give a clear indication of the number of items retailed, while box office figures signal the gross revenue that a film has achieved. It is also usually possible to find out the production costs of a film and thus make some estimates regarding its profits. In comparison, *Billboard* in the United States and the Official Charts Company in the United Kingdom do not publish a record's sales figures or streaming data as part of their charts. The only indicator in both cases is a symbol to indicate that a record that has achieved a gold, platinum, silver or diamond award. It is as though any sales figure between zero and award status is not worth noting. In addition, the recording industry is reticent about disclosing the costs of any given recording, as well as the differing royalty rates its artists receive.

It is perhaps obvious why the book and film industries do not hand out sales awards. The two art forms have a financial and generic diversity that would render the idea absurd. This obviousness should make us think again about the recording industry: is it really so homogenized that sales awards can work fairly for all? The rules for receiving these awards are statistically rigid: all artists working within a territory have the same target to work towards; these targets are published freely; there is one local governing body that oversees them. At the same time, there is an elasticity about these awards that hints at the wider diversity of the recording industry: the numbers needed to achieve award status have differed between territories and have shifted over time. The awards have also been adapted to encompass new recording formats, such as downloads and streams. The incorporation of streaming raises a further question. Why does the industry continue to issue awards based on the sales of singles and albums when the consumption of streamed music utilizes a different model?

In the following I shall highlight some of the standards and variables relating to the gold disc and its elementary partners. I shall look at the history of these trophies and examine the rules by which they can be acquired. I shall also examine the record company accounting that the sales awards tend to obscure. In addition, I shall address the continuing use of these awards in the digital age. Finally, I shall look at the musical culture that the awards endorse, examining their impact upon artistic creation and audience reception. To explore these themes I will address the recording industries in the United States and the United Kingdom. The sales awards are both local and global in nature. The International Federation of Phonographic Industry (IFPI) lists over 50 territories that operate an award scheme. It also acknowledges the different criteria that each territory utilizes (IFPI 2018: 133). Therefore, while much that follows can be applied broadly, regional differences should also be borne in mind.

The origins of the gold disc

Joseph Murrells, in his history of the gold disc, states that the 'exact point in time when a golden disc was first given by a company to an artist has not been established' (1974: 7). His own candidate for the original recipient is the violinist Marie Hall, who in 1905 was awarded a 'presentation charm bracelet [that] was made of gold and pearls and displayed a minute violin, a tapered gramophone arm, and seven tiny *golden discs*, representing her seven best selling records' (1974: 7, original emphasis). Later awards have not featured miniaturized discs but have instead been copies of actual records. The first award to bear a similarity to those issued today was presented on 10 February 1942, marking 1,200,000 sales of Glen Miller's 'Chattanooga Choo Choo'. Miller was given a master copy of the record, which was painted gold and framed. Attached to the presentation box was a plaque that noted the sales that had been amassed.

While Miller was the first artist to receive a gold disc, it was Elvis Presley who did most to institutionalize the award. Ed Ward has claimed that the singer received his first gold record in April 1956, stating that it was 'an award RCA invented especially for him' (1986: 120). This is not true. RCA Victor was after all also Glenn Miller's record company. What is nevertheless certain is that Presley increased the currency of the gold disc. In 1958 he became one of the first popular music artists to have their hits gathered together on a long playing record. This release was given a significant title: *Elvis' Golden Records*. There is a simple reason why Presley was RCA Victor's golden artist: he was selling a huge quantity of discs. Five months after his first RCA Victor release he was responsible for half the company's popular music revenue, and a decade later he was still making up a quarter of RCA Victor's record sales (Jorgensen 1998: 48; Chapple and Garofalo 1977: 210). More broadly, the rock 'n' roll era was the point at which the recording industry gained a firm ascendancy over the music publishing industry (Garofalo 2005: 70). This transformation had already been underway[1]: the arrival of singles charts based on the sales of recordings had been indicative of the trend (in America, *Billboard*'s 'best sellers in stores' chart began in 1940; in Britain, the first singles chart was published in 1952). The success of Presley and his contemporaries confirmed the change. This was the case in America, where in 'the new order of rock'n'roll, sheet-music sales and public performances followed a successful recording' (Millard 1995: 257), as well as in the United Kingdom, where *Record Mirror* reported, '[i]f there has been a decline in sheet music sales in 1957 then some of the blame must be laid at the door of the R and R craze' (Conley 1957: 84).

The Recording Industry Association of America (RIAA) formalized the award programme on 14 March 1958, when Perry Como, another RCA Victor artist, received their first official gold disc for his single 'Catch a Falling Star' (RIAA's first gold album was the cast recording of *Oklahoma!*, which was given its award four months later). Como's record company were celebratory of his achievements: in 1958 they released an album titled *Como's Golden Records*. RIAA have wished to associate their award with other forms of music, however. In 2008, they chose to celebrate the fiftieth anniversary of their golden records, not with Como's music, but instead with Presley's 'Hard Headed Woman', which on 11 August 1958 became the singer's first single to receive the trade body-authorized gold disc (RIAA 2008). It was rock 'n' roll and not Como's easy listening that placed the record centre stage. While 'Catch a Falling Star' worked well as print music, 'Hard Headed Woman' did not. In 1957 the *Melody Maker* reported that 'the successful Rock-'n'-Roll numbers were only hits on a record and just didn't mean a thing so far as sheet music was concerned' (David 1957: 10), and in 1958 the publisher

Bill Phillips stated '[s]ure, rock sells records – *but not music*' (Nicholl 1957: 8, original emphasis). More than other genres, it made sense to represent rock 'n' roll success with a gold disc. This was the starting point for new forms of popular music where the golden record could serve as a business model as well as an award.

IFPI has been keen to perpetuate the idea that recording is at the centre of the music industries. Biannually from 2010 until 2016, the organization published reports titled *Investing in Music*. These reports denigrate the importance of live music income as well as the ability of artists to go the DIY digital route (IFPI 2012: 4, 5). IFPI argue that 'if an artist wishes to sell their music in significant volume and attract large audiences, they need the support of a major or independent record company' (IFPI 2012: 5). Their mention of 'significant volume' is important. IFPI define 'commercial success' as 'breaking an artist to Gold or Platinum status in an individual market' (IFPI 2012: 11). We need to examine what this status is, before considering why IFPI's criterion of success is set so high.

The gold standard

There has been more than one gold standard. There is confusion, in fact, about the amount needed to acquire the first official awards. RIAA state that '[i]n the beginning, there was only a Gold® album award for the sale of 500,000 copies' (2014a). In contrast, Murrells believes that gold discs were first certified by RIAA for '1,000,000 single sales and a gross of 1,000,000 dollars for album sales' (1974: 7). The difference in procedure for singles and albums is indicative of the fact that albums used to sell in fewer numbers than singles but were more highly priced; thus, it would be easier for them to achieve a million dollars in revenue than a million copies sold. This measurement nevertheless demonstrates how the quantities sold to achieve award status have fluctuated.

Although they do not readily admit it, RIAA have shifted their standards several times. In 1976 the organization introduced its platinum award, which could be gained by achieving one million album sales or two million singles sales. To achieve a gold record for an album, an artist now had to sell 500,000 copies of their release. In 1989 the figures for single sales were halved. Artists had to sell 500,000 copies to achieve gold status and one million for platinum. This reflected an overall downturn in the importance of this format in America. In comparison, album sales continued to grow. Consequently, in 1999 the diamond award was introduced, celebrating records that achieved ten million sales (RIAA 2017).

In the United Kingdom the qualifying sales tallies have also changed. The British Phonographic Industry (BPI) was set up in 1973, launching its own awards in the same year. At first its scheme shared the same split between singles (copies sold) and albums (gross revenue received) as the United States. An artist would have to achieve sales of 500,000 singles to receive a gold disc and 1,000,000 for platinum. For albums they would have to generate £150,000 to receive a gold disc and £1 million for platinum. The gross-revenue figure for albums shifted several times in the 1970s before being switched to a copies sold target in 1979. This manoeuvre was qualified by the fact that differently priced LPs needed to sell different amounts: those with a dealer price below £2.24 had to sell 200,000 units to achieve gold and 600,000 to achieve platinum; for LPs priced above this the targets were halved. These dealer prices have been altered periodically and so has the tally for singles. In 1989 it was reduced to 400,000 to achieve gold and 600,000 to achieve platinum. Indicative of the fact that the United Kingdom is a smaller market than the United States, there is no diamond award. BPI have instead created a lower silver award, which artists could originally achieve by selling 250,000 singles or £75,000 worth of LPs. As of January 2019, the criteria for achieving this trophy were set at 200,000 singles or 60,000 full-price albums.

Writing in 1974, Murrells stated that the differing amounts between territories were derived by 'taking into consideration the total population of the country concerned, these being their equivalent of a "million" sales' (1974: 8). Curiously, the figures do equate for the United States and the United Kingdom today: if we take recent population figures, to achieve a gold album in each country that record would have to be bought by approximately 0.16 per cent of the population (the census figures for the United States from 2010 give a population total of 308,745,539, while those for the United Kingdom from 2011 have its population at 63,181,775). Nevertheless, the changing tallies throw into question any clear link between population size and the awards given out. These differing amounts also cast doubt on the idea that commercial success can be equated with 'Gold or Platinum status in an individual market'. A record does not cost less to create and to promote just because you are in a smaller country. The recording industries' economies of scale do not work this way (MMC 1994: s. 285).

Breakeven points

The crucial determinant in calculating the profitability of a record is its breakeven point: the amount of copies it needs to sell (or the number of times it needs to be played) to generate a profit. The recording industry has a maxim: 'revenue is vanity, profit is sanity' (Sutherland 2019). Yet this is a factor that the sales awards obfuscate. It is also a factor that is hard to calculate, as breakeven points have varied across time and between releases.

Writing about the UK music industry in 1978, Simon Frith suggested that '[t]he average single costs about £2,000 to make, the average album £15-20,000', while 'costs of promotion and advertising start from about £2,000 a record' (1978: 117). This was an era in which artists used professional studios to make their recordings and major record companies controlled the manufacturing and distribution processes. Consequently, expenditure on each release remained fairly consistent. Frith equated the breakeven point for singles with Top 30 chart success, meaning that a 45rpm disc of this era would have to sell around 20,000 copies to achieve a profit. For albums he leant towards IFPI's model of equating commercial success with sales awards. However, he selected the lower silver award, which in this era was set at £100,000 in sales, or roughly 30,000 LPs (1978: 118).

The late 1970s was nevertheless a period in which new business strategies were being employed. Some UK independent record labels were making records that were relatively cheap to produce and market. Dave Laing suggested that

> By dispensing with the need for expensive productions, promotional staff and the other overheads of chart-oriented companies, Stiff and the other small record labels which set up from 1977 onwards to release punk rock and new wave material, could work to 'break-even' figures which could be as low as 2000 copies for a single.
>
> (1985: 10)

This represents only ten per cent of Frith's target.

The reason for the discrepancy between Frith's and Laing's figures is the different business ideals that the major and independent companies were operating. While the smaller companies wanted (and needed) to achieve profitability with the majority of records they released, the major record companies had been adopting a 'mud-against-the-wall approach' to their release schedules, issuing a large variety of records into the marketplace in the hope that some would stick around as 'hits'. Estimates of the success rate for this approach have varied, but the most commonly cited ratio is one-in-ten. The major labels' policy could be witnessed in a fatalistic belief that there 'are no formulas for producing a hit record' (Hirsch 1971–72: 664). Paul Hirsch noted that '[u]nder these conditions it apparently is more efficient to produce many "failures" for each success than to sponsor fewer items and pretest each on a massive scale to increase media coverage and consumer sales' (1971–72: 652). This is not to say that the majors spent less money on promoting each individual record than the independent companies. The reverse is the case (MMC 1994: s. 6.30, s. 10.49, s. 12.150; Dannen 2003: 264).

The seemly democratic sales target of the gold disc has hidden a bias towards the major labels' way of doing things. If the tallies are supposed to equate to commercial success, then this is success as defined by the larger companies' breakeven points. A cheaply made record might be more profitable than a high-profile release even if it is selling fewer copies, yet this has meant nothing when it comes to the awards, which have been based on total sales or gross revenue only (Jones 1997: 61–62; MMC 1994: s. 2.135). Moreover, it is not just the bottom line for the record companies that these trophies have obscured. They provide no indication of the share of sales revenue that an artist might receive.

Artists' income

There are two times in an artist's career when they are most likely to be photographed alongside recording industry personnel. One is when they are signing their contracts; the other is if they are lucky enough to be presented with a sales award. The lack of evidence of interaction between these two parties at other times is telling. Few pictures have been taken of A&R staff or marketing teams in action. In particular, it is unusual to see them working together with artists in the creation of the final product. This could, in part, be due to romantic ideals: the audience wants to feel that musicians and singers are the principal authors of the music. It could also be reflective of high rates of failure. Responsibility for the product is placed squarely with the artists. Unless the record happens to be a success, that is, at which point industry personnel re-enter the frame.

If one aim of sales award photographs is to emphasize the industry's contribution to artistic success at the moment of triumph, another is to pronounce the artist's share of the company's success. The gold disc symbolizes an industry in which an artist's income is tied to the number of records they sell for their label. However, just as with the breakeven point, this is a playing field that is skewed. Although gold disc status should at least ensure profitability, it does not mean that there is parity among recording deals.

One important discrepancy is royalty rates, which can vary widely. Some independent and production companies offer 50/50 contracts, whereby an artist gains 50 per cent of the profits once costs have been recouped. In contrast, many artists who have exclusive recording contracts with major companies will receive half that percentage for record sales at most, albeit that royalty rates have varied in accordance with different types of product and they have also generally improved over time. The independent contract might offer an artist a more profitable contract, but in the 50/50 deal all costs need to be covered before royalties are paid. In contrast, recoupment in many exclusive contracts is restricted to recording costs, video costs and personal advances (Harrison 2017: 88).

Record contracts have also differed when it comes to deductions and reductions. In relation to physical product (and sometimes to digital product too), money has been deducted from artists' royalties in order to account for special packaging and to cover the record companies in the case of breakages and faulty products. While the amounts charged have been fairly standard, they have varied according to contract and the format of release. It has also been possible for some artists to demand their removal. Moreover, as we progress through the twenty-first century such deductions are finally becoming a thing of the past (Harrison 2017: 98). Artists' royalty rates have been further reduced if their recordings are advertised on television or sold at a budget price. In many cases they will have little control over these promotional decisions. Although these policies have been adopted to gain a sales boost, the trade bodies have paid little attention to them when handing out awards. RIAA and BPI have not been particularly stringent when it comes to accounting for the budgeting of records by major record labels and they have not taken into account product that is advertised (RIAA 2019b).

Regarding physical products, the award schemes have received criticism for being based on the amount of records shipped to retailers rather than using sales-based evidence derived from barcodes (RIAA 2019b). In America the award calculations factor in records that have been returned to record companies by retailers, thus rendering moot the old industry joke that a record has 'shipped gold and returned platinum' (Dannen 2003: 167–68). They do not, however, take into account the number of records that sit unsold on store shelves (RIAA 2019b). In Britain the rules are looser: to qualify, a record company merely has to provide evidence of 'firm, invoiced sales to the trade' (BPI 2009).

The trade organizations in the two countries differ when it comes to factoring in promotional copies. According to RIAA's audit requirements '[p]romotional radio and press copies, cut-outs, inventory sell-offs, and surplus sales are not included toward certification' and neither are 'promotional track downloads' (RIAA 2019b). BPI qualifying criteria make no mention of these factors. Record contracts are usually clear on this point, however, commonly deducting as much as fifteen per cent of a record's sales from royalty calculations to factor in a 'free goods' allowance (Harrison 2017: 98). The labels claim that this allowance is 'irrelevant' for the majority of artists because 90 per cent of them fail to reach breakeven points and therefore are not receiving royalties anyway (MMC 1994: s. 12.161). They fail to point out that the imposition of this allowance makes it harder for artists to recoup.

Record companies are able to request award certification quickly. In America, sales of physical albums become eligible 30 days after a product is released (RIAA 2019b). In Britain it used to be the case that companies could apply when their recording had reached 'the appropriate level of sales' (BPI 2009).[2] Awards have therefore been granted before the true retail profile of a record has been established. In comparison, when it comes to an artist's royalties, it has been common practice for record companies to hold a reserve against possible returns. Donald S. Passman provides the example that 'if a company ships 100,000 records of an artist, they may only pay the artist on 65,000 of these and wait to see if the other 35,000 are returned' (2014: 79). Here, rather than establishing a sales record after 30 days, the record company can wait up to two years to pay the artist for the proportion of the reserve that has actually been sold (Passman 2014: 79–80).

Despite differences between recording contracts, all artists working within a territory are judged according to the same sales award rules. As with the costs of recordings, little information about recording contracts is made publicly available. The apparent simplicity of sales award criteria hides the complexity of record companies' financial and contractual operations. Moreover, these operations have only grown more complex and diverse in the digital age. There are many oddities about the perpetuation of sales awards based on physical products in the era of downloads and streaming, and in some ways these awards are now performing more of a cover-up operation than they did before. In the remainder of this chapter, I will explore the awards' transformation in the modern era. Just as significantly, I shall look at ways they have remained the same. I shall close by looking at the reactions of artists and consumers to the golden ideal.

Embracing change in the digital era

BPI and RIAA have made efforts to keep up with digital trends. BPI has allowed downloads to contribute to sales figures for their awards since 2004. RIAA also incorporated downloads in 2004, introducing a new 'Digital Single Sales Award' in this year. The two organizations have additionally incorporated streaming data in their awards calculations. Reflecting the lack of physical single sales in the United States, RIAA's awards for singles are now wholly digital: 'on-demand audio and/or video song streams' have been tabulated along with downloads since May 2013 (RIAA 2017). RIAA also include streams alongside downloads and physical sales for their album awards. BPI has included streams for its singles awards since July 2014, and for its album awards since June 2015.

If RIAA and BPI had not incorporated this data, their awards would have become outmoded. They would have been ignoring the most popular ways of consuming music and it would have been hard for artists to reach unit thresholds on the sales of physical products alone. However, while the purchase of downloads is akin to the purchase of vinyl records and CDs, streaming works on a different model. Songs and albums are not paid for on a per-item basis.

Consumers either pay a monthly subscription to access the 'premium' versions of the streaming sites or alternatively no fee is paid if they elect 'advertising-supported' versions instead.

RIAA and BPI have nevertheless chosen to view each stream as a sale. RIAA's initial calculation for singles was that 100 streams would equal one download sale (RIAA 2014b). In January 2016, this was increased to 150 streams per download (RIAA 2019a). This was reflective of the increased popularity of streaming, rather than indicating any change in breakeven points or royalties paid to artists. BPI's ratios are based on those established by the Official Charts Company for its singles chart. They began with a 100:1 streams-to-sale ratio, which was increased to 150:1 in January 2017, and was subsequently recalibrated in June 2018 to a rate for subscription services of 100:1 and for ad-supported of 600:1 (BPI 2019). The organizations have different criteria for album awards. RIAA's calculation is '1,500 on-demand audio and/or video song streams = 10 track sales = 1 album sale' (RIAA 2019). BPI quantify the twelve most-streamed tracks from the standard version of an album; the two most popular songs are then 'down-weighted' and made equivalent to the average figure of the ten remaining tracks; the total is then divided by 1000 and added to the physical and download sales of the album to determine the award (BPI 2017). Ignoring the fact that many listeners consume streams via playlists rather than in the form of older recording formats, this convoluted methodology has been introduced in the United Kingdom in an attempt to distinguish between the consumption of streams as 'singles' or as 'albums'. RIAA and BPI also diverge when it comes to video streaming. RIAA includes 'official label/company videos' towards certification, but 'user-generated videos' do not qualify (RIAA 2019a). As of January 2019, BPI does not incorporate video streams in their certifications.

As these fluctuating and diverging criteria make clear, there are problems in equating sales with streams. Nevertheless, there are ways in which download and streaming data provide a more accurate picture of the sales and usage of music than has previously been available. When it comes to downloading, no reserves can be held against sales; thus, the tally that goes towards the sales award is more in keeping with royalties that artists receive. In respect of streaming, the access-based figures help to remove some doubts that might previously have been held about the use value of a record. This factor is somewhat negated, however, due to the fact that if a song is played for at least 30 seconds and then skipped it will still count towards the sales awards (Official Charts Company 2017). There are also new problems to consider. Is the consumption of audio streams via playlists passive? Does the inclusion of YouTube figures in RIAA's tally reflect music usage or are some videos clocking up viewing figures because they offer some mild curiosity or titillation to the consumer? In addition, the omission of user-generated videos hints at the digital world that escapes copyright and royalties.

Ultimately, while the trade bodies have embraced digital formats, it can be argued that they have done so without acknowledging the major changes these technologies have entailed. Moreover, they continue to honour both the sales and streams of intangible digitized music with an award that is physical in nature and which celebrates the mass reproduction of singles and albums.

Ignoring change in the digital era

The sales awards have become deliberately old fashioned. During the 1980s and 1990s most of the awards handed out were framed compact discs, appropriately so as this was the leading format for much of this period. Today, despite the fact that vinyl record sales are dwarfed by streaming activity and remain lower than the sales of compact discs, it is this format that is being used for the awards. Many of the trophies look similar to those given to Elvis Presley in the 1950s. They feature vinyl discs that have been metalized, tinted and framed. This peculiarity is being taken to extremes in America, where some artists are being awarded vinyl albums to mark the popularity of digital single releases.[3] The awards have always been symbolic rather than functional objects,[4] representing an industry that is focused on the sales of recordings and in which the record company is the locus of power. In the digital era this symbolic function has been extended: in the return to the vinyl record, the sales awards imply continuity in a world that has changed.

One striking thing about IFPI's definition of commercial success as 'breaking an artist to Gold or Platinum status in an individual market' is that it is being applied in the twenty-first century. The awards are derived in concept and appearance from the physical record, yet since the early 2000s overall sales of physical records have been in decline and recordings have formed a decreasing share of total music industry revenue. The latter transformation is, of course, one of the reasons why IFPI is upholding the sales award. They wish to perpetuate the idea that recording remains at the centre of the popular music industries.

As record sales have declined in importance, their breakeven point has become more variable. Although it was possible for Frith and Laing to suggest figures in the 1970s, there can be no such certainty today. It is possible to make and distribute recordings cheaply. On the other hand, because of the openness of the digital environment, huge expenditure can be involved in trying to ensure that a new record is heard. According to IFPI, a newly signed artist can cost up to $2 million promote (IFPI 2016: 6). With an average dealer price for an album of $8, this would mean that 250,000 copies (and streaming equivalents) would need to be sold for the project to break even. Some records have to sell far more than this. For example, it has been suggested that Lady Gaga's record label Interscope spent between $25 and $30 million on the production and promotion of her 2013 album *Artpop* (Houghton 2013b). With such a figure it would be virtually impossible for an artist to earn back their recording advance through sales alone, even if reaching gold or platinum status.

The widely publicized 360° deal is indicative of the fact that record companies have searched beyond recordings for sources of revenue. In return for providing marketing, promotion and touring support for an act, the record company expects a share of an artist's profits from areas such as merchandising, brand sponsorship and ticket sales. In these instances, it is particularly problematic to equate 'commercial success' with a sales tally, as breakeven points are spread across a broad spectrum of activities (Pakinkis 2015: 15). These 360° deals obviously affect the incomes of artists too: the sources of revenue have diversified, but artists are paying back money from more areas as well.

This is not the case for all performers, however. Some of them have gained increased control of their careers. Here too, we can witness a turn away from a concentration on record sales. In 2007, Prince's album *Planet Earth* was not sold in record stores or via websites in the United Kingdom; it was instead given away free with the *Mail on Sunday*. In return Prince was reported to have earned £250,000 from the newspaper (Forde 2012: 39). In 2013, Jay-Z distributed one million copies of his album *Magna Carta Holy Grail* for free to Samsung customers. His fee for doing so was a rumoured $5 million from the company. While these 'sales' were ruled out of his *Billboard* chart placing, they were said to have earned him a 'multi-platinum award for his wall' (Houghton 2013a).

Some artists have reduced the bottom line. Released in 2007, Radiohead's *In Rainbows* was first issued according to a 'pay what you want' basis. The album is reported to have turned a profit on these initial sales alone, largely because Radiohead had few production and distribution overheads, while the novel sales tactic generated a considerable amount of free publicity (Wikström 2013: 113). In 2013, another innovative method of release received widespread attention. Amanda Palmer was dropped by her label for selling only 25,000 copies of an album, a figure far below sales award status (Palmer 2013). She was nevertheless able to generate large revenues for her subsequent album, *Theatre is Evil*, by approaching customers directly. Rather than buying a ready-made CD, they were asked to donate funds towards its creation, and would eventually receive a copy when the album was complete. Palmer managed to raise $1,192,793, constituting 'the biggest music crowd-funding project to date' (Palmer 2013). The money came from 24,883 fans, roughly the same number that led to her being dropped (Palmer 2013).

It has therefore been possible for some artists to escape the gold and platinum standard. In some instances they have not needed to sell their recordings to make money; in others they have not needed to attain award status to generate a profit. For other artists, the maintenance of these awards is problematic. They further the recording industry's inference that downloading and streaming are akin to the sale of a physical product. This, in turn, has helped the companies to uphold traditional contractual policies. While some new signings, independent acts and superstar artists might be able to set their terms in accordance with the digital environment, this is not the case for the majority of artists who were contracted before downloads and streaming were popularized (Ingham 2018). Despite the fact that their record companies' manufacturing and distribution overheads have been vastly reduced and their digital products should not warrant deductions, they will be receiving the same royalty rates for downloads and streams as for physical releases.

While the sales awards provide a mask of continuity, there is also some truth in IFPI's arguments. The revenue generated by recordings might be declining in importance, but recording itself remains primary in the music industries. In most cases, live tours and merchandising follow on from the creation of new records, rather than the other way around. In these circumstances, it is not surprising that these sales awards continue to be embraced by the majority of artists who are in a position to attain them. RIAA and BPI have created Facebook pages for their trophies, providing photographs of winners receiving their tinctured discs. Moreover, it can be argued that as well as there being a commercial need for records to achieve golden status, there is a cultural one as well.

The golden audience

The large sales and streaming tally required to receive a sales award is, in part, a result of the poor success ratios of the recording industry. This is a business that requires vast returns from its successful artists to offset losses from its failures. It is centred on hits: records that are ideally successful on a global scale. When it comes to audiences, there are both pessimistic and optimistic ways of reading this situation. The pessimistic view is that the bigger a hit becomes, the more it is forced upon the public. The recordings that receive gold awards are the ones that are most enmeshed within the capitalist system. What is selected for this process is music that, rather than challenging capitalist ideology, renders it safe. Classically, this is the 'hypodermic syringe' model of culture in which popular music acts as an opiate of the people (Abercrombie and Longhurst 1998: 5).

The optimistic way of looking at this situation is to suggest that the public is active in its response to popular music. It is even possible to argue that the more successful a recording is, the more it becomes the people's music. Contrary to the belief that the public is injected with the biggest hits, it is when a record attracts a large audience that it escapes the chicanery of the recording and media industries. Although records can be hyped into the charts, they can only become hits on a golden scale if they genuinely connect with the public (Dannen 2003: 15; Smeaton 2015).

What happens when a recording receives a mass audience? Some artists have talked with enthusiasm about the ways their work is taken over and reworked by the public. Manfred Mann claimed that 'the more people buy a record, the more successful it is – not only commercially but artistically' (Frith 1978: 202), while Imogen Heap has stated 'unless somebody else hears it, music is like a joke without a punchline' (Kappala-Ramsamy 2010). It has been suggested that the more successful a recording is, the more it becomes public property. Speaking of their hit 'One Day Like This', Mark Potter of Elbow has stated, '[w]e don't own that song any more [...]. It's grown legs and it's doing its own thing' (Lynskey 2014: 41). Danny Boyle was able to convince Mike Oldfield to perform *Tubular Bells* at the London Olympics in 2012 because this platinum record 'does belong to Britain' ('Tubular Bells' 2013).

This leaves us in a peculiar situation. The gold disc is reflective of a recording industry that sets the bar for success at what can be regarded as an artificially high level. Yet when it comes to audiences the consequences can be viewed positively. It results in music that has a dynamic public life. By the same measure, some of the twenty-first century business models cannot be viewed as being successful. The album releases by Amanda Palmer and Prince, for example, are better known for their economic strategies than for their music; they have had little public resonance. The gold disc may be bogus, biased, duplicitous, capitalistic and out-of-date, but perhaps it also results in something that is good. What if the most useful popular music comes from stars who are golden and whose record sales are huge?

NOTES

1. Undertaking a copyright study for the US government, William M. Blaisdell reported that, '[b]etween 1951 and 1955, while sheet music royalty payments fell by 44 percent in volume, the volume of mechanical royalty payments by record producers to music publishers increased by 60 percent' (1960: 94).
2. Downloading and streaming work differently, resulting in the fact that titles are 'automatically certified' when they have 'reached the appropriate level of sales as measured by the Official Charts Company' (BPI 2019).
3. For examples see the website for the official framing company, 'Jewel Box Platinum': http://jewelboxplatinum.com.
4. It has never been possible to play a gold disc: they are rendered inert by their coating and due to the fact they have been framed. In addition, the awards have usually housed the

wrong record: the disc in the frame rarely corresponds with the disc whose sales are being honoured: a close look at its grooves gives away this fact.

REFERENCES

Abercrombie, Nicholas and Longhurst, Brian (1998), *Audiences: A Sociological Theory of Performance and Imagination,* London: Sage.

Blaisdell, William M. (1960), *The Economic Aspects of the Compulsory License,* Washington: United States Government Printing Office.

British Phonographic Industry (BPI) (2009), *Certified Awards – Rules for Eligibility*, London: BPI.

——— (2017), 'BPI's iconic album awards to include audio streams', 11 June, http://www.bpi.co.uk/home/BPIs-Iconic-Album-Awards-to-Include-Audio-Streams.aspx. Accessed 11 June 2018.

——— (2019), 'Award levels', https://www.bpi.co.uk/brit-certified/award-levels/. Accessed 25 January 2019.

Chapple, Steve and Garofalo, Reebee (1977), *Rock 'n' Roll is Here to Pay: The History of Politics of the Music Industry*, Chicago: Nelson-Hall.

Conley, Len (1957), 'The big trend: Return of the ballad ... Sheet-music sales back to normal', *Record Mirror*, 28 December, pp. 84–85.

Dannen, Fredric (2003), *Hit Men: Power Brokers and Fast Money Inside the Music Business,* London: Helter Skelter.

David, Hubert W. (1957), 'Songsheet', *Melody Maker*, 19 January, p. 10.

Forde, Eamonn (2012), 'Loss leaders', *The Word*, April, pp. 38–39.

Frith, Simon (1978), *The Sociology of Rock,* London: Constable.

Garofalo, Reebee (2005), *Rockin' Out: Popular Music in the U.S.A.*, Boston: Prentice Hall.

Harrison, Ann (2017), *Music: The Business: The Essential Guide to the Law and the Deals,* 7th ed., London: Virgin.

Hirsch, Paul (1971-72), 'Processing fads and fashions', *American Journal of Sociology*, 77:4, pp. 639–59.

Houghton, Bruce (2013a), 'Billboard reminds how antiquated their charts are with rejection of 1M Jay-Z Samsung albums', *Hypebot.com*, 21 June, https://www.hypebot.com/hypebot/2013/06/billboard-reminds-how-antiquated-their-charts-are-with-rejection-of-1m-jay-z-samsung-albums.html. Accessed 25 January 2019.

——— (2013b), 'Fumbled Lady Gaga release could cost Interscope $25 million', *Hypebot.com*, 18 November, http://www.hypebot.com/hypebot/2013/11/lady-gaga-sales-slump-could-cost-interscope-25m-and-what-that-says-about-the-record-biz.html. Accessed 25 January 2019.

Ingham, Tim (2018), 'Spotify's direct distribution deals: What do artists get paid?', 23 September, https://www.musicbusinessworldwide.com/spotifys-direct-distribution-deals-what-do-the-artists-get/. Accessed 12 February 2020.

International Federation of the Phonographic Industry (IFPI) (2012), 'Investing in music: How music companies discover, nurture and promote talent', http://www.ifpi.org/content/library/investing_in_music.pdf. Accessed 25 January 2013 [no longer available].

——— (2016), 'Investing in music: The value of record companies', http://www.ifpi.org/investing-in-music.php. Accessed 25 January 2019 [no longer available].

——— (2018), *Global Music Report 2018: Full Report: Data and Analysis*, London: IFPI.

Jones, Michael (1997), 'Organising pop: Why so few acts make pop music', Ph.D. thesis, Liverpool: University of Liverpool.

Jorgensen, Ernst (1998), *Elvis Presley: A Life in Music*, New York: St. Martin's Press.

Kappala-Ramsamy, Gemma (2010), 'Imogen Heap: "Unless somebody else hears it, music is like a joke without a punchline"', *Observer*, 7 November, https://www.theguardian.com/music/2010/nov/07/imogen-heap-interview. Accessed 25 January 2019.

Laing, Dave (1985), *One Chord Wonders,* Milton Keynes: Open University Press.

Lynskey, Dorian (2014), 'Happy landing', *Q*, 333, pp. 34–42.

Millard, Andre (1995), *America on Record: A History of Recorded Sound*, Cambridge: CUP.

Monopolies and Mergers Commission (MMC) (1994), *The Supply of Recorded Music: A Report on the Supply in the UK of Prerecorded Compact Discs, Vinyl Discs and Tapes Containing Music*, London: HSMO.

Murrells, Joseph (1974), *The Book of Golden Discs*, London: Barrie & Jenkins.

Nicholl, Gee (1957), 'R. 'n' roll brings sheet music slump', *Record Mirror*, 16 February, p. 8.

O'Casey, Matt (2013), *Tubular Bells: The Mike Oldfield Story*, UK: BBC.

Official Charts Company (2017), 'Meeting the chart rules', http://www.officialcharts.com/getting-into-the-charts/meeting-the-chart-rules/. Accessed 25 January 2018.

Pakinkis, Tom (2015), 'The death of the million seller?', *Music Week*, 6 February, pp. 14–16.

Palmer, Amanda (2013), '"The art of asking", TED: Ideas worth spreading', http://www.ted.com/talks/amanda_palmer_the_art_of_asking.html. Accessed 25 January 2019.

Passman, Donald S. (2014), *All You Need to Know About the Music Business*, 8th ed., New York: Free Press.

Recording Industry Association of America (RIAA) (2008), 'RIAA celebrates 50 years of Golden Records', http://www.riaa.com/newsitem.php?id=7B0D4A07-0D23-A750-0BE1-22882C5C2F13. Accessed 25 January 2015 [no longer available].

——— (2014a), 'History of the awards', http://www.riaa.com/goldandplatinum.php?content_selector=historyx. Accessed 25 January 2015 [no longer available].

——— (2014b), 'New "combined" digital', http://www.riaa.com/goldandplatinum.php?content_selector=new-combined-GP. Accessed 25 January 2015.

——— (2017), 'Gold and platinum: Story of gold and platinum', https://www.riaa.com/gold-platinum/story/. Accessed 25 January 2018.

——— (2019a), 'About the awards', https://www.riaa.com/gold-platinum/about-awards/. Accessed 25 January 2019.

——— (2019b), 'RIAA and GR&F certification audit requirements RIAA album award, http://www.riaa.com/wp-content/uploads/2017/06/ALBUM-AWARD-RIAA-AND-GRF-CERTIFICATION-AUDIT-REQUIREMENTS.pdf. Accessed 25 January 2019.

Smeaton, Bob (2015), *How to Make a Number One Record*, UK: BBC.

Stratton, Jon (1982), 'Capitalism and romantic ideology in the record business', *Popular Music*, 3, pp. 143–56.

Sutherland, Mark (2019), 'Never mind the revenues, profit is the real key to music biz revival', *Music Week*, 25 March, http://www.musicweek.com/opinion/read/never-mind-the-revenues-profit-is-the-real-key-to-the-music-biz-revival/075711. Accessed 3 April 2019.

Ward, Ed (1986), 'The fifties and before', in E. Ward, G. Stokes and K. Tucker (eds), *Rock of Ages: The Rolling Stone History of Rock and Roll*, Harmondsworth: Penguin, pp. 17–246.

Wikström, Patrik (2013), *The Music Industry: Music in the Cloud*, 2nd ed., Cambridge: Polity Press.

3

'I am a One in Ten': Success Ratios in the Recording Industry

Richard Osborne

There is a ratio that record companies repeatedly state: they claim that theirs is a business in which only one in ten succeeds. This figure was cited at least as early as the 1950s and is still in use today. It masks a great deal of human fall-out. Artists' dreams are shattered and projects come to nought. It could also be considered poor business practice: how have record companies managed to be so profligate for so long? Michael Jones has argued that '[w]e do not have to ask why the music industry lives with such a high failure rate; the answer is, simply and quite brutally, because it can afford to' (Jones 1997: 28). The industry works to a simple formula, calculating that 'as little as 10% of new material must make a profit large enough to offset losses on the majority of releases' (Vogel 2011: 261).

Yet this failure rate is worth probing further. What I wish to underline in this chapter is the extent to which record companies can afford failure because of failure itself. They do not verify the one-in-ten statistic, but instead employ it rhetorically. It is combined with a further trope: the companies claim to be risk-taking investors in new music. In doing so, they cast their one-in-ten statistic in a benevolent light. Artists are not failing because record companies are bad at their jobs; they are failing because record companies dare to push boundaries. This rationale has been employed for a fundamental cause, defending the economic base upon which the recording industry has been built. It has been used in justification of stringent aspects of recording contracts and it has underpinned the record companies' claims to ownership of sound recording copyright.

This chapter explores the evolution of this rhetoric. It begins by outlining the origins of the one-in-ten statistic, before tracing its prevalence within the recording industry and its analyses within academia. It next examines the uses of the ratio when coupled with the employment of 'new' music. Finally, this chapter looks at the promotional literature of the International Federation of the Phonographic Industry (IFPI), which has recently deployed these tropes for a new cause. They are defending the purpose of record companies in the digital age.

The origins of the one-in-ten statistic

The success ratio is tied to the risks of novelty. How do you attract consumers to a song they have not heard before? How do you interest them in a nascent performer? In the first half of the twentieth century these tasks were as likely to be undertaken by music publishers as they were by record companies. Giving evidence ahead of the UK's 1911 Copyright Act, the publishers argued that they bore the chief responsibility for finding and popularizing hit songs. As a result, they had 'all the big percentage of failures, and the small extent of success' (Gorrell Committee 1910: 70). The record companies, in contrast, would 'never take a thing unless it is popular already' (Gorrell Committee 1910: 53). John Drummond Robertson, head of the leading British manufacturer, the Gramophone Company, could only cite a single composition that had been 'specially composed for the gramophone' and he could not state for certain whether this 'class of composition' would grow (Gorrell Committee 1910: 53).

The publishers used their low success rate tactically during these debates. A new right was being introduced for the use of compositions in 'mechanical' devices, such as phonographs, gramophones, piano players and music boxes. They argued that because of the high risks of their business they should be entitled to set their own royalty rates and choose which manufacturers could feature their compositions. The rhetorical tactic was not successful in this instance. The record companies campaigned successfully for a compulsory licence, resulting in a standard royalty rate and the removal of the publishers' veto on the recording of their copyrighted compositions.

In 1928, at a subsequent UK inquiry into mechanical licensing, the publishers continued to maintain that they played the most 'important role in bringing out and popularizing a work' and that, conversely, record companies 'seldom if ever bring out a new work or procure its initial popularity' (Report of Committee 1928: 9). William Boosey of Chappell & Co. claimed 'only one song in forty which his firm published could really be described as a success' (Peacock and Weir 1975: 43). The record companies admitted that publishers bore the primary 'expense of making a work popular', but were now stressing their own slim chances of making 'more than two or three "hits" in a year' (Report of Committee 1928: 19). They argued that there were 'about 5,000 Copyright titles in their catalogues' and it 'would be idle to suggest that all these are or have been popular successes' (Report of Committee 1928: 19).

In Britain and America it was not until the 1950s that record sales overtook sales of sheet music (Garofalo 2005: 70). Counter-intuitively, it was at this point that it began to be suggested that 'the real money is in the publishing' (Stanley 2011). The publishers' gains from recording royalties compensated their losses from sheet music revenue. In addition, their marketing costs were considerably reduced, as record companies increasingly took on the major costs of promotion. Correspondingly, while there is less evidence hereafter of publishers talking about success ratios, it was in this period that the recording industry's one-in-ten statistic emerged. An early use can be found in *Billboard*, 21 July 1958. Bob Rolontz calculated that there were about 100 singles released in the American market each week, a figure that he regarded as 'overproduction':

> Since less than 10 per cent of all records released become hits, and the figure is closer to 5 per cent than 10 per cent, the majority of them hardly sell at all. Possibly 60 per cent of all released sell 2,000 to 3,000. Another 20 per cent sell up to 25,000. And another 10 per cent sell 50,000 or more. The hit 10 per cent sell the 100,000 to 1,000,000 records. In other words 80 per cent of all records released are a loss for all concerned.
>
> (Rolontz 1958a: 1–4)

From the outset we can witness two characteristics of the recording industry's success ratio. First, it can be measured in different ways. Rolontz begins by examining the ratio of hits to releases but then addresses the profitability of records. The second is that it can vary. His article alternates between five per cent, ten per cent and twenty per cent. It is nevertheless the one-in-ten statistic that the business has most commonly employed. Rolontz used it in relation to albums in the following week's *Billboard*, arguing that 'true money making LP's are certainly no more than 10 per cent of all released' (1958b: 10). These early instances of the statistic are restricted to journalistic investigations where it is used somewhat disparagingly. However, just as the publishers had done before them, the record companies would utilize failure for their own ends.

The prevalence of the one-in-ten statistic

The one-in-ten statistic has been employed in different territories and across different time periods. By the 1960s, it was being used in Britain. The *Melody Maker* asked, '[i]f, as the record companies now admit, nine out of ten singles fail to make the Top Fifty, what can the aspiring popper do to shorten the odds against his getting that elusive hit record?' (Anon. 1966: 8). It was still being employed in the United Kingdom 30 years later. In 1994, the government's Monopolies and Mergers Commission (MMC) was informed by major record labels that 'only one in ten of the pop artists with whom they sign contracts turns out to be successful' (MMC 1994: s. 2.102). As we shall see, a great deal rested upon this statement, but it remained unchallenged and unverified by the MMC. British politicians were similarly biddable. In 1997, Chris Smith, who was then the Labour Party's Culture Secretary, echoed industry claims that '[o]n average, 80-90 per cent of artists signed to record companies will not succeed' (1997: 81).

Meanwhile, the ratio maintained its presence in the United States. Its usage can be traced into the 1970s, when it was argued that 'only 10 percent [of records] smelled "break even"' (Denisoff 1975: 5). It was still being employed in the 1990s, when it was suggested that '[n]ine out of ten acts signed to record contracts are losers' (Goodman 1987: 232). Writing in 2014, Simon Napier-Bell summed up the statistic's persistence: 'the ratio of success is what it always was – for every ten artists signed, nine will get nowhere. A contract with a major record company was always a 90 per cent guarantee of failure and it still is today' (2014: 285).

The endurance of the statistic could be considered remarkable. It has survived despite significant changes in recording industry practice. Three factors, in particular, should have affected its consistency. The first is that the industry has gone through peaks and troughs. The common reaction of record companies during leaner times is to cut the size of their artist rosters and introduce more cautious signing policies. As a result there should be a higher ratio of hits to releases during hard times, at least if measured in relation to chart entries. The second is that the industry has moved from a model in which a major label was defined as an organization that had its own pressing plants and distribution networks, to one where there is less physical manufacture, most of which is undertaken by outside companies (Laing 2003: 621). In the 1970s, the majors' manufacturing interests were viewed as a cause of overproduction, as these companies needed to generate sufficient product to keep their pressing plants busy (Denisoff 1975: 97–98). Manufacture also provided a platform from which to experiment. The majors pressed and distributed records for smaller companies, thus gaining a steady stream of revenue that safeguarded them against the 'adverse financial impact resulting from the considerable risk involved in speculative investment in new recording artists' (Hill 1978: 32). Following on from this, some commentators have maintained that the majors took greater artistic chances when they were in the manufacturing business (Harrison 2017: 178). The third factor is that record companies have become increasingly sophisticated when it comes to consumer data. From an industry that did little audience analysis, we now have one that conducts detailed market research, taking full advantage of the digitization of consumer activity (Frith 2001: 34). Despite this wealth of data, the one-in-ten statistic has endured.

The ratio is variable nonetheless. As we have moved through this time period it has less regularly been employed in relation to the ratio of hits to releases, which is just about quantifiable. Instead, it has been more commonly applied to the proportion of records that are profitable, or the number of artists whose contracts are renewed because they are providing sufficient returns. When it comes to profitability, we have to trust the record companies' own calculations. They do not publicize precise sales figures for individual titles, nor do they detail the breakeven points of releases, which can vary widely. There has also been variation regarding which breakeven point they use. Sometimes they employ the statistic in relation to the recoupment of an artist's personal, recording and video advances. At others they apply it to the overall expenditure on a release, adding in the costs of manufacture, distribution, marketing and promotion. What also gets obscured is the fact that artists and record companies have different breakeven points. A 'failed' record for an artist may be profitable for their record company. Interviewed in 1971, Warner Bros. executive Joe Smith admitted that his artists received a lower share of profits than his company did; therefore, their debts took longer to pay off. He calculated that it would take sales of 100,000 albums for an artist to recoup 'their advance and recording costs, and from then on they're making money. But only 10 to 15 percent of the albums sell that well' (Sanjek and Sanjek 1991: 212).

Some academics have questioned the veracity of success ratios. Writing in the 1990s, Keith Negus reported an industry belief that only 'one in eight' artists recoup their advances. While arguing that this is 'an elusive figure, hard to verify and as mythical as it is statistical', he noted that some genres have a higher hit rate than others (1999: 47–50). In 2013, Lee Marshall listed a number of one-in-ten citations. He questioned their 'seeming truism' and suggested 'the failure rate may not be as high as conventionally perceived' (2013: 583, 584). Other academics have tested the ratios out. In the early 1970s, Simon Frith quantified 'A year of singles in Britain', finding a success rate of 'about one in eleven' (1974: 40). Jones undertook a similar exercise in 1995, tracking a week's worth of single releases to monitor how many made the charts (1997: 38–48). His main concern, however, was with the overall profitability of acts. Although he discovered a high rate of failure, he noted:

> Without knowing the extent of the recording and the promotional budgets for a new act; or the extent of recoupable debt for an 'established' act, we cannot know the sales target figure for a release by that act. Without knowing the sales target figure, and with no access to actual numbers of records sold, we can't judge whether the act in question is regarded by their label as either succeeding or failing. (1997: 47)

Although the statistic has remained much the same, the academic accounts of it have changed. In the 1970s and 1980s it was used as evidence of the 'mud against the wall' approach to releasing music, whereby labels issued a large array of titles hoping some would stick as hits (Chapple and Garofalo 1977: 14). Bernard Miège drew pessimistic conclusions from this scenario, claiming that it resulted in job insecurity and impecuniosity for artists (1989: 89–90). In contrast, Frith saw it as evidence of consumer sovereignty (1978: 97). David Hesmondhalgh added a further view, arguing that the signing policies of these decades resulted in 'a substantial degree of artistic innovation and experimentation' (2013: 249).

By the 1990s the costs of recording, promoting and marketing records had increased considerably (Negus 1992: 40). This was also the era in which more sophisticated methods of audience and sales analysis took hold. Negus detailed how this resulted in 'a straightforward reluctance to experiment, a reduction in risk-taking and a propensity towards a partial view of the world' (1999: 52), while Jones suggested that record companies were no longer involved in 'overproduction'; they were instead 'over-signing' new acts (1997: 313). This policy was considered to be more cost-effective. Although record companies would 'initiate the commodification of a number of commodities' they would 'choose to concentrate marketing and promotional resources on only a proportion of these on the basis of "intelligence" garnered from the market place' (Jones 1997: 149). The essential point of analysis was no longer what happened once a record was in the market, but the system of prioritization that had taken place before it was released.

Building on these studies, some writers have suggested that record companies have a systematic approach to failure. By 2001, Frith was viewing success ratios in a new light. He asked, '[w]hat if a record's failure reflects not the irrational activities of musicians and consumers but the perfectly rational activities of record companies themselves?' (2001: 47). In contemplating why a record company would choose not to promote some of its artists, he outlined the following areas of policy:

> the development of the portfolio management structure; the carefully orchestrated programme of global release and promotion; the calculation of what budgets are available for what products when; a sense at any one moment of to which project it makes most sense to devote energy.
>
> (Frith 2001: 47)

Marshall has gone further, stating that 'the high failure rate associated with the record labels can [...] have some beneficial aspects for labels' (2013: 584). He points out that it 'serves important rhetorical purposes in relation to governments, policy makers, and consumers, and [...] in contractual negotiations with its artists' (2013: 584).

Uses and abuses of the one-in-ten statistic

Marshall is correct; the one-in-ten statistic has been tactically employed. In Britain, the MMC's 1994 report *The Supply of Recorded Music* provides a rare insight into industry policy. Here the statistic is used in defence of the record companies' ownership of sound recording copyright and their restrictive contractual clauses. The report states at its outset that '[c]opyright is central to the operations of the record industry' (MMC 1994: s. 1.4). The International Managers Forum (IMF) pointed out to the MMC that 'the copyright catalogues of the record companies are their most valuable asset' (MMC 1994: s. 8.35).

The companies' claims upon sound recording copyright were contestable, however. In British law, ownership is awarded to the 'producer', defined as 'the person by whom the arrangements necessary for the making of the sound recording are undertaken' (Copyright, Designs and Patents Act 1988: s. 9.2aa). The record companies argued that

> [t]he courts had held that the word 'undertake' meant 'be responsible for', especially in the financial sense but also generally. It could therefore be assumed that [...] Parliament had intended that copyright should vest in the person who had undertaken the financial responsibility for making the recording. The ownership of that copyright was the reward for the risk they had undertaken.
>
> (MMC 1994: s. 12.108)

It is nevertheless rare for record companies to undertake the financial risk or organizational responsibilities on their own. Artists' recording budgets are usually issued in the form of advances. The record companies claw these advances back from the artists' royalties: they are 'recoupable'. In addition, artists will regularly make their own arrangements for recording projects. They will source independent studios and independent record producers. They will also select session musicians themselves. If the companies' own interpretation of the law is correct, then it is possible to interpret it as positing recouped recording artists as at least the co-owners of copyright in sound recordings. They have contributed to the general and financial arrangements.

The record companies provided one further rationale for their ownership of sound recording copyright, however. They argued to the MMC that only one in ten of their artists would achieve profitability, while the remaining 90 per cent would have their losses written off (MMC 1994: s. 2.102). Highlighting this statistic, the companies suggested that they bore the responsibility for financing the *totality* of sound recordings. As such, they deserved the copyrights of the few successes to compensate for the losses of the many failures.

The companies' claims did not end there. They maintained that, in compensation for the low success rate, their artists should be tied for long contractual periods and should not be entitled to record for rival record companies (MMC 1994: s. 2.41). After hearing evidence from each of the major record companies, the MMC agreed with their claims that

> [i]t was only by concluding contracts which embodied such terms as retention of copyright, exclusivity and a reasonable length of contract term that the companies could reap the necessary long-term benefits for those few artists who succeeded and that the artists who succeeded could reap the long-term benefits in their development and career.
>
> (MMC 1994: s. 12.99)

Yet record companies bear much of the responsibility for this rate of failure. One reason why the majority of signings have failed to recoup is because advances have been high. The labels have escalated these payments as a means of outpacing their competitors. Jeff Ayeroff of Warner Bros. has stated, '[i]f there's a band that we want, that Interscope want or that DreamWorks wants, we want it really badly [...] and we will pay the money to get it, making the risk higher' (Stahl 2013: 164). Speaking to the MMC, one of the labels spoke of setting advances at a level 'necessary to persuade the artist to accept the offer in preference to a rival record company' (1994: s. 11.5). The companies suggested that, for artists, high advances and copyright ownership should be considered mutually exclusive. This argument was nevertheless reliant on the failure of the majority of artists to recoup.

Another reason why so many recordings have failed to achieve profitability is because of the high costs of marketing and promotion. Yet these costs are high because there are so many records. Broadcasters, journalists and other intermediaries are faced with a plethora of releases. One way to filter them is to assess marketing expenditure. Marshall notes that 'failing to spend substantial amounts on independent promoters makes it look like the label is not serious about a record, thus dooming it to failure' (2013: 583). This expenditure has enabled major record companies to exercise their power. In America, for example, there have been times when promotion has become so expensive that only the largest labels can afford it, thus providing 'a means to keep small companies off the charts' (Dannen 2003: 264).

It is the major record companies, ultimately, who have set the bar for the success ratio so high, but they have argued that they deserve compensation for its effects. In doing so, they have received ample rewards. In Britain, their contractual policies garnered official approval from the MMC, while their ownership of copyright has received scant investigation. To achieve this, however, they have had to make their failure rate appear noble. This is where the rhetoric of new music has come in.

New music

New music and success ratios have long been considered in tandem. As an example, they are brought together in the 21 July 1958 *Billboard* article cited above. Rolontz believed that overproduction had a negative effect on new acts, arguing that record companies provided them with little 'staying power' as they were constantly looking for acts that were newer still (1958a: 4).

Overproduction came to be viewed more positively. *The Supply of Recorded Music* includes a benevolent self-portrayal of the record companies' contracts and copyrights. The labels defended their economic system on the grounds that it would facilitate the sponsorship of new British performers:

> If material modifications were made to the key provisions in recording contracts, dealing in particular with the extent of copyright acquired by the record company, the length of the contract and the exclusivity provisions imposed on the artist, then the companies would be forced to take a much more short-term view of their relationship with artists, which would not only be detrimental to the long-term development of those artists, but which would inevitably mean that the companies would not be able to invest as widely in new UK artists as they did at present.
>
> (MMC 1994: s. 12.103)

This line of reasoning was promoted further in the 1990s, as dialogue between British record companies and governments increased. Writing about this period, Martin Cloonan noted that 'key people in the popular music industries came to realize that politicians needed to be lobbied' (2007: 21). In part, this was because their industries were being addressed (*The Supply of Recorded Music* was one of a number of official investigations). It was also because governments were keen to open discussions. Their interest was reflective of an era in which the profits of heavy industry had declined while those of the cultural industries had grown (Cloonan 2007: 39).

Cloonan argues that the record companies were in need of 'an image-building exercise', adding that '[c]learly at a time when cultural policy was increasingly becoming part of economic policy and when the music industries seemingly felt some unease about stressing pop's cultural value, the pragmatic response was to make the economic case' (Cloonan 2007: 75). The argument they made was nevertheless balanced between the two. While the record companies promoted their economic worth, they also sought protection. In doing so, their talk of new music leant more towards its artistic qualities than to financial policy. There was no mention of portfolio management or budget calculations; instead there was an emphasis on the risk-taking nature of supporting the new. There was less talk about the search for the next blockbuster acts than there was about promoting the marginal, the challenging and the forward-looking. The companies stressed they were signing 'creative' artists, issuing 'innovative music' and sponsoring acts with 'minority appeal' (MMC 1994: s. 11.29, 12.79, 12.105).

As Cloonan states, the 'music industries' commonsense view of the world' began to permeate British governments (2007: 41). Research undertaken by Negus and Jones in the late 1990s suggested a system of tight financial control and restricted musical innovation. It was in this same period, however, that the record companies stressed they were risk-taking. This tactic was employed in one of the first investigations into the record business in this era, the National Heritage Committee's 1993 inquiry into CD prices. However, when the major companies suggested they were involved in 'a high risk business', the Committee would only concede that this could sometimes be the case (Cloonan 2007: 70). *The Supply of Recorded Music*, published the following year, evidences a new level of accord with the recording industry. There is agreement that it is a 'high-risk business', driven by the search for new artists (MMC 1994: s. 1.13).

The record companies had much to gain by highlighting their audacious deeds. Risk-taking was used in defence of their ownership of sound recording copyright: the MMC conceded that 'since the record companies take the risk of investing in artists when they are unknown, they should not have the rewards taken away on those occasions when their investment turns out to be successful' (MMC 1994: s. 2.140). It also supported their system of exclusive, long-term contracts: the companies argued that they provided the platform from which 'to take the very significant risks in investing in new artists' (MMC 1994: s. 12.99).

Although the MMC endorsed these claims, the record companies' suggestions did not go uncontested. Giving evidence to the Commission, the IMF questioned the record labels' quantification of success. They argued that the one-in-ten success ratio was based on a short-term analysis of an artist's profitability, pointing to the fact that a record company would retain copyright in a sound recording for 50 years, regardless of whether an artist remained signed to them throughout the whole of that period.[1] Therefore, it could accrue revenue long after an artist had been dropped on account of non-profitability. They noted that, whereas the losses from 'unsuccessful' artists would be detailed in company balance sheets, the value of their copyright catalogues would not appear there (MMC 1994: s. 8.35). The IMF proposed a shorter duration for the record companies' control of sound recording copyright, suggesting a period of ten years, after which the rights would 'return' to the artist (MMC 1994 s. 10.49). This, they believed, would give artists greater bargaining power in their negotiations with the industry, as the value of these copyrights would reduce the need to 'obtain capital [...] on disadvantageous terms' (MMC 1994: s. 10.50).

The record companies' benevolent self-portrayal has been questioned elsewhere. Miles Copeland, who has had a successful career as a manager and as a head of independent record labels, suggests that '[i]f you're trying to build a record company, and you're trying to build an asset, what you really try to do is you try to find a young artist that you can sign and develop' (Stahl 2013: 155). For Copeland, these are 'the riskiest ones', but they are also 'where you're going to get the most return. When I go to the marketplace to try to borrow additional money, or get investment in my company, they're going to look at what are the potential returns of [my] company' (Stahl 2013: 155).

New artists have offered good returns because they have been contractually weak. In a competitive business, in which only a small proportion of artists are successful and an even smaller proportion is signed, prospective artists have had little bargaining power. Until recently, those who managed to secure record company interest would generally be on lower royalty rates than established artists and their contracts would contain a greater number of restrictive clauses (Dannen 2003: 79; Negus 1992: 149–50). Leslie F. Hill, while a director at EMI, conceded that new artists had 'the greatest profit potential for the company' (1978: 35).

In their dialogue with governments, record companies have claimed that their ownership of copyright and restrictive contractual system support the creation of new music. The reverse is also true. The rhetoric of new music supports the record companies' system of ownership and control. A measure of the companies' faith in this rhetoric is that it has been adopted by IFPI, their global trade body. Moreover, investment in new music is now being used for an all-encompassing cause: to explain the continued need for record companies themselves.

Investing in new music

In the twenty-first century, the profitability of record companies has fallen. IFPI has charted a decline in global revenue from US$27.3 billion in 1999 to US$19.1 billion in 2018 (IFPI 2012b: 7; 2019: 13). The organization has nevertheless argued that if an artist wants to achieve success, the best chance of doing so is to sign with a record company. This claim has been made most forcibly in IFPI's *Investing in Music* reports, issued in 2010, 2012, 2014 and 2016. Ann Harrison believes that the aim of these documents has been to 'debunk suggestions that an artist can develop careers in the business without needing a label' (2017: 61). The reports admit as much, maintaining '[t]here has been a mistaken belief among some that the role of labels would be diminished in the digital age' (IFPI 2014: 6).

In making their case, IFPI have stressed that new artists are at the heart of record companies' concerns; each report stresses they are the 'lifeblood' of the industry (2010: 6–7; 2012a: 7, 9; 2014: 6; 2016: 10). They offer daunting figures about the amount of money it costs to break a new act. A spend of 'between US$200,000 and US$500,000' in 2012 had risen to 'between US$0.5 million and US$2 million' by 2016 (2012a: 11; 2016: 6). Marketing is shown as taking the lion's share of industry expenditure, reaching US$200,000–700,000 per new act in 2016 (2016: 6). What remains unstated is that these high costs can be partially attributed to the companies' promotional wars, which are in turn related to the fact that more artists are signed than will succeed.

There is one concession to previous practice, however. The one-in-ten ratio has been revised. Left as it was, it could have been taken as evidence that record companies are not viable. Why sign with them if there is only a slim chance you will succeed? Consequently, the 2012 report tells us 'the most common estimate cited by senior music company management is a success ratio of one in five. This is more than the commonly estimated one-in-ten ratio of a decade ago, reflecting a generally higher success rate than was previously the norm' (2012a: 11).[2] However, just as record companies provided little evidence for their earlier statistic, this revision is offered without proof.

The ratio is balanced with the idea that record labels support a 'wide community of artists, many of whom will not be commercially successful' (2010: 5). Failure is employed as a means of demonstrating altruistic ways. IFPI claim that, while '[c]ontinually investing in new talent is a hugely risky business', it is record companies who 'shoulder the financial risk inherent in trying to break a new act' (2010: 6; 2014: 5). According to Nick Raphael, president of Capitol Records UK:

> We put just as much effort and money, if not more so, into the acts that don't succeed as with those that do. There may be any number of reasons why they don't connect with the audience, but it is not for lack of effort and support from labels that want them to succeed.
>
> (2014: 9)

There is no mention of the strategic prioritization of acts. The reports claim instead that 'long-term' contractual involvement is of benefit to artists, as it allows them 'to develop their own brand identity and earn a living from different sources' (2010: 7).

It is not just prospective artists who are expected to read these reports, but also policy-makers. To this end, IFPI claim that investment in new music benefits 'the economy as a whole' and that record companies have 'sustained their investment in artists despite the significant fall-off in overall sales revenue' (2010: 5, 7). The reports boast how record companies invest more money in 'research and development' than the pharmaceutical and biotechnology sector (2012a: 9; 2014: 9).

In order to continue this practice, the companies' ownership of copyright must be maintained:

> It is copyright that makes investment in music possible. It is copyright that allows the industry that helps artists gain a return on its investment, and therefore plough back new funds and resources into the next generation of talent. And it is copyright which underlies the endeavours, the risks and the successes that fill the pages of this report.
>
> (2014: 4)

The 2014 *Investing in Music* report comes close to declaring the record companies' self-interest. Placido Domingo, Chairman of IFPI, states that 'instead of calling this report *Investing in Music*, it could also be titled *Investing in Copyright*' (2014: 4). For the most part, however, this investment is not discussed as resulting in something that the record companies will profit from or own. The suggestion, instead, is that revenues derived from copyright will be ploughed back into the future. IFPI claim that the majority of record companies' copyright earnings are spent on new music, as labels 'reinvest the proceeds of successful campaigns in the discovery and nurturing of the next generation of talent' (2012a: 7). In reaching this formulation, they provide a phrase that record companies have grasped for in each of their campaigns and reports. What they are peddling is a 'virtuous cycle of investment' (2010: 5). This honourable inflection has been implied whenever they have combined the rhetoric of their success rate with their rhetoric of newness.

Conclusion

The economic wellbeing of record companies has been aided by their employment of two rhetorical tropes. The first is that only one in ten artists succeeds; the second is that they are supporters of new music. Both are problematic. The labels' success ratios require verification and their nurturing abilities can be questioned. Artists who are not prioritized for promotion would hardly recommend their companies' virtues, while those who do succeed can find themselves paying for the losers. Moreover, record companies might be signing new artists, quantitatively, but this does not mean that their music is new, qualitatively. In the current century, for example, theories of 'retromania' have taken hold (Reynolds 2011).

This is not to say that either trope is baseless. The careers of most artists will end in failure and the record companies will write-off these artists' losses. There is also an element of truth in the companies' risk-taking propaganda. Until recently it has been hard to test their claims because there have been few alternatives to their policies. This hegemony is finally being challenged. The past decade has witnessed the rise of service companies, such as Kobalt, who perform many of the functions of a traditional record company but do not own their artists' copyrights. How can they afford this? The charge originally levelled against them was that they could only do so because they were not taking risks; they were forgoing copyrights because their deals were reserved for 'heritage' artists with proven track records (Anon. 2015: 9). Nevertheless, it is now becoming possible for new performers, on a variety of types of record deal, to own their own copyrights. Some of them are also reversing previous practice by gaining better royalty rates than the artists who have preceded them (Ingham 2019). The reason why they can do this, however, is because they are not exactly new. These artists have established their dedicated coteries of followers (both online and in person) *before* contracting with a record company. It is these levels of experience that provide them with their negotiating power.

These changes do not negate the need to monitor record company practice. The vast majority of artists remain on long-term, exclusive contracts and they do not own their sound recording copyrights. The record companies have upheld this position via arguments about failure and novelty. One reason why they have not received sufficient questioning is because of the high success rate of their rhetoric.

NOTES

1. In 2011 the European Union issued a directive that increased the term of sound recording copyright in member countries to 70 years. In their efforts to achieve this result, British record companies made much of their risk-taking investment in new music (Osborne 2017: 404–06).
2. The 2010 report states that '[e]stimates of the success ratio vary between one in five and one in ten' (2010: 7). Curiously, the 2016 report returns to this state of uncertainty, stating, '[s]ome labels estimate the ratio of commercial success to failure as 1 in 4; others consider the chances to be much lower – less than 1 in 10' (2016: 10).

REFERENCES

Anon. (1966), 'If the odds against having a hit are 10-1, what difference does a Beatle song make?', *Melody Maker*, 27 August, p. 8.

——— (2015), 'Years of service', *Music Week*, 16 January, pp. 8–10.

Chapple, Steve and Garofalo, Reebee (1977), *Rock 'n' Roll is Here to Pay: The History of Politics of the Music Industry*, Chicago: Nelson-Hall.

Cloonan, Martin (2007), *Popular Music and the State in the UK*, Aldershot: Ashgate.

Copyright, Designs and Patents Act 1988 (1988), 'Legislation', http://www.legislation.gov.uk/ukpga/1988/48/pdfs/ukpga_19880048_en.pdf. Accessed 26 January 2019.

Copyright Royalty (Mechanical Musical Instruments Inquiry) Report of Committee 1928 (1928), London: His Majesty's Stationery Office.

Dannen, Fredric (2003), *Hit Men: Power Brokers and Fast Money Inside the Music Business*, London: Helter Skelter.

Denisoff, R. Serge (1975), *Solid Gold: The Popular Record Industry*, New Brunswick and London: Transaction.

Frith, Simon (1974), 'A year of singles in Britain', in C. Gillett (ed.), *Rock File 2*, Frogmore: Granada, pp. 37–46.

——— (1978), *The Sociology of Rock*, London, Constable.

——— (2001), 'The popular music industry', in S. Frith, W. Straw and J. Street (eds), *Cambridge Companion to Pop and Rock*, Cambridge: Cambridge University Press, pp. 26–52.

Garofalo, Reebee (2005), *Rockin' Out: Popular Music in the U.S.A.*, Upper Saddle River: Prentice Hall.

Goodman, Fred (1987), *The Mansion on the Hill: Dylan, Young, Geffen, Springsteen and the Head-On Collision of Rock and Commerce*, London: Jonathan Cape.

Gorrell Committee (1910), *Minutes of Evidence Taken Before the Law of Copyright Committee*, London: His Majesty's Stationery Office.

Harrison, Anne (2017), *Music: The Business: The Essential Guide to the Law and the Deals*, 7th ed., London: Virgin.

Hesmondhalgh, David (2013), *The Cultural Industries*, 3rd ed., London: Sage.

Hill, Leslie F. (1978), 'An insight into the finances of the record industry', *Three Banks Review*, 118, pp. 28–45.

Ingham, Tim (2019), 'Records labels are spending more and more on signing (and paying) artists . . .', *Music Business Worldwide*, 26 May, https://www.musicbusinessworldwide.com/record-labels-are-spending-more-and-more-on-signing-and-paying-artists/. Accessed 7 November 2019.

International Federation of the Phonographic Industry (IFPI) (2010), 'Investing in music: How music companies discover, develop and promote talent', http://www.ifpi.org/content/library/Investing_In_Music.pdf. Accessed 26 January 2011 [no longer available].

——— (2012a), 'Investing in music: How music companies discover, nurture and promote talent', http://www.ifpi.org/content/library/Investing_In_Music.pdf. Accessed 26 January 2013 [no longer available].

——— (2012b), *Recording Industry in Numbers 2011: The Definitive Source of Global Music Market Information*, London: IFPI.

——— (2014), 'Investing in music: How music companies discover, nurture and promote talent', http://www.ifpi.org/content/library/Investing_In_Music.pdf. Accessed 26 January 2015 [no longer available].

——— (2016), 'Investing in music: The value of record companies', http://www.ifpi.org/content/library/Investing_In_Music.pdf. Accessed 26 January 2017 [no longer available].

——— (2019), 'Global music report 2019: State of the industry', https://www.ifpi.org/news/IFPI-GLOBAL-MUSIC-REPORT-2019. Accessed 3 April 2019.

Jones, Michael (1997), 'Organising pop: Why so few acts make pop music', Ph.D. thesis, Liverpool: University of Liverpool.

Laing, Dave (2003), 'Major', in J. Shepherd, D. Horn, D. Laing, P. Oliver and P. Wicke (eds), *Continuum Encyclopedia of Popular Music of the World. Volume I: Media, Industry and Society*, London and New York: Continuum, p. 621.

Marshall, Lee (2013), 'The structural functions of stardom in the recording industry', *Popular Music and Society*, 36:5, pp. 578–96.

Miège, Bernard (1989), *The Capitalization of Cultural Production*, New York: International General.

Monopolies and Mergers Commission (MMC) (1994), *The Supply of Recorded Music*, London, HMSO.

Napier-Bell, Simon (2014), *Ta-Ra-Ra-Boom-De-Ay: The Dodgy Business of Popular Music*, London: Unbound.

Negus, Keith (1992), *Producing Pop: Culture and Conflict in the Music Industry*, London: Arnold.

——— (1999), *Music Genres and Corporate Cultures*, London: Routledge.

Osborne, Richard (2017), 'Success ratios, new music and sound recording copyright', *Popular Music*, 36: 3, pp. 393–409.

Peacock, Alan and Weir, Ronald (1975), *The Composer in the Market Place*, London: Faber.

Report of Committee (1928), *Copyright Royalty (Mechanical Musical Instruments Inquiry)*, London: His Majesty's Stationery Office.

Reynolds, Simon (2011), *Retromania: Pop Culture's Addiction to Its Own Past*, London: Faber and Faber.

Rolontz, Bob (1958a), 'Too many disks spoil the broth', *Billboard*, 21 July, pp. 1, 4.

——— (1958b), 'Package output spirals for real industry headache', *Billboard*, 11 August, pp. 1, 10.

Sanjek, Russell and Sanjek, David (1991), *American Popular Music Business in the 20th Century*, New York and Oxford: Oxford University Press.

Smith, Chris (1997), *Creative Britain*, London: Faber and Faber.

Stahl, Matt (2013), *Unfree Masters: Recording Artists and the Politics of Work*, Durham and London: Duke University Press.

Stanley, Bob (2011), 'Copyright extension: Good for Cliff and the Beatles, bad for the little guys?', *Guardian*, 15 September, http://www.theguardian.com/music/2011/sep/15/copyright-extension-cliffs-law-beatles. Accessed 26 January 2019.

PART II

POLICY

4

The Global Music Report: Selling a Narrative of Decline

David Arditi

The ability of trade organizations to collect and report data pertaining to the industry that they represent enables these organizations to shape the image of their industries in the eyes of variously invested actors from legislators to the public and prospective artists. In these circumstances, collecting and reporting data are neither economically nor politically neutral projects; the production of knowledge is intimately bound to power. In this chapter, I explore the relationship of knowledge and power through a critical interpretive reading of *Recording Industry in Numbers* (RIN), an annual text produced by the International Federation of the Phonographic Industry (IFPI), which IFPI changed to *Global Music Report* (GMR) in 2016. Currently headquartered in London, IFPI was founded as the recording industry's global trade industry organization in Italy in 1933, with the principal aim of promoting performing rights in recorded performances (Frith 1988: 57). A number of state-based institutions fulfil the same objectives as IFPI at a domestic level, including the Recording Industry Association of America (RIAA) and the British Phonographic Industry (BPI). As I will demonstrate, IFPI's annual report is a tool used by major record labels to sell a vision or 'ideological set' to legislators and the public (Harker 1997: 46), which has led to the creation of a regulatory framework that favours corporate conglomerates over independent producers. Increasingly, IFPI's ideological aims affect not only music industry policy, but also the structure of contemporary capitalism.

IFPI first published RIN in 1992. Before 1992, they released periodic *IFPI World Sales* and press releases to demonstrate data, but RIN proved a more 'consistent' explication of annual recording industry data as reported by the national trade associations. With the tagline 'The definitive source of global music market information', RIN provided a snapshot of the recording industry's view of itself from year to year. In 2004, IFPI began releasing a separate, freely available *Digital Music Report*. Then, in 2016, they began combining both reports under the name *Global Music Report*. GMR has been made available in different formats: a free pdf, which can be downloaded from IFPI's website; and a lengthier version that is priced differently for different consumers (the 2018 edition costs £500 for the academic package, £1000 for the 'recorded music industry buyer' and £5000 for the premium package [IFPI 2019]).

Because of the sometimes-candid nature of RIN and GMR, the reports are an essential resource for recording industry researchers in respect of the data they offer. They are also worth investigating in relation to the information they ignore and the language IFPI uses to describe the data. In this chapter, I first describe the relationship between access to the documents and the relative candour displayed in them. Second, I provide a description of the major themes in RIN and GMR to demonstrate the position of the reports in the construction of ideology. Finally, I discuss how IFPI uses these reports to construct their narrative of the proper way to consume music.

Access and candour

After beginning as a comb-bound report, IFPI later bound RIN in a format that resembles a school yearbook. This is fitting, as the reports contain a year-in-review for the major record labels of the global recording industry. The visual appearance of RIN and GMR have changed in accordance with developing publication technology and also with what appears to be a changing audience for the publications. As a result, RIN and GMR have evolved from dry documentation of data with little explication, to colourful publications with extensive commentaries. As RIN transitioned to the free GMR, IFPI went from an apparently straightforward assessment of the recording industry to an articulation of its ideological positions.

The binding of the reports is important because the full versions are not readily available in digital formats, which makes it difficult for researchers to access them. Interestingly, other data reports produced by IFPI are available digitally on its website. First appearing in 2004, the *Online* (later *Digital*) *Music Report* aimed to 'raise awareness of the developments in the online music market, and in doing so, help accelerate them' (Berman 2004: 1). The tendency of the *Digital Music Report* was to overstate the harm done to the recording industry by file-sharing and to highlight the virtues of using online retailers. Additionally, IFPI released biennial reports entitled *Investing in Music* between 2010 and 2016, which emphasized the investment that record labels make in artists. These two publications have provided the organization with a free public platform to portray record company benevolence and to campaign about the malfeasance of pirates, as well as the need to close the 'safe harbours' of companies such as YouTube (Arditi 2014a, 2014b). Access to RIN and the full GMR has been more difficult. I argue below that this is because these reports have sometimes problematized the dominant narrative of the recording industry that has been perpetuated in the press.

In my first attempt to use RIN, I obtained the reports via interlibrary loan from libraries across the United States. A number of reports were not available in any libraries. This created my first barrier to in-depth research because some libraries have a 24-hour checkout limit on the reports. Where IFPI has aimed to make transferring music online impossible with the use of Digital Rights Management (DRM), they have been equally active at making RIN and GMR 'wired shut' (Gillespie 2007). For example, the pdf for the 2013 RIN was only made available from IFPI's website at expensive prices (£750 for 1–3 users: £1500 for 4–10 users; and £2250 for 11+ users). The hard copy could be purchased for an additional £150–£300, and excel data at a further cost. These prices are similar to those of the full 2019 GMR. They are too high for most individual researchers.

Fortunately, after an extended negotiation, my university, the University of Texas at Arlington (UTA), was able to purchase hard copies of the report from 1994 to 2012 and later the 2017 GMR. However, IFPI would not sell pdf versions of RIN to UTA because the trade organization does not want the reports readily available online, even if behind a university library firewall, at least in the United States. At the same time, IFPI made the UTA library sign an agreement that it would not allow university members to take the RINs off campus. In one conversation I had with IFPI, the representative I spoke with compared a university library with an IFPI member like Apple by stating that Apple employees are not allowed to remove RINs from Apple's 'campus'. These limitations have the practical effect of RIN being under-analysed within academic research in the United States because it is difficult to obtain the entire archive for close research. Why is it so hard to get this information? It could be because there are moments of candour in RIN that have directly contradicted what the recording industry was conveying through press releases, congressional testimony and news interviews. This candour tends to disintegrate in the public editions of GMR, but remains evident in its more restricted versions.

Publicly, RIAA claimed that the decline of the compact disc format in the early 2000s (see Figure 4.1) was a direct result of file-sharing. However, at the height of RIAA's public rhetoric, RIN was more nuanced about the decline of the CD (IFPI 2002). IFPI acknowledged in 2002 that there was reason to believe that 'the recent fall in CD sales [could be attributed] to a maturation of the "CD-replacement cycle" in the largest markets, whereby consumers have repurchased albums on CD that they had previously bought on cassette or LP. The amount of direct replacement of titles purchased on CD has never been researched and is unknown' (IFPI

2002: 8). In the North American market, IFPI also claimed that the CD's decline was linked to 'uncertainty about the economy' and 'increased competition from a revived gaming industry and DVD video' (IFPI 2002: 24). In the introduction to the 2005 edition of RIN, IFPI's Market Research Director, Keith Jopling, candidly asserted:

> The music business is emerging from a period frequently described in recent years as a 'crisis'. The year 2004 was the industry's best year-on-year performance for five years – and while tough times lay ahead, the industry has clearly turned a corner [...]. Demand for music, in all forms, is higher than it has ever been before. And entertainment sectors related to music, or that use music, are growing. But there are big challenges for the music market too. Internet piracy is the greatest of them, but it is by no means the only obstacle to growth. Consumers are spending more on other, newer entertainment products such as DVD and games. They are also spending more on mobile phones, internet and other 'subscriptions'.
>
> (IFPI 2005: 3)

While IFPI and domestic recording industry trade associations publicly blamed file-sharing as the *only* culprit for the decline of CDs, in these more private reports IFPI acknowledged that competition in the entertainment market, a recession and a buying cycle all contributed to the format's decline. Jopling's quote reveals the complexity of the recording industry's challenges in respect of digital media, albeit that he encourages industry readers to keep piracy at the front of their minds.

Although RIN allowed space for candour, it could be argued that IFPI was only forthright in these reports because of their circumscribed distribution. Due to their pricing and policy restrictions there was limited access to the discourse in the reports. These limitations allowed the authors to construct and report a non-ideological picture of the status of the recording industry. In the following section, I will highlight the data and methodologies deployed by IFPI in these reports.

A look at the data

As the self-described 'definitive source of global music market information', RIN provides sales information about music revenues from 1992 to 2016. This allows the researcher to track this history across sales categories. In addition, the reports' global scope provides opportunities to understand variegated music consumption patterns in different countries. The RIN reports exhibit information at three levels – world, regional and national – with data gathered from local trade industry groups such as RIAA in the United States and BPI in the United Kingdom. They synthesize national reports of sales figures at the regional and global levels, whereby nation-based trade organizations provide a narrative that IFPI appropriates. However, the transition to the publicly available GMR in 2016 coincided with a demonstrable change in data from previous years, which exposes the industry's rhetorical tactics in publications made available to the public.

While the media format of the recorded commodity has changed over time, RIN reflects these shifts inconsistently. In early editions of RIN, sales data is limited to vinyl albums, cassettes and CDs. In subsequent editions, IFPI includes everything from music videos to streaming audio and performing rights to sync revenue. However, from year to year there can be significant changes in the commodity information present in a given edition. At the end of each decade, IFPI provides detailed data on the previous ten years, which allows the researcher to see broader trends. For instance, the short-lived minidisc, which some hailed as the CD's successor, first appeared in the 2000 edition, but was no longer included by the 2002 edition. In 2002, music videos made their first appearance in RIN, but in subsequent years IFPI classified them variously as music videos, as 'other', or further broke them down into VHS and DVD. While singles have been a consistent sales category in all editions of RIN, IFPI added online singles to this category beginning with the 2004 edition. The following year, they began reporting on digital singles and digital albums. However, in some years the data is unclear about what constitutes a single.

In previous research projects, I have used data from RIN as a source to demonstrate the growth and decline of the recording industry over the past two decades. Each year, I enter the data in an excel sheet, noting inconsistencies that have occurred due to inflation (IFPI adjusts the data for inflation based on US dollars) and because of slight changes reported by each country's affiliate organizations. I adjust the previous years' data up or down according the changes made in the newest edition. However, in the 2015 edition, I noticed an obvious problem with the data. IFPI began repeating the phrase 'first year of growth': 2012 first year of growth … 2014 first year of growth … 2015 first year of growth. Each year they have readjusted graphs to demonstrate this development. For instance, in the 2015 RIN, IFPI showed $14.96 billion revenue for 2014, but in the 2016 GMR they reported $14.5 billion for 2014 and $15 billion for 2015. By 2017's GMR report they showed $14.3 billion for 2014, $14.8 billion for 2015 and $15.7 billion for 2016.

While slight inconsistencies existed in RIN, the publication of GMR in 2016 marked the wholesale remaking of data that had previously been consistent. In fact, this report notes a major change in methodology in its fine print: 'IFPI has amended its measure of performance rights revenue to include performers' and record company collections. Historical revenues have been restated to provide equivalent year-on-year comparisons' (IFPI 2016). This brief note alludes to a change without specifying the material of the change (the first year that performance rights were reported by IFPI was 2005, when they released global performance rights information dating back to 2000). Later in the report, IFPI specifies some of the sources of revenue now included as performance rights without providing data for them, although from the information provided it is clear that all revenues should increase as a result. However, as described above, the report details a yearly decline in revenue. The inclusion of performance rights demonstrates just one of the ways in which IFPI has manipulated its data. What follows is a more detailed analysis of particular aspects of the reports.

Unit shipments vs. unit sales

The reporting strategy of IFPI for physical products is based on shipments as opposed to sales. A shipment includes all units sent to retail outlets for sale, but retail outlets do not necessarily sell all of the units that the labels send to them. As a result, record labels buy back the unsold units. These buyback programmes are vital to music retailers because there is no way for them to predict how much product to purchase ahead of a release. However, the number of units left unsold is not included in IFPI's data.

In the United States, the discrepancy between actual sales and unit shipments can be obtained by referring to Nielsen SoundScan. Unlike IFPI, Nielsen SoundScan gains its information by using a point-of-sale (POS) system that uses barcodes and computer technology to log each purchase of an album. SoundScan was initially developed to circumvent the survey methodology that *Billboard* magazine had used to obtain information by speaking with record store clerks to determine its sales charts. Under the survey methodology, record labels would give record store clerks promotional goods in return for them telling the *Billboard* survey they had sold more of a particular album or single (Watkins 2005). *Billboard* used the surveys because they realized that shipment data were inaccurate, but with SoundScan they recognized they could get even more accurate data on sales. This new system was met with resistance by the recording industry because it revealed that some of their purported best sellers were not as popular as had been portrayed, therefore disrupting their marketing strategies.

Figure 4.1 shows a striking distinction between the RIAA shipment data that feeds into IFPI's reports and the Nielsen SoundScan data on CD sales from 1995 to 2008. The graph shows a consistently higher assessment on behalf of RIAA and a shrinking gap between their figures and Nielsen's figures as time progresses: from a high of 330 million units in 1996 to 24.7 million units in 2008.

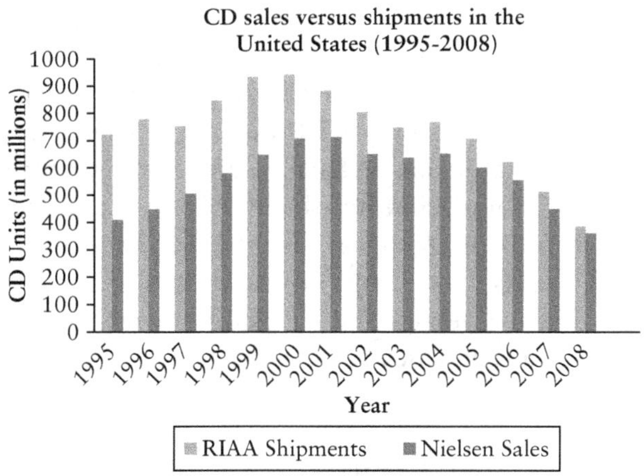

FIGURE 4.1: CD sales versus shipments in the United States (1995–2008). Sources: IFPI (1996, 2000, 2002, 2004, 2005, 2007, 2008, 2010); Nielsen (1997, 1999, 2001, 2003, 2005, 2007, 2011).

Beyond these discrepancies between recorded music shipped and recorded music sold, IFPI's reports also have variance about what counts as a unit of music. In the glossary page of each edition of RIN, there is a description of how the numbers are calculated. Between 1994 and 2005 it states, '[t]otal units: calculated as the total album equivalent – three singles are counted as one album. Sales in all formats included' (IFPI 2004: 2). However, in the 2006 RIN there is no mention of how unit sales are calculated. Then, when the unit sales description re-emerges in the 2007 edition, it reads '[u]nits: measured in "packages" i.e. a double disc CD is counted as a single product' (IFPI 2007: 1). This change is not contextualized in the text. While using an entirely arbitrary number (three singles = one unit), it was at least clear prior to 2006 how units were calculated. If three million singles were sold in 2004, IFPI calculated this as one million units sold. Beginning with the 2007 report it is no longer possible to gather how they count sales of singles.

The elasticity of information demonstrates how the numbers in RIN and GMR can be manipulated in support of IFPI's narratives. The organization has presented a picture of an industry in decline as a means to facilitate the production of an ideology about piracy on the Internet. More recently, figures have been employed to highlight a 'value gap', the idea that digital streaming services (especially YouTube) do not compensate artists fairly. These narratives have been fostered in order to engender the support of the public and governmental bodies to change laws and practices (Arditi 2014a, 2014b).

Retail value

IFPI has an idiosyncratic way of defining units, one that does not reflect retail prices (for example, three singles do not equal the price of a CD, and a collection of CDs recorded as a unit does not equal the purchase cost of a standard CD). As a result, one of the more elusive and least helpful aspects of RIN and GMR is the calculation of retail value. Two overarching questions are left unanswered in these reports. How much money is actually spent on recorded music each year? How does that number relate back to record label profits?

IFPI give information based on suggested retail price and shipment of units. In most editions of RIN and GMR they define retail value as an 'estimate of the final value paid by the consumer for the purchase of a music product, inclusive of relevant sales taxes. For US sales, dollar value reflects shipments at suggested retail list prices as per RIAA published statistics' (IFPI 2005: 2). However, in respect of physical sales of music, the suggested retail price of music is a notoriously inaccurate measurement because stores rarely sell music at the retail value and they regularly sell promotional albums they have received for free from record labels.

Despite the fact that IFPI calculate total world revenue based on an inaccurate 'average' retail price multiplied by an overinflated estimate of record sales based on record shipments, they still use the revenue data in RIN and GMR to construct a story about the recording industry. While they show an overall decline, IFPI overinflate their numbers to obscure sales. This may seem counterintuitive, but my point is that the data is not connected to material reality. It is used to create a narrative that does not reflect the actual condition of the recording industry.

While IFPI put a significant emphasis on recording industry revenue, there is no information on recording industry profit. Profit for the recording industry is equal to the revenue earned from the sale of music minus the costs that go into producing, distributing and selling the music. Since the revenue data is based on a certain amount of speculation, it would be impossible to ascertain profits from these figures. Additionally, the major record labels are divisions of larger corporations that only share some information about their overall corporate profits and revenues, but do not elaborate on their divisions. No data collection/interpretation strategy exists that will enable a transparent understanding of recording industry profit.

There is a deficiency of information on the costs of production in RIN and GMR, including at least six significant areas: (1) personal and recording advances for recording artists; (2) royalties for recording artists; (3) royalties for songwriters and publishers; (4) manufacture; (5) distribution; (6) marketing and promotion. Without this information, even from the industry's own estimates, it is impossible to calculate the profit of the recording industry. However, this is the task that music industry researchers must embrace to understand the dynamics of the broader music business and its relationship with the recording industry.

For close to fifteen years, the recording industry constructed a crisis narrative about ever-shrinking revenue, but because of inadequate data collection, no evidence was provided to establish shrinking profits. Some cite mergers, lay-offs and shrinking record contracts as evidence of decline, but as I argue elsewhere, these are standard practices in capitalism to increase profits (Arditi 2014b, 2017). By creating a narrative about loss, IFPI has used its position to create knowledge that has enhanced the major record labels' power in the broader music industry.

Performance rights and synchronization licenses

At the beginning of this chapter, I quoted Frith saying that IFPI was created to promote performance rights in recordings. However, they did not begin to report data on performance rights until the 2005 edition of RIN, over 70 years after the organization's foundation. The 2005 edition of RIN reads:

> IFPI is publishing global performance rights collections for the licensing of sound recordings and music videos. Licensing income from both radio and TV broadcasting and public performance – such as the use of music or videos in nightclubs, bars, restaurants and hotels – is an increasingly important revenue source for record companies.
>
> (IFPI 2005: 20)

The inclusion of performance rights reflects the increased use of synergy in the cultural industries over the past decade. Nightclubs, bars, restaurants, hotels, television, radio and movies have licensed music from record labels since the early days of the recording industry, but the process accelerated as a result of large corporations using their different divisions to cross-promote one another (Hesmondhalgh 2007: 166). Each time a recorded song is played, performance rights must be paid to the rights holder, albeit that the categories for payment vary by territory. In order to utilize these changes, IFPI has become more interested in tracking how music is being used across media. Various European countries have collected this revenue for a considerable period, but for other countries, including the United States, this is a relatively new area of revenue. It is the global expansion of performing rights that has made it such a key issue for IFPI.

Furthermore, these synergistic activities do not stop at the boundary of the corporation, but rather record labels increasingly deploy music across media formats. This is a conscious strategy on the part of record labels that I describe elsewhere as the 'digital music trap [...] the expansion of the means of music consumption using digital technology' (Arditi 2017: 3). IFPI is well aware of these changes, and the newer editions of RIN and GMR demonstrate an attempt on the part of the recording industry to quantify the increased revenue stream from performance rights.

In addition to reporting performance rights, IFPI now provides some limited information about 'synchronization', the term used by the industry for the licensing of music in videos, television programmes, games and movies. These licences are a significant source of revenue for the major record labels, but the public reporting of this data has generally been non-existent or partial at best. In 2009, RIAA began publishing information about synchronization revenues in its own reports, documenting over $200 million in licensing revenue (RIAA 2013). However, it is unlikely that revenues went from zero to $200 million overnight and there is no attempt to account for synchronization prior to 2009. IFPI began reporting synchronization data in 2011 and reported $324 million that year, but again have given no indication of the revenue generated in previous years.

Copyright enforcement

Beyond the rise of synergy, in recent years there has been an increased interest in copyright enforcement as it pertains to recorded music. Copyright infringements are one explanation given by the industry for shrinking profit margins, as part of its crisis narrative. IFPI wants to ensure that any business that uses music for profit pays for this usage as required by copyright. For instance, the 2011 RIN states,

> [b]usinesses that use recorded music to attract and retain customers drive productivity and motivate employees increasingly pay a fair price for doing so wherever they are located. Music is used in a vast range of commercial contexts, from bars, shops and nightclubs to radio and television broadcasts.
>
> (2011: 28)

Hidden underneath this rather banal statement is a desire, on the part of IFPI, to hunt down the people who exploit music for profit without compensating record labels. In the next paragraph, IFPI remind us that these 'businesses are required by law in most countries to pay performers and producers when they use their work' and follow this statement by implying that the United States' exception for analogue radio and the Japanese exception for entertainment venues must be changed to adhere to this basic principle (2011: 28). It is vital for culture industry researchers to observe these statements within RIN and GMR and relate them to broader policy. At these moments in these reports, IFPI propagates ideology by making moral appeals about how laws work in other countries without situating the reasons why one country may have laws that differ from another's.

The broader music industry

As mentioned above, IFPI periodically includes a section on 'the broader music industry' in its reports. The following categories are generally included in this section to provide side-by-side comparison: radio-advertising revenues, recorded music retail sales, the live music sector, musical instrument sales, portable digital sales (hardware that plays digital music), audio home systems, songwriter musical copyright, music TV/magazines advertising revenue, music-related video games sales, and the performance rights market. These categories are of interest to researchers because they demonstrate what IFPI considers as its competitors and allies. For instance, by providing information on consumer electronics (hardware), record labels can calculate the media format for which they should produce their music. On the other hand, radio-advertising revenues loom large and there has been a consistent message that analogue radio stations in the United States should pay performance rights for sound recordings. Meanwhile, information about the live music sector, which for instance 'increased by 4 per cent globally in 2009' (IFPI 2010: 24), provides an indication why the recording industry became interested in 360° deals during the 2000s. In the 2008 edition of RIN, the broader music industry section indicates that IFPI was paying special attention to music video games by including a picture from *Guitar Hero* in the issue (2008: 13). Furthermore, IFPI asserts that recorded music 'is part of, and the driver of, a much broader music sector comprising a range of commercial activity based around music' (IFPI 2011: 26). By claiming that recorded music is the 'driver of' the broader music industry, IFPI declares that all other types of music commodities derive from the recorded music commodity. In recent years, IFPI has also claimed that social media derives its value from the music industry because recording artists provide some of the most popular accounts across social media platforms (IFPI 2015, 2016, 2017). These seemingly minor sets of data within RIN and GMR provide some of the more useful information because they illuminate how IFPI situates itself within the wider music industries.

World rankings and global data

Each edition of RIN and GMR contains a section entitled 'World Rankings', which ranks each country included in the reports in relation to their percentage of total world sales based on retail value. However, some years both the ranking by retail value and ranking by volume are included in tandem. When both data sets are presented together, it has demonstrated variation between the two sets of values. For instance, the 2001 edition of RIN demonstrates that the United States accounted for 38 per cent of the retail value of music in the world, but that same year only accounted for 31 per cent of the total units sold (volume) (2001: 10–13). These discrepancies can have an effect on rankings. In 2000, the United Kingdom ranked third in retail value with Germany in fourth, but when measured in terms of volume these two countries reversed ranks (IFPI 2001: 10–13). By looking more closely at this data, researchers may begin to discern systemic patterns in recorded music sales.

Throughout the 1990s Dave Laing wrote a series of critical reports in the 'Middle Eight' section of *Popular Music*, which focused on some of the problems of tracking global data for the recording industry. In 1997, he pointed to three problems with IFPI's reports (Laing 1997). First, each nation's recording industry trade group reports different data to IFPI. Second, the counting of 'parallel imports' ('copies of recordings imported by retailers or wholesalers from countries where prices are lower') distorts sales, as some countries do not include them in their figures (Laing 1997: 312). Finally, he demonstrates how these numbers get conflated with world music sales, but this conflation ignores the 'composer's rights market', which for 1996 would increase the overall revenues by $5 billion (Laing 1997: 312).

The majority of any given issue of RIN or GMR is dedicated to country-specific data. This presents researchers with information varying from unit and retail value to population sizes and income per capita. Each year IFPI presents slightly different data, but it consistently reports unit sales (usually shipments) and retail values. An important part of this information for the recording industry is hardware penetration. In different years this could be anything from CD player penetration to broadband penetration, depending on the hardware that the industry is most concerned with at that moment. A consistent part of the country-specific data is per capita unit sales and per capita money spent on music. While this data falls short because of inequality within a country (for example, if the average person spend is $50, some people may spend $0 on music while others spend $100), it provides interesting statistics for culture industry researchers to explore.

'Legitimate music'

'Legitimate music' is a term that consistently appears in these reports. However, there is no standard definition for what counts as 'legitimate'. For instance, I discussed above how IFPI feels that US analogue radio stations exploit the use of recorded music, but it is not clear whether they would label this use of music as illegitimate. What is legitimate? IFPI clearly believe that music sold and/or authorized by IFPI members is legitimate, but it is not so clear if they believe that music sold and/or authorized by non-member record labels or recording artists can be considered in the same manner. Overall, this is another area where IFPI has used RIN and GMR to propagate ideology to transform definitions and knowledge about the rules that govern record production, distribution, retail and consumption. They have constructed a binary between legitimate/illegitimate music in order to advance an ideological position about digital music distribution.

As early as the 1996 edition of RIN, IFPI was using the term 'legitimate': 'PIRACY is measured as the level of piracy as a percentage of total (legitimate and pirate) sales' (IFPI 1996: 2). However, this definition is circular because it defines 'piracy' as that which is not legitimate: piracy = illegitimate. What is piracy? Law professor Jessica Litman defines it as being 'about folks who made and sold large numbers of counterfeit copies' (Litman 2006: 85). Another legal scholar, Lawrence Lessig, defines commercial piracy as 'unauthorized taking of other people's content within a commercial context' (Lessig 2004: 62). In both cases, there is an emphasis on unauthorized reproduction of copyrighted material through commercial exchange. We can perhaps assume this is IFPI's own definition, but they are not explicit. Furthermore, in the 1990s RIN's main goal, in general, seems to have been to increase awareness of commercial piracy in the Global South.[1]

The individual country profiles provide information on the consumption of recorded music through industry-authorized channels. In other words, if we take the per capita sales data seriously, in some countries (primarily in the Global South) this number is artificially low because instances of large-scale piracy are much higher. Because of global inequality, there is a demand for cheap music on black markets supported by the unauthorized reproduction of copyrighted material. By labelling this material as illegitimate, IFPI have hoped to compel states and intergovernmental organizations, such as the World Trade Organization, to intercede in the music black market on their behalf.

IFPI's discussion about legitimate music consumption took a sharp turn in the 2000s as they began to focus on 'illegitimate' file-sharing. The 2000 edition of RIN points out that the 'internet is emerging as a vitally important medium for disseminating recorded music. Legitimate sales of music over the internet were at a very low level in 1999, despite an exponential increase in unauthorized music files' (IFPI 2000: 6). IFPI identify 'legitimate' as the opposite of 'unauthorized music files'. Who is the authorizing authority? We can get an idea from Lessig and Litman that authorized content is licensed by the copyright owner, but there is not always a clear delineation under laws that the non-commercial distribution of music violates copyright (Litman 2006). Additionally, IFPI includes practices such as the use of recordable CDs as piracy, which are illegal to use only in specific cases. Beginning with the 2001 edition of RIN, they became fixated on developing 'legitimate' outlets for online music consumption.

The issue of legitimacy is important because of the position this question plays both in the popular imaginary and the policy arena. In the United States, as the Congress prepared to debate copyright policy in 2013, the copyright green paper made extensive use of the term 'legitimate' in a manner derived directly from RIN (IPTF 2013). In fact, this green paper uses the term 'legitimate' 36 times without any explanation of what the term means in context (IPTF 2013). However, from the Internet Policy Task Force's language, it is clear that their use of the term was influenced by IFPI. This unquestioned acceptance of industry thinking enabled IFPI to advance its agenda to rewrite laws so they would benefit its members' interests.

Conclusion

By providing a protected space for the recording industry to communicate, RIN and GMR have facilitated the production of ideology. Through the dissemination of these reports, the recording industry has constructed narratives about music sales and copyright without having to share corporate information such as revenue and profits, which has enabled IFPI to use and abuse its data. This information has been repackaged and sold to politicians and the public in order to create laws that benefit major record labels (Arditi 2014b). The laws and regulations passed because of this information affect the production of culture and communication networks. Therefore, trade association data must be examined as a site of knowledge production and power.

NOTE

1. The term 'Global South' refers to relatively poor countries that tend to be further south than wealthier countries. These countries have also experienced the harmful effects of colonization.

REFERENCES

Arditi, David (2014a), 'Downloading is killing music: The recording industry's piracy panic narrative', *Civilisations,* 63:1, pp. 13–32.

——— (2014b), *iTake-Over: The Recording Industry in the Digital Era,* Lanham: Rowman & Littlefield Publishers.

——— (2017), 'Music everywhere: Setting a digital music trap', *Critical Sociology* (published online ahead of print 31 August), https://doi.org/10.1177/0896920517729192. Accessed 31 August 2017.

Berman, Jay (2004), *Online Music Report*, London: IFPI.

Frith, Simon (1988), 'Copyright and the music business', *Popular Music*, 7:1, pp. 57–75.

Gillespie, Tarleton (2007), *Wired Shut: Copyright and the Shape of Digital Culture*, Cambridge, MA: MIT Press.

Harker, Dave (1997), 'The wonderful world of IFPI: Music industry rhetoric, the critics and the classical marxist critique', *Popular Music*, 16:1, pp. 45–79.

Hesmondhalgh, David (2007), *The Cultural Industries*, 2nd ed., Los Angeles: SAGE.

International Federation of the Phonographic Industry (IFPI) (1996), *Recording Industry in Numbers*, London: IFPI.

——— (2000), *Recording Industry in Numbers*, London: IFPI.

——— (2001), *Recording Industry in Numbers*, London: IFPI.

——— (2002), *Recording Industry in Numbers*, London: IFPI.

——— (2004), *Recording Industry in Numbers*, London: IFPI.

——— (2005), *Recording Industry in Numbers*, London: IFPI.

——— (2007), *Recording Industry in Numbers*, London: IFPI.

——— (2008), *Recording Industry in Numbers*, London: IFPI.

——— (2010), *Recording Industry in Numbers*, London: IFPI.

——— (2011), *Recording Industry in Numbers*, London: IFPI.

——— (2015), *Recording Industry in Numbers*, London: IFPI.

——— (2016), *Global Music Report 2016*, London: IFPI.

——— (2017), *Global Music Report 2017*, London: IFPI.

——— (2019), 'About the report', IFPI, https://gmr.ifpi.org/about-the-report. Accessed 3 April 2019.

Internet Policy Task Force (IPTF) (2013), *Copyright Policy, Creativity, and Innovation in the Digital Economy*, Washington, DC: The Department of Commerce Internet Policy Task Force.

Laing, Dave (1997), 'World record sales', *Popular Music* 16:3, pp. 311–12.

Lessig, Lawrence (2004), *Free Culture: The Nature and Future of Creativity*, New York: Penguin.

Litman, Jessica (2006), *Digital Copyright*, Amherst: Prometheus Books.

Nielsen (1997), *1996 Year-end Music Industry Report*, New York: Nielsen.

——— (1999), *1998 Year-end Music Industry Report,* New York: Nielsen.

——— (2001), *2000 Year-end Music Industry Report,* New York: Nielsen.

——— (2003), *2002 Year-end Music Industry Report,* New York: Nielsen.

——— (2005), *2004 Year-end Music Industry Report,* New York: Nielsen.

——— (2007), *2006 Year-end Music Industry Report,* New York: Nielsen.

——— (2011) *2010 Year-end Music Industry Report,* New York: Nielsen.

Recording Industry Association of America (RIAA) (2013), 'Year-end industry shipment and revenue statistics', *RIAA Shipment Database,* http://www.riaa.com/chartindex.php. Accessed 24 July 2013 [no longer available].

Watkins, Craig S. (2005), *Hip Hop Matters: Politics, Pop Culture, and the Struggle for the Soul of a Movement*, Boston: Beacon Press.

5

Popular Music Funding in Canada

Shain Shapiro

This chapter concerns popular music funding in Canada, where an extensive public subsidy for popular music has existed since 1971, when the Canadian Radio, Television and Telecommunications Commission (CRTC) introduced Canadian content quota regulations on publicly owned airwaves, now generally known as CANCON. This quota is at the core of popular music policy in the country. Recordings are assessed in terms of the writers of the music, the lyricists, the artists and where the music was produced. To qualify for the quota, there must be Canadian contributors amongst at least two of these four categories. Beginning at 25 per cent of broadcast content, the quota has steadily increased; in 2019 it was set at 35 per cent of the content for English-speaking Canada and 65 per cent for French-language content in Quebec. This quota has been accompanied by subsidizing systems, including the Foundation to Assist Canadian Talent on Record (FACTOR), the first national fund to support English Canadian content producers, which was established in 1982. FACTOR is financed by a levy on the private radio industry. In addition, the Canadian government introduced the Canada Music Fund (CMF) in 2000, providing substantial support for the breadth of the music industry, from small and medium enterprises through to Canada's most well-known music companies. The system of funding has expanded so that it now infiltrates every level of the Canadian music business, from a new band recording a demo to a major music conference recruiting international buyers.

More broadly, Canada has one of the most extensive systems of any country for funding of the arts and is viewed as a model case by other nations. The Canadian system has been discussed in the United Kingdom and Australia (Spalding 2008: 155), and in recent years music industry and government representatives from Bulgaria, Ireland, Scotland, Israel, France, South Africa, Switzerland and Denmark have approached Canadian policy-makers and funding administrators to consult on policies (McKie 2012). Canada's funding system is shaped by a unique question, nonetheless: what does Canadian culture represent? Canadian cultural identity has been influenced by various dynamics, including close proximity to the United States, sparse population density and the promotion of federalism in a country that has two official languages and popular cultures. Defining what Canadian culture is, and subsequently how to protect, enrich and promote it, has therefore been at the core of arts funding.

This chapter documents a change of orientation in policy. Where the funding of popular music had initially leant towards promoting and protecting Canadian culture, developments in the 2000s saw a move towards enriching its makers. This was most manifest with the Radio Starmaker Fund (RSF) and FondsRadiostar, but was also present in debates concerning support for 'emerging artists'. It is these developments that will be addressed. The use of numbers runs throughout this history. Quota percentages are established, thresholds for participation are defined and measures are put in place to quantify success.

Radio Starmaker Fund and FondsRadiostar

The Radio Starmaker Fund (RSF), covering English language Canada, and FondsRadiostar, covering Quebec, were created in 1997 but not launched until 2000, with the first round of funding being awarded to over a dozen acts in 2001. This funding was markedly different to previous systems in Canada. The term 'starmaker' is indicative of its objective. RSF/FondsRadiostar was commercially focused and designed exclusively for established artists. In addition, this funding system did not support content creation, breaking with the core objectives of CANCON and previous state policy. In its first year, just under Can$3 million was guaranteed, with a cap placed at Can$50m (CAB 1998). For FondsRadiostar in 2001–2002, the fund distributed over Can$1.5 million, 20 per cent of the total amount available for the fund that year (FondsRadiostar 2002). The funding was accrued through half of the six per cent tax that was levied on broadcaster mergers and acquisitions, as mandated in the 1998 commercial radio review. While it was initially planned that the fund would conclude in 2010, it remains operational as of 2019, with four rounds of funding available per year through RSF, and a rolling programme through FondsRadiostar.

Gary Slaight of Standard Broadcasting and Ross Davies of CHUM, members of the Canadian Association of Broadcasters (CAB), initiated the funds. In the 1990s, broadcasting regulations were loosened so that if a company owned two FM stations in a given market, they were also allowed to purchase one AM station, or vice versa (Roman 2012). According to the executive director of RSF, Chip Sutherland, '[t]he broadcasters knew such consolidation of ownership would have an effect on culture, in theory, so they accepted a tax on such agreements, which was arbitrarily decided at six per cent' (Sutherland 2012). This tax, which Sutherland suggests as being readily accepted, was in fact subject to intense negotiation. There were debates concerning who would administer the allocation and how much the allocation should be. In the initial discussions, FACTOR lobbied to have control of the funding, while the Canadian Independent Record Production Association (CIRPA) argued that only independent labels should have access to it. Initially, CAB members argued for an overall three per cent tax, while the music industry lobby aimed for percentages as high as ten per cent. In the agreement with the CRTC, a compromise of six per cent was reached, albeit begrudgingly. Out of this six per cent tax, three per cent was to go towards the new fund, two per cent to FACTOR, half a per cent to community radio programming and the final half per cent was discretionary, ultimately being used as marketing reinvestment for the stations themselves. The money for the new fund was divided, with fourth-fifths going to RSF and a fifth to FondsRadiostar. In a speech that was recorded at The Empire Club in Toronto in 2001, Michael McCabe, then President of CAB, stated:

> Private radio broadcasters accept the public-policy goals underpinning the Canadian-content requirements. But many in our industry are concerned about the continued shortage of high-quality Canadian music that appeals to a mass audience. In other words, Canada does not have enough music stars. This is a serious challenge, and one that cannot be overcome through government regulation. Statistics prove this beyond any doubt.
>
> (McCabe 2001)

RSF/FondsRadiostar was more in tune with the commercial desires of broadcasters than any previous culturally focused initiative. To defend this shift, McCabe argued that Canada did not need more music per se, but more music stars and commercial successes. It can be argued, however, that this framework contradicted the initial objectives of CANCON. Canadian content regulations had not been written to assist the building of a star system. Moreover, while the Canada Music Fund had expressed a desire to facilitate greater commercial success, achieving stardom was not a pre-requisite for support. Instead, what mattered was being Canadian and creating content as a Canadian. For RSF/FondsRadiostar this was not the case. The support was privately delivered and the requirements to meet such guidelines were determined by the broadcasters. There was a focus on international success over local content development. Their argument was that while more music may not beget more stars; more stars may beget a stronger, more sustainable sector:

> The concept behind these two funds is very simple: they are going to seek out and identify the most promising musical artists, and then provide them with the marketing and promotional support needed to help them become stars. Our business goal is very straightforward: we want to increase the supply of Canadian music that Canadians want to listen to. It's a revolutionary concept, I know: we intend to do nothing less than give the people what they want.
>
> (McCabe 2001)

Previous policies had not focused on giving people 'what they want'. Instead, they focused on giving people Canadian content, albeit that how that content reflected national characteristics was never clearly defined.

RSF/FondsRadiostar outlined Canadian sales quotas that each act had to meet in order to qualify for support. These were separated by genre, with pop/rock requiring the highest sales levels and world, jazz and classical requiring the lowest. Support was delivered to acts that had already achieved a certain degree of success. It was not stipulated that the funding had to go towards the creation of new music.

The rules insisted that '[y]ou do not qualify for funding if the royalties and revenues from the Canadian sales of your records flow directly to a corporation outside of Canada. You must receive your royalties from Canadian sales directly through a Canadian company' (RSF 2001). This did not mean that international major record companies could not partake of the funding, however, as each of them had stakes in Canadian companies. CIRPA argued that allowing major labels to access RSF/FondsRadiostar was unfair to independent record companies. In response, RSF/FondsRadiostar opened up applications to individual artists, regardless of what labels they were signed to, but insisted that major label artists meet higher sales quotas. This created the first instance where multinational entities could access funding for their projects in Canada. It did not matter how an artist accumulated their success and which businesses they worked with; it mattered more that they had success, regardless of the business infrastructure.

RSF/FondsRadiostar's rules were outside of state control. Once CAB members had agreed to the levy, further regulations were up to the funders themselves. The CRTC was not mandated to control the manner in which the money was allocated, but only to ensure that support was available for Canadian content development. The CRTC did not mention how the money was to be spent. It stated simply that of the six per cent allocation, half should be 'allocated to a new Canadian music marketing and promotion fund' (Canadian Radio-Television and Telecommunications Commission 1998). In explaining what marketing and promotion meant in this context, the report concluded, 'the purpose of the Canadian music marketing and promotion fund will be to support co-operative activities by broadcasters and the music industry to market and promote Canadian music, including new talent'

(CRTC 1998). Given that such new talent would have to sell between 2500 and 10,000 units in Canada to qualify, a level was established that, in some ways, eliminated a significant number of new artists from applying. It was likely, in fact, that any qualifying new act would have been established with the backing of a major label.

By 1998, RSF had been created but no programme for distributing the funds existed, leaving Can$8m in reserves (Sutherland 2012). By the end of 2001, after a series of mergers and acquisitions amongst radio broadcasters, the fund had Can$23m in capital, but only committed to paying out Can$1m (Sutherland 2012). In fact, it was nearly four years after its initiation that the programme delivered its first support to artists. According to Catherine Saxberg, the second executive hired by Sutherland to run the fund, '[t]he broadcasters sat on the money for four years' (2012). Nevertheless, RSF's annual reports reveal that the amount of support that acts have received has been substantial. In one round with RSF in 2010, the Ontario-based singer-songwriter City and Colour received Can$143,004.77. Two rounds later in the same year, he received Can$41,845.08 (RSF 2011). For the most part, acts that were more successful, and therefore had higher touring and marketing costs to consider, were more likely to achieve a positive response to their applications. It was also the case that, to a point, the more successful an act was, the more support they received. In addition, while this is not presented in the annual reporting on financial data, RSF and FondsRadiostar have assisted labels, sector associations, music festivals and conferences (Johnston 2012). Labels that qualified for FondsRadiostar, similar to the Radio Starmaker Fund, had to meet sales thresholds to be included.

This support has enhanced acts' ability to market their recordings and to tour domestically and internationally. This support is provided, however, through a non-renewable structure that will conclude if no more consolidation amongst broadcasters occurs in Canada. RSF/FondsRadiostar presents a peculiar case in comparison to other Canadian popular music-funding initiatives. Previously, support had been delivered through a complex structure encapsulating both public and private support. In contrast, this was the first privately run and directed fund. While CANCON and the requirement to air a percentage of Canadian music on radio initiated the discussions leading to RSF, the fund itself is distanced from the wording in the *Broadcasting Act of Canada*, which states that programming should

> encourage the development of Canadian expression by providing a wide range of programming that reflects Canadian attitudes, opinions, ideas, values and artistic creativity, by displaying Canadian talent in entertainment programming and by offering information and analysis concerning Canada and other countries from a Canadian point of view.
>
> (Department of Justice 2012)

RSF/FondsRadiostar and the industry

As RSF/FondsRadiostar increased its disbursements, the domestic artists' market share of Canadian content remained stationary, hovering between fifteen per cent and 22 per cent (Department of Canadian Heritage 2007: 5). Meanwhile, overall music sales dropped. Between 2006 and 2008, Canada's trade value of music sales declined by eight per cent (Department of Canadian Heritage 2007: 5). This situation was not unique to Canada, as the trade value of global music sales declined in this period from US$24b to US$18.4b (Department of Canadian Heritage 2007: 6). Despite this decline, the amount of albums released by Canadian artists remained almost stationary: 2562 were released in 2004 compared with 2465 in 2008 (Department of Canadian Heritage 2007: 9). Therefore, there is little statistical evidence to demonstrate that financial support led to the creation of stars and their concomitant blockbuster releases.

Throughout this period, funding continued to increase in Canada, through greater RSF/FondsRadiostar availability and the introduction of a series of regional funding structures. Nevertheless, the amount of support allocated and its impact on its recipients in the current music industry had yet to be measured. For example, the 2007 *Canadian Music Industry Profile*, published by the Department of Canadian Heritage, did not mention this subsidization (Department of Canadian Heritage 2007: 5). The funding was being questioned, however. When interviewed in 2008, Slaight revealed that the increase of support had had unintended consequences. He stated that 'there's too much cash available from governments and broadcasters (through FACTOR, Radio Starmaker, VideoFACT and Arts Councils) but no grand game plan as to how the cash can be best used' (Quill 2008). This was the first time in Canadian funding history that a complaint of this nature had been noted publicly.

The amount of media consolidation occurred faster than the CRTC anticipated. Acts thus received substantial contributions from RSF/FondsRadiostar because money was available to be given to them. Moreover, applicants had a good chance of receiving funding. In comparison with FACTOR's tour programmes, which were often oversubscribed with the result that applicants had a twenty per cent success rate in achieving funding (FACTOR 2011: 5), RSF applicants had an 85–90 per cent success rate (RSF 2009: 4). The major restricting factor for artists to receive RSF/FondRadiostar funding was the sales quotas required. Therefore, there were cases whereby artists petitioned the board of directors to be reclassified under genres with lower ratios. Dan Mangan, for example, successfully gained reclassification as folk rather pop/rock and as a result his sales figures qualified for the fund in 2011 (Mangan 2012).

While not reported in official literature, these tactics meant that the number of qualifying artists increased, thus ensuring that the funds were allocated as required.

This meant that an increased number of acts were provided with subsidies for expensive touring costs, but it also produced a false economy that will eventually disappear in the event there is no further media consolidation. However, while the fund itself might be temporary, its influence on Canada's music sector could have lasting effects. There has been a shift towards supporting commercial development and away from providing cultural support.

The 2006 commercial radio review and defining emerging artists

On 23 January 2006, Canada held an election. The Conservatives won, ending twelve years of Liberal leadership. Before the election, a CRTC commercial radio review was announced. The review was originally intended to take place in 2005, but was delayed because of the election and parliamentary debates concerning the rollout of digital and satellite radio. On 31 January 2006, the CRTC released a 'call of interest' in respect of hearings set to take place in Ottawa on 13 May and 15 May of that year (CRTC 2006b). These hearings were intended to debate the financial stability of the private radio sector in accordance with its demographic reach, contributions to developing Canadian content requirements and the issue of licence renewals. The review provoked disagreement between CIRPA, the Canadian Music Publishers Association (CMPA), its partners and CAB, with each providing different recommendations to amend the regulations. Rulings that had been made in 1998 were addressed first, outlining the financial benefits of these decisions to CAB members:

> Canadian commercial AM and FM radio stations, as a group, experienced an average annual growth in total revenues of 5.5% between the broadcast years 2001 and 2005. Increases in the limits on the number of stations that a licensee may own in a single market established by the 1998 Commercial Radio Policy resulted in a consolidation of radio ownership, enhanced operational synergies and improved profitability.
>
> (CRTC 2006b: 10)

All parties who submitted recommendations argued that CANCON should be changed. Music industry representatives viewed the 35 per cent quota level as too low, while CAB thought it too high. CIRPA argued that 45 per cent would better suit emerging Canadian content, while the Canadian Association of Songwriters argued for 55 per cent (CRTC 2006a). The broadcasters argued that the quota must reflect market conditions, with 'data from Statistics Canada indicating that Canadian recordings only comprised 17% of total sales of recordings in 1998 and 16% of total sales of recordings in 2000 and 2003' (CRTC 2006b: 52). In addition, they pointed out that Canadians were listening to less analogue radio in 2006, compared with 1998, because new media, such as Internet and satellite technology, was competing with traditional radio. Opportunities to listen to foreign content, via online sources and satellite radio increased, leading CAB members to argue that consumers were, in fact, listening to more foreign content. They argued in their submission that traditional radio consumption had decreased on average by 1.25 hours per week (CRTC 2006b: 8).

Debates about how much of the CANCON quota should be used to serve emerging Canadian content were equally polarizing. CAB submitted a statement titled 'The issues of requiring commitment to the airplay of emerging artists':

> CAB strongly believes that the purpose of establishing an industry-wide definition for each of the French and English radio markets is to ensure fairness, predictability and consistency when assessing the level of airplay of music by emerging artists on commercial radio. It should not in any way shape or form be viewed or used as a way to impose additional regulations on the private commercial radio sector. A new level of quota or condition of license based on commitments made by applicants either through the renewal of their license, through a competitive licensing process for attributing new radio licenses or transfer of ownership of existing radio stations is unnecessary and unworkable in an era in which regulated commercial radio is competing with other, less-regulated or unregulated music delivery platforms.
>
> (Smith 2008: 8)

CIRPA, the Society of Composers, Authors and Music Publishers in Canada (SOCAN), CMPA and its partners objected to this statement, as CAB did not clarify what they meant by the term 'emerging'. CAB's response was to suggest a bonus system for playing CANCON between six in the morning and six at night, where each play of a defined emerging artist would count for 125 per cent of CANCON requirements. This would lower the CANCON requirement for the station in exchange for a promise to air an emerging artist during peak broadcasting hours, a rule not guaranteed under CANCON. CIRPA argued that while CAB members generally abided by the quota requirement, most of this quota was aired during off-peak hours. This was not a new argument, as similar accusations had been raised since the mid-1970s.

Two years after these debates, the CRTC offered a definition of 'emerging artist' as referring to performers who had had Top 40 status for less than a year:

> 'Top 40, less than one year' definition appears to have the most advantages since:
> - o Current and historical chart information is relatively easy for all to obtain;
> - o Some of the relevant charts combine airplay and sales data, two important measures of popularity; and

> The 'Top 40, less than one year' definition may strike an appropriate balance between ensuring name recognition on the part of radio listeners and music consumers and the exposure of an ever-renewing roster of emerging talent.
> (CRTC 2008: 8)

This was similar to the definition offered by CAB in 2006, which stated that 'for the English-language markets, a performer could be considered as an "emerging Canadian artist" up until 12 full months after the date the artist's first selection reaches the Top 40 on Broadcast Data System (BDS) or Mediabase all-format charts, or becomes gold certified for the first time' (CRTC 2006a: 64).

This is an economically focused definition, bypassing many performers simply because Top 40 artists, whatever genre they are, tend to need strong business infrastructures behind them. In fact, this definition of 'emerging' favoured artists who had already 'emerged'. How the definition of 'Top 40' was assessed was through the Broadcast Data System, by which stations independently monitored their programming. This was a private initiative, controlled by the broadcasters.

The independent music sector rallied against this definition. In its recommendations, CIRPA claimed, 'there are more than 20,000 tracks released each year in Canada and on average radio stations add less than 70 of them. It is highly unlikely that the other 19,930 of them are unfit for radio airplay' (Ferguson 2006a: 1a). While this statistic has not been verified, it outlines CIRPA's frustration on behalf of the independent labels. CIRPA's own recommendations to the CRTC reveal their position:

> Let's face it: Canadian radio isn't interested in breaking new acts or new music. They are asking to receive extra credit for playing music they should already be playing. They just don't want to play it unless it means they can play less Canadian music overall, which is the ultimate goal of their proposed bonus system.
> (Ferguson 2006: 7)

CIRPA did not offer a viable alternative to define the concept of an emerging artist, other than one who fits within its independent member base. As a result, the Commission did not come to a definable and acceptable decision for what an emerging artist was in Canada or how they would be treated by Canadian radio. In the dissenting arguments section, commissioner Stuart Langford stated:

> Imaginative is the absolute last word that springs to my mind when I review paragraphs 32 to 96 of the majority decision. In essence, with exceptions so minor as, in my opinion, to be practically inconsequential, the majority's view of an appropriate future approach to promoting Canadian content and talent

> appears to have been envisaged by looking in a rear-view mirror. What they believe they saw there, though, is anyone's guess.
>
> (CRTC 2006b: 220)

By 'looking in a rear-view mirror', Langford was arguing that the CRTC was administering CAB in a manner that allowed them to satisfy the regulations in whichever way they saw fit; therefore, most decisions made by the commission were inconsequential. He claimed that the protection and promotion of Canadian culture were being ignored:

> They [the broadcasters] meet the 35% level but they do so by playing just a few marquee artists over and over again. That's great for big names like Shania Twain and Avril Lavigne, but not so good for lesser-known performers.
>
> (CRTC 2006b: 220)

By not defining the concept of an 'emerging artist' concisely, CANCON became, for many broadcasters, a means by which to air the content most suitable to them, even if this was comprised of a few select artists. Here too, Canadian cultural policy was being utilized to legislate and regulate economic objectives. In her Robarts Lecture at the University of Toronto in 1996, Joyce Zemans had predicted this state of affairs, suggesting that the 'evidence of this shift lies in the transformation in the focus of Canadian cultural policy away from a nationalist, public service, market corrective approach towards a growing emphasis on a market ideology' (Zemans 1996).

Conclusion

It can be argued that from the introduction of the RSF/FondsRadiostar in 1998 through to the development of the Canada Music Fund (CMF) in 2001 and the commercial radio review in 2006, policies in Canada concerning popular music shifted from supporting and protecting content itself to a more economically focused, international perspective. The core objectives enshrined in Canadian cultural policy, such as the protection and enrichment of Canadian content as written in the *Broadcasting Act of Canada* (Department of Justice 2012) and the retention of CANCON quota remained, but the tactics taken to support them did not align with such policy objectives.

From the wording in *From Creators to Audience,* issued by the Department of Canadian Heritage in 2001, to the initial disbursement from RSF/FondsRadiostar, a new focus emerged that shifted policy from simply ensuring the production of Canadian music to positioning Canada as a global, commercially successful brand.

While Canadian content creators benefitted from these program introductions, the ones who benefitted most fitted into a policy that valued content in terms of commercial success and stardom rather than for its diversity and plurality. Priority treatment was given to those who qualified for RSF or the Music Entrepreneur Component (MEC) of the Canada Music Fund (which provides approximately Can$500,000 to each of the top twenty revenue-generating music businesses each year). For example, only one jazz label, Justin Time, qualified for MEC during this period compared with over a dozen indie, rock and commercial labels, such as Last Gang, Arts & Crafts or Nettwerk. The organizations debating, enacting and refining these policies – the music sector, broadcasters and the state – shifted concern away from the protection of Canadian music to focus more on the amounts of financing that they could utilize. For the broadcasters, this financing came in the ability to buy and sell each other and control more than two stations per market, while for the music sector, the focus honed in on the amount of money available for their represented businesses.

Such changes occurred during a marked global shift in how music was recorded, manufactured, distributed and sold. By the mid-2000s, bricks and mortar retail outlets were no longer the primary source of revenue generation for labels and content creators; music was now widely available, often for free, through peer-to-peer downloading and streaming. In addition, listening options for consumers burgeoned, with online and satellite radio altering listening habits and limiting the impact that terrestrial radio could have on commercial success. Artists were not confined to relying on large-scale distribution structures to support their music. Through the Internet, a global audience was emerging that did not rely on national borders or boundaries to find content.

As a result, nationalistic, protectionist cultural policy such as CANCON was impacted. The broadcasting and music industry sectors both noticed this. For the broadcasters, the ability to consolidate produced leaner, more profitable companies that could compete with international competitors, especially those in the United States. For music makers and labels, the legislated protection of Canadian content was deprioritized. In its place came the provision of finance to develop content that could compete internationally. The most supported Canadian content, in terms of popular music development, was comprised of internationally successful, commercial pop, rock and MOR acts. Artists like Avril Lavigne, Shania Twain, Celine Dion and Nickelback were all supported by funding mechanisms at one stage in their career and 'enhanced' the Canadian brand abroad through their continued success. However, this success did not always trickle back to Canada's domestic businesses, ones that these programs were designed to support. For example, the *Canadian Music Industry Profile* of 2008 states, '[a]lthough music is gaining in popularity, it is also under significant pressure. Pervasive unauthorized downloading presents numerous challenges for the industry, which is diversifying its activities and changing its business models to adapt to new realities' (Department of Canadian Heritage 2009: 6). The report continues, 'Canadian-controlled record labels experienced an increase in operating revenues; however, their profit margin remained smaller than that of foreign-controlled major labels' (Department of Canadian Heritage 2009: 8).

Why then have music companies of other countries looked towards the Canadian funding system as a source of inspiration? The Canadian music industries have had a more concerted and prolonged dialogue with their governments than those of other nations, and they have secured greater protection and greater sources of funding. Yet these policies have not always safeguarded Canadian businesses and they have not developed recognizably 'Canadian' performers. Maybe the answer to the question lies in these results. The music companies that lobby governments most concertedly are usually the multinational corporations. They seek localized developments in funding and policy but their economics and repertoire are global in nature.

REFERENCES

Canadian Association of Broadcasters (CAB) (1998), *Radio Starmaker Fund*, Canadian Association of Broadcasters, http://www.cab-acr.ca/english/radio/starmakerfund/default.shtm. Accessed 1 October 2011.

Canadian Radio-Television and Telecommunications Commission (CRTC) (1998), *Commercial Radio Policy Review*, Government of Canada, http://www.crtc.gc.ca/eng/archive/1998/pb98-41.htm. Accessed 8 January 2012.

——— (2006a), 'CRTC announces results of its commercial radio policy review', Government of Canada, 15 December, http://www.crtc.gc.ca/eng/archive/2006/n2006-1.htm. Accessed 6 February 2012.

——— (2006b), 'Public notice 2006-158: Commercial Radio Policy 2006', Government of Canada, December 15, http://www.crtc.gc.ca/eng/archive/2006/PB2006-158.htm. Accessed 6 February 2012.

——— (2008), 'Diversity of voices', Government of Canada, http://www.crtc.gc.ca/eng/archive/2008/pb2008-4.htm. Accessed 24 November 2013.

Department of Canadian Heritage (2001), 'From creators to audience: New policy directions for Canadian Sound Recording 2001 Report', Government of Canada, http://www.pch.gc.ca/eng/1289312410707/1289312410708. Accessed 6 February 2012 [no longer available].

_______ (2007), 'The Canadian music industry – 2006 economic profile', Government of Canada, www.pch.gc.ca/pgm/fmusc-cmusf/pubs/prfl/index-eng.cfm. Accessed 13 September 2013 [no longer available].

——— (2009), 'The Canadian music industry – 2008 economic profile', Government of Canada, www.pch.gc.ca/eng/1289313312537/1289313312539. Accessed 6 March 2012.

Department of Justice (2012), *Broadcasting Act of Canada*, Government of Canada, http://laws-lois.justice.gc.ca/eng/acts/B-9.01/page-2.html#h-4. Accessed 6 March 2012.

Ferguson, Cori (2006a), 'Notice of public hearing: Review of commercial broadcasting policy – Letter submitted to Ms. Diane Rheaume', *Canadian Independent Music Association Archives*, 15 April.

——— (2006), 'Broadcasting Notice 2006-1: Review of commercial radio policy', *Canadian Independent Music Association Archives*, 12 June.

FondsRadiostar (2002), *Annual Report: 2001–2002*, FondsRadiostar, https://www.fondsradiostar.com/sites/default/files/ra-01-02-fr.pdf. Accessed 28 October 2013.

Foundation Assistant Canadian Talent on Recordings (FACTOR) (2011), *2010–2011 Annual Report,* Foundation to Assist Canadian Talent on Record, https://www.factor.ca/aboutthefoundation/annualreports#.UqSmMmRdWSE. Accessed 21 April 2012.

Johnston, Stuart (2012), email to author, London, UK, 13 May.

Mangan, Dan (2012), telephone interview with Shain Shapiro, London, UK, 4 April.

McCabe, Michael (2001), 'Canadian music at a crossroad: "10 reasons why Canada's music industry needs a new policy framework"', *The Empire Club of Canada*, 28 March, http://speeches.empireclub.org/62858/data. Accessed 13 February 2020.

McKie, Duncan (2012), telephone interview with Shain Shapiro, London, UK, 23 April.

Quill, Greg (2008), 'What's wrong with Canadian music: On Juno Sunday', *Toronto Star*, 6 April, https://www.thestar.com/news/2008/04/06/whats_wrong_with_canadian_music_on_juno_sunday.html. Accessed 11 February 2019.

Radio Starmaker Fund (RSF) (2001), *Annual Report: 2000–2001*, Toronto: Radio Starmaker Fund.

——— (2009), *Annual Report 2008–2009*, Radio Starmaker Fund, Toronto, https://www.starmaker.ca/reports/RSF_2008-2009_Annual_Report.pdf. Accessed 28 October 2013.

——— (2011), *Annual Report 2010–2011*, Radio Starmaker Fund, Toronto, https://www.starmaker.ca/annualreports/2011. Accessed 28 October 2013.

Roman, Duff (2012), email to author, London, UK, 8 February.

Saxberg, Catherine (2012), email to author, London, UK, 6 January.

Smith, Pierre Louis (2008), 'Broadcasting Public Notice 2008–16: Call for comments on the definition of emerging Canadian artists on commercial radio', *Canadian Association of Broadcasters*, 28 June, http://www.cab-acr.ca/english/research/08/sub_may2608.pdf. Accessed 29 October 2013.

Spalding, Eric (2008), 'Twice born: The origins of FACTOR, 1982–1986', *Journal of Canadian Studies*, 2:42, pp. 140–59.

Sutherland, Chip (2012), telephone interview with Shain Shapiro, London, UK, 10 April.

Zemans, Joyce (1996), 'What is here? Canadian culture in a globalized world', *Tenth Annual Robarts Lecture*, York University, Toronto, Canada, 13 March.

PART III

LIVE MUSIC

6

Stop Making Census! Some Experiential Reflections on Conducting a Live Music Census

Adam Behr, Matt Brennan, Martin Cloonan and Emma Webster

This chapter discusses the challenges and opportunities for researching live music through the method of a census. It draws on our experience of running the United Kingdom's first national Live Music Census (the project was named the UK Live Music Census) in March 2017 and falls into six parts: (1) the background to our work in live music research; (2) a review of previous censuses; (3) lessons learned from previous censuses; (4) the context for the UK Live Music Census; (5) experiences of running the census; and (6) issues for discussion arising from the census. Our conclusion suggests that such projects are likely to remain part of the research landscape for the foreseeable future, but also cautions that they are not for the faint-hearted or the methodologically nervous.

Part one: Background

The origins of our census can be traced back to research conducted in Scotland in 2002, which, amongst other things, highlighted the importance of live music to the nation's music economy (Williamson et al. 2003). Subsequent work by Frith et al. (2010, 2013) as part of an Arts and Humanities Research Council (AHRC)-funded enquiry into the history of the United Kingdom's live music industry kick-started a series of related projects in academic live music research and knowledge exchange (Frith and Cloonan 2019). For us, it included the establishment in 2012 of the Live Music Exchange (Behr et al. 2019), which has since provided a focus for debates on aspects of live music and acted as a *nom de guerre* for several projects, consultancies and reports to which we have contributed in various capacities.

This work has engendered increasingly close cooperation with parts of the live music industry, including two projects examining cultural value, both funded by the AHRC. The first involved working with the Queen's Hall in Edinburgh to examine the relationship between different promotional practices and the cultural value that audiences place on live music (Behr et al. 2016a). The second investigated different models of venue funding in Glasgow, Leeds and Camden, working with industry-related bodies: PRS for Music, UK Music and the Musicians' Union (Behr et al. 2014). Although primarily qualitative work, this can be seen retrospectively to have carried the kernel of the later UK-wide census project in looking across cities as well as across venue types.

By 2015, then, we found ourselves amongst the vanguard of research into the United Kingdom's live music sector. However, we were also aware of other attempts to conduct such exercises and so to provide the context for our work there follows a brief overview of comparable exercises undertaken prior to our own census.

Part two: Previous work

Some previous surveys were linked to broader attempts to intervene in the local music industries, others arose from local campaigns and sometimes the two motives were combined. The biggest specific inspiration for our census, the 2012 Victorian Live Music Census, arose indirectly from local activism that began in 2010 and came to centre on the Save Live Australia's Music campaign which yielded a commitment by local policy-makers to discover the true picture of the city's live music scene (Homan 2014). The subsequent census was undertaken on Saturday 13 October 2012, when volunteers visited Melbourne's venues, gathering information on such things as the maximum number of people expected to attend, the number of musicians (including DJs) and other staff employed on the night, and how the venue operated. Volunteers also distributed flyers containing links to online surveys for musicians and audiences, forming the second part of the data collection methodology. The report usefully includes the statistical assumptions that allowed the researchers to estimate annual figures for attendances and spend (Music Victoria/City of Melbourne 2012: 24–25). This provided a starting point for calculations for our pilot study in Edinburgh and thus a useful template for the UK Live Music Census. While the language of the Melbourne census report is often more informal than academic, its aspirations to be as methodologically rigorous, comprehensive and transparent as possible struck a chord.

An alternative is provided by the Austin Music Census (Titan Music Group 2015) which was a local survey with a wider remit. Part of the report deals specifically with live music in the form of '[m]usic venues and nightlife establishments' but the Austin Census is essentially a survey of local music industries personnel (Titan Music Group: 5). While this survey does not focus on live music per se, it does provide some useful ideas for those wishing to research their local music industries and some recommendations for policy-makers, for example 'minimizing venue regulations' while recognizing the need for a mixed economy of private sector, non-profit and public sector investment (Titan Music Group: 6). As the methodology lacks a dedicated live music census, the Austin report's main influence on our work was in terms of rigour rather than methodology.

Australia has been at the forefront of several developments in live music policy, including the provision of a federal Live Music Office and the development of music industries strategies in major centres like Sydney and Melbourne (City of Melbourne 2014; City of Sydney 2014), as well as a survey of live music in South Australia (Live Music Office 2015). The Adelaide Live Music Census of May 2015 provided a snapshot of 'live music in licensed premises in greater Adelaide' (Music SA/Live Music Office 2015: 2). The methodology was relatively informal, with data gathered across the month from venue websites and social media, gig guides, word of mouth, phone calls and industry contacts. Overall this report provides some baseline information on what sorts of gigs took place where, and whether they had special licences. It largely consists of details of the venues rather than an analysis of income, trends, issues and so on. Thus, while it contains some useful information, there are also methodological limitations. The Adelaide methodology was largely replicated in 2016 with a follow-up that both covered a larger geographical spread and allowed for some comparative analysis, supported by the South Australia State Government's Music Development Office and the National Live Music Office. Alongside the existence of a city Live Music Action Plan (City of Adelaide 2017), this illustrates the potential – indeed, often the necessity – for communication with the policy-makers who are a key part of a city's live music ecology in the research process (Behr et al. 2016b).

The Live Music Office was also involved with research on the economic, social and cultural contribution of the Australian live music industry, which surveyed consumers nationwide alongside surveys of venues in Hobart, Melbourne, Adelaide and Sydney (Live Music Office 2014). The report contains a useful literature review of the social and cultural value of live music (Live Music Office 2014: 10–11) and discusses the various forms of live music capital (Live Music Office 2014: 34–38). However, as in Austin, the methodology did not contain a snapshot live music census and therefore did not provide a direct methodological model for our own census exercises.

Prior to our UK-wide census, we conducted the aforementioned Edinburgh pilot census on Saturday 6 June 2015. Our team visited 45 venues and collected information about the events taking place, with thirteen more venues added in afterwards via information gathered from various sources. Based on the Melbourne model, this was the first exercise of its kind in the United Kingdom. As with Melbourne, in addition to visiting venues on the night we conducted online surveys of venues and musicians in what became something of a blueprint for the later UK-wide census.

The Edinburgh report is the most 'academic' in tone of the ones reviewed here, in that it had the greatest awareness of other reports and the widest context within which the research was taking place. We erred on the side of caution with some of the figures, something also apparent in other surveys, such as in Melbourne and Adelaide. While we too produced a 'big number' on annual spend on live music, our findings were generally couched in terms of minimum numbers and somewhat qualified throughout (Behr et al. 2015: 39–40).

We argued in the Edinburgh report that such research is 'an ongoing task', acknowledging the need to refine our own methodology (Behr et al. 2015: 25). We also noted methodological differences across previous work and the updating of such methodologies within annual publications such as UK Music's *Measuring Music* reports (2018a) and those previously undertaken by PRS for Music (Page and Carey 2010, 2011). This pointed towards the importance of considering studies 'in specific locations and by specific organisations [...] against their wider context' (Behr et al. 2015: 11). While acknowledging the logistical constraints on providing comprehensive data about the city, we suggested that the findings still illustrated 'the value of live music to Edinburgh and of the [...] Census approach to appraising it' (Behr et al. 2015: 1).

Importantly, the Edinburgh Census fed into local policy. The impetus for it partly emerged from a City of Edinburgh Council working group which had been established in order to address concerns about venue closures and a clause in local licensing policy that amplified music should be 'inaudible' in neighbouring premises. Adam Behr and Matt Brennan were on the working group and suggested a live music census to assess the scale of the problem. Our eventual recommendation to amend the clause was adopted after lengthy and occasionally contentious consultation. The potential for such work to make a concrete difference boosted our plans for a UK-wide project.

As well as addressing the 'inaudibility' clause, we observed that a significant proportion of venues reported noise, planning or development issues with the local authority (Behr et al. 2015: 4), recommending that the city adopt the 'Agent of Change' principle and that the local authorities should 'recognise the economic and cultural value of live music to the city' (Behr et al. 2015: 5).[1] Overall, our pilot study offered an iterative refinement of the Melbourne approach, also helping to introduce the concept of a live music census to the United Kingdom.

The final local census before our own UK-wide one was the Bristol Live Music Census, based on a survey night of Thursday 22 October 2015 and seeking to explore 'the live music ecosystem in Bristol' (Bucks New University/UK Music 2016: 5). It gathered information from 23 venues on the night and included online surveys of venue operators, musicians and audiences (Bucks New University/UK Music 2016: 16). The economic analysis and production of a 'big number' for live music revenue (Bucks New University/UK Music 2016: 5) were carried out by Oxford Economics, the consultants who worked on UK Music's *Wish You Were Here* reports (2017). Nearly a quarter of the report is taken up with the economic methodology and the obvious complexity involved suggests that the search for a big number quantifying the value of music can be a major issue for censuses, as well as for policy-makers and the media. It is simply easier to digest a number than to process qualitative data on the lived experiences of those working in the industries. Problems caused by planning regulations were also noted – and adoption of Agent of Change recommended – along with the lack of comparative UK data (Bucks New University/UK Music 2016: 15), something we hoped to address in our own work.

Part three: Reporting the reports

The reports covered above provided a number of lessons that informed our work. One key issue was the choice of the census night. One of the methodological matters we negotiated in Edinburgh was the paradoxical nature of a live music census itself, in that it cannot take place on a 'non-typical' night for live music but also 'there is no such thing as a "typical" night of live music activity' (Behr et al. 2015: 23). For example, the Melbourne and Edinburgh snapshots took place on a Saturday night. This bears upon the outcome, Saturdays often being the busiest night of the week for live music. The Bristol census was on a Thursday, while Adelaide opted for a survey over a month. Our choice of a Thursday for the UK Live Music Census was an attempt to avoid extremes, while also capturing part of any 'the weekend starts here' feeling.[2] Furthermore, any census night will be affected by such factors as whether the local arena/stadium (should they exist) is hosting a music event, what competing events there might be (for example, a big sporting match), time of year and so on. It is possible to raise legitimate concerns about the choice of any particular night and all the responsible researcher can do is to justify their choice, try to take into account any mitigating factors that might affect the outcome and highlight these in the final report.

This typicality (or not) of the snapshot census date for live music means that such censuses tend to err on the side of caution for any economic analysis, particularly those which gross up to annual estimates of spend from one 24-hour period. In Melbourne, for example, readers are told that while 'the findings associated with the Census [...] are the most comprehensive and authoritative estimates so far reported [...] [t]he figures should be viewed with obvious caution' (Music Victoria/City of Melbourne 2012: 7, 16). Given these challenges, it is unsurprising that the census reports we reviewed (and our own) came laden with such caveats, generally along the lines of 'we have tried to be as accurate and comprehensive as possible but it's really rather complicated'.

In addition to their differing methodologies, a number of other factors warrant mention regarding previous live music surveys to the UK Live Music Census. The first is that, as noted above, they are often the result of local issues that have attracted political attention, often via activist campaigns. This was certainly the case in Melbourne and became so in our work in Edinburgh and UK-wide. As such, music census findings have sometimes informed the development of cities' music strategies that can have important impacts on their live music scenes. Consequently, a census has the potential to be politically controversial, while also serving to raise questions about the status of live music within a city.

It is important, then, that those undertaking a census realize that research does not take place in abstraction but in material realities shaped by several factors, including the researchers' own backgrounds and politics, the prevailing economic and political climate (both in their widest senses) and relationships with (and the current health of) the contemporary music industries. If negotiating such contextual factors can be time consuming, not negotiating them can be the kiss of death: the text of any census means little outside its wider context.

Part four: The context for the UK Live Music Census

With the above in mind we set out to design and fundraise for a live music census that would maintain the local/regional micro level focus of previous censuses but also combine it with national data to obtain a broader, macro level, understanding of the state of live music across the country. The UK Live Music Census was made possible by a grant from the AHRC, the project running from September 2016 to February 2018. Our work began at a time when the United Kingdom's live music sector was facing something of a dichotomy. On the one hand, there were reports of a live music 'boom' as the sector continued to out-perform the previously dominant recording sector, which was still adjusting to the impact of digitization. Successive reports from 2009 onwards showed the value of the live music sector exceeding that of the recorded sector and that the gap was growing (Page and Carey 2010, 2011; UK Music 2015, 2016, 2017, 2018a). This was apparent in both sets of reports, despite the different definitions adopted and methodologies utilized within them, including the fact that they account for overall value differently across recorded and live music such as, in some cases, calculating gross value to an area to include hotel nights, travel and other ancillary spend. On the other hand, however, if such reports suggested a healthy live sector at a macro level, then other accounts indicated that our research was taking place at a challenging time at the micro level, particularly for small venues and clubs (Davyd 2016).

Recent years have seen numerous media reports of British music venues closing due to factors such as property development and the gentrification of once lively musical neighbourhoods, including the Boardwalk in Sheffield, which closed in 2010, and the Cockpit in Leeds, which closed in 2014. Working with the consultancies Nordicity and Sound Diplomacy, the Mayor of London's Music Venues Taskforce found similar problems in the UK capital (2015). Closures are due not only to diminishing audiences and the conversion or even demolition of some venues, but also development around venues and the ensuing noise complaints from new residential neighbours. Such accounts suggested that it was becoming ever more difficult to make the provision of live music economically viable in certain places.

In undertaking the UK Live Music Census we were determined to get behind these stories of 'boom and bust' to provide insight into the actual situation. We went in believing that the potential benefits of a live music census apply not just to academic researchers but also in terms of the potential impact on how policy-makers – local, national and international – understand, value and ultimately encourage live music in cities to flourish.

To mitigate the politically sensitive nature of the work, we knew we had to get major players from the United Kingdom's music industries on board with the research. This entailed getting relevant letters of support for our funding bid.[3] We were aided here by having previously worked with UK Music (the UK music industries' representative and lobbying body) and the Musicians' Union, both of whom were formal partners on the project alongside the campaign group for 'grassroots' music venues, the Music Venue Trust. We also secured the participation of groups such as Julie's Bicycle (an environmental advisory group for the creative industries), Attitude Is Everything (lobbyists for access to live music for the Deaf and disabled) and PRS for Music (the UK collecting agency for songwriters and composers).

Seeking such support had some practical implications. For example, when consulting about online questionnaires we were often asked to include questions relating to representatives' particular interests, such as access to venues or environmental policies. This was entirely understandable, yet also jarred with the necessity to keep the length of the questionnaires to a minimum. There were additional complications surrounding UK Music's scheme for working with Higher Education Institutions (HEIs), its Music Academic Partners (MAPs) (UK Music 2019). As part of our collaboration with UK Music, we wrote MAPs (and consequently their cities) into the project's consultation process and as ancillary/satellite censuses that could add to the dataset should those HEIs be able to conduct a snapshot within the project timeframe, some of which did so. In sum, while working with music industries' organizations can be extremely worthwhile, it can also lead to demands with important methodological and time implications. Support from the music industries for the census was vital, however, and, if nothing else, shows the potential for common interests between researchers who value impartiality and organizations that need to promote their own interests (Williamson et al. 2011).

Part five: The UK Live Music Census in practice

Following consultations with focus groups comprising key music industries stakeholders, we developed a five-part methodology consisting of:

1. Mapping local live music ecologies via desk research of event listings, venues' websites and social media.
2. Snapshot censuses over a 24-hour period in three cities carried out by the central research team, plus further censuses carried out by MAPs.
3. Nationwide online surveys targeting musicians, venues, promoters and audiences.
4. Shorter follow-up venue surveys.
5. Semi-structured profile interviews with venues, promoters and musicians to provide narrative for the final report.

A detailed breakdown of what was done – or rather an idealized version of what we recommend *should* be done – is available in the open source toolkit on the project website, with a 'how to' guide for others wishing to carry out a census (Webster et al. 2018b). This was produced as part of the project's goal of providing a replicable methodology and, hopefully, encouraging data gathering to allow for the possibility of more longitudinal and geographically comparative work. An outline of the methodology follows.

We *mapped* local live music ecologies by constructing venue lists in each snapshot city, taking care to include those spaces used for live music that are not 'venues' per se, and also lists of events taking place on the snapshot census date. This was a particularly time-consuming aspect of the research, involving scraping event listings sites using web-based tools, checking venues' social media pages and trawling the Internet for information. Nevertheless, the lists proved invaluable for planning the snapshot censuses and later allowed for analysis of local live music ecologies in terms of the number and spread of venue types.

Snapshot censuses were coordinated by members of the central research team in the primary case-study cities of Glasgow, Newcastle-Gateshead and Oxford, with affiliate censuses of varying scale coordinated by members of MAP institutions in Brighton, Leeds, Liverpool and Southampton. Working in shifts, volunteers visited venues hosting live music over one 24-hour period in March 2017 (and June in Liverpool). The volunteers completed short surveys comprising of: (a) audience interviews with questions about spend, motivation for attendance and frequency of attendance; and (b) venue observations, wherein volunteers estimated the number of patrons in the venue at the time, genre of music playing and the maximum number of patrons expected (obtained from speaking to members of staff). From identifying which venues were hosting live music on the census date to recruiting and training volunteers, to actually running the census on the night, this was the most resource-intensive section of the project.

The *online surveys* contained a combination of quantitative and qualitative questions asking the four types of respondent for a variety of data around economic, social and cultural value. The majority of the research team has backgrounds in the social sciences and humanities and so perhaps the most difficult issue facing us was how to deal with the sector's economic value. There is a particular pressure on researchers to come up with a definitive figure for economic value – the aforementioned industry- and media-friendly 'big number' – something that is, in fact, methodologically complex. This partly emanates from political and media pressure to have easily digestible, bite-size chunks of knowledge. The result of this is often to downplay complexity and nuance and to highlight the big number, often used to both publicize the overarching value of music, and lobby for supportive measures.[4] Realizing, nevertheless, the importance of such figures, we employed a consultant statistician, Professor Jake Ansell, on the project whose role evolved into more of a co-investigative than purely consultative one because of the complexities of these issues.

To calculate economic value and in order to be able to estimate Gross Value Added (GVA), we attempted to collect data via the survey on venues' and promoters' annual income and expenditure, as a possible alternative to the method used in the Edinburgh Census, which only examined audience spend. However, income and expenditure data were unfortunately not always forthcoming, summed up best in this response to the question from a venue: 'We are not sharing financial info with people we don't even know'. Reluctance to give such data appears to be a sector-wide issue. We therefore had to use a method of calculating economic value based on audience spend, using data from the snapshot census date combined with venue data about average audience attendance on the snapshot census date, average frequency of venue opening per week and a ratio for seasonal behaviour (explained in full in our report [Webster et al. 2018c] and the toolkit [Webster et al. 2018b]). We have since refined the questions about financial data in the venue and promoter surveys to match more closely those used by the Europe-wide group Live DMA, to hopefully increase the response rate in any future censuses.

Unlike previous studies, one of our aims was to provide a more holistic understanding of the value of live music in the United Kingdom. To better understand the social and cultural value of live music, then, we included various quantitative and qualitative questions in all four surveys. For example, we asked both audiences and musicians to name a significant venue and give reasons for its importance to them, yielding data that was probably the richest (and most enjoyable) to analyse. The venue and promoter surveys asked tickbox questions about respondents' 'cultural activities' such as charity work and formal/informal links with educational communities, as well as asking what respondents believe that they bring to their locale.[5] While time consuming to analyse, and sensitive to researchers' own subjectivities, the data from such qualitative questions enabled us to identify broad themes about the social and cultural value of live music. However, there remains the wider question of whether a survey-based approach is the most appropriate for understanding notions of social and cultural value, particularly since these are slippery and difficult to categorize neatly into tickbox categories. As Eleonora Belfiore and Oliver Bennett have argued, 'a "toolkit approach" to arts impact assessment [...] demands excessive simplifications' (2010: 121). Nevertheless, we believe that the advantages outweigh the disadvantages in this context and have mitigated such simplification by using both tickbox and open-ended questions.

Because of the issues apparently facing venues in the United Kingdom, it was imperative that we obtained enough venue data to be able to draw reasonable conclusions. Completing surveys, however, is rarely a priority for venue staff and so the fourth component of the methodology had to be deployed. In addition to the online surveys, then, we also conducted *venue follow-up surveys* either by phoning venues or visiting them in person.

Finally, we conducted eighteen semi-structured *profile interviews* to provide some detailed narrative and examples of best practice alongside the drier, more statistical parts of the report. The interviews also allowed us to fill in some of the gaps in our research data, most glaringly a smaller return from Northern Ireland and Wales than we had hoped for, as well as data from BAME groups and from genres such as grime and hip-hop.

The main findings were that music has significant economic, social and cultural value. We also found that venues often played much wider roles than hosting live music, such as being sites of volunteering, charity and educational work. We highlighted the importance of policy-makers valuing venues, especially smaller ones, and made calculations of the value of live music in each city (based on seven categories of spending) and of the employment that live music sustains in each city (drawing on UK Music 2017b) (Webster et al. 2018c: 14–16). In addition we noted a number of ongoing issues, making recommendations to various levels of government (local authority, devolved institutions and United Kingdom) about the best way forward. In sum an enormous amount of information, of the sort that should provide food for thought for lobbyists and policy-makers alike, was produced via a methodology that had the support of representatives from major players within the United Kingdom's music industries.

Part six: Issues and discussion

After completing our report of findings for the UK Live Music Census, we identified seven key issues that warrant further discussion: (1) our cross-genre approach; (2) defining live music; (3) defining venue types; (4) survey length; (5) local versus national issues; (6) nomenclature issues; and (7) the quest for a 'big number'. At over 100 pages in length, it is not possible to reproduce our report findings within this book chapter. However, we recommend reading the discussion below alongside the report itself, which is freely available on the project website (Webster et al. 2018c).

While previous censuses in Australia and the United States focused on popular music, the UK Live Music Census, like the Edinburgh pilot study, attempted to capture data *across all genres and venue types*. The advantages of this approach were that we avoided the criticism of 'ignoring' forms of music such as classical, folk and jazz, that we did not have to negotiate definitions of what counts as 'popular music' for the purposes of the census and that we were able to include as many forms of live music practice as possible. The disadvantage was that by attempting to address all forms of practice, we risked homogenizing what is a very diverse sector and therefore making generalizations across 'art worlds' (Becker 1982) that perhaps face different issues. However, by examining the United Kingdom's live music sector as a whole we have attempted to understand issues that appear to be affecting multiple art worlds, like the lack of suitable venues and the prevalence of musicians working for free. But defining genres was not straightforward. While we developed a list of 21 genres that we believed covered most broad types of music, the 'other – please specify' option was well used by respondents for whom our categories did not suffice.

Defining what counts as live music was also complicated. For our purposes, a live music event is one at which musicians (including named DJs) provide music for audiences and dancers gathering in public places where the music is the *principal purpose* of that gathering. Even this was not clear-cut, however, as questions arose as to whether a dance workshop accompanied by a live band counted as a live music event (answer: no) or whether a ballet performance fitted the description (answer: no).

Furthermore, as we found with the Edinburgh study, *defining venue types* was also difficult because many spaces for live music have more than one function. Although a glossary of venue-type definitions was provided for the census, it is clear that respondents' own definitions did not always tally with our own. The use of 'small music venue' by respondents, for example, did not necessarily equate either with our definition or with the Music Venue Trust's definition of a 'grassroots music venue' (Mayor of London's Music Venues Taskforce 2015: 34–37), but was instead broader and more inconsistent. In Edinburgh we had included an 'other' category for venues like student unions and social clubs but the 2017 census highlighted the significance of such venue types as distinct categories, and so the venue typology has since been modified and increased to nineteen categories (Webster et al. 2018a). Other survey questions have been similarly tweaked following the 2017 Census, as some were in use for the first time and have now been improved. As our review of prior reports showed, census taking and the development of an appropriate methodology is an iterative process. As this was the first attempt to run a national live music census, the methodology will doubtless be developed and refined over time.

As noted above, one challenge was to try to keep the *length of the surveys* to a minimum. However, it is apparent from the number of respondents who did not complete their survey – for example, only 141 completed promoter surveys out of 367 started – that our surveys may have been too extensive and thorough for some. With this in mind, we have published the full-length updated surveys in our toolkit but suggest that future live music census coordinators may wish to exclude those questions that are not relevant to their area, particularly those identified as 'additional'.[6]

There is also the question of whether a UK-wide census is appropriate and, particularly, how a national overview works in relation to local censuses. Previous censuses have been mostly local or regional and this was the first time in the world, we believe, that an attempt had been made to combine a local and national live music census exercise in this way. The advantage of undertaking a local live music census is that it can galvanize, or be galvanized by, the locale in which it takes place, particularly if, as with the examples above, there is a local issue that needs addressing, as was the case with noise control in Edinburgh. The disadvantage is, of course, its locality, in the sense that it can only offer a local perspective rather than a national one, and hence is of less interest to national policy-makers. The advantage of undertaking a *national* census is that it garners national interest, including national media attention. However, one corresponding disadvantage is that the local focus can get diluted.

There is also the issue of *nomenclature*. The advantage of the word 'census' is that for most adults, a census is something of which they have experience, and they understand that it involves counting and data. However, in statistical terms, a census means that everyone in the population is included, which was obviously not the case here. Indeed, and particularly with the audience surveys, there will always be an element of self-selection regarding participation in this type of project.

Finally, we were always conscious of the desire for a 'big number', which politicians, policy-makers and the media can easily digest and use as a barometer for the health of any sector. We did not wish to produce a figure for the value of live music across the United Kingdom – such figures are produced annually by UK Music – but we did want to do so for the three census cities, which was part of the reason for engaging a statistician. We are aware of the pros and cons of producing such figures, but also conscious that the interest of the parties mentioned earlier might be limited without them.

Conclusion

As we can attest, a live music census is a time-consuming, resource-intensive project. Added complexities arise from its reliance on volunteers to collect the data and members of the public to fill out the surveys. Furthermore, venue staff and promoters are busy people and not always inclined towards filling out survey forms. There is also the related matter of 'survey fatigue' in which surveys are so commonplace that overall participation declines.[7]

Data collection for a live music census involves a substantial amount of preparation and follow-up work, which requires a dedicated local census coordinator with sufficient time and resources. Another consideration is whether data from one night of the year can be grossed up to represent the whole year. In truth, one would need resources beyond what are realistically available to conduct a census that was able to collect all listings data about a locale, to send sufficient volunteers to every single venue on the snapshot census date, and to collect detailed data on every musician, venue and promoter after the event. Our results are therefore, and necessarily, conservative rather than overly optimistic since we obviously could not collect data from every audience member, venue, musician or promoter who was active on the snapshot census date. As with previous census exercises, then, we too have to say that we have done the best we can, given the time and resources available.

To conclude, our experience of live music censuses is wide-ranging, from reviewing other efforts to conducting our own projects across multiple cities and, for the first time, working to combine these into a national picture. As will be evident from this chapter, the process is far from straightforward. Attempting to balance geographical, sectoral and – perhaps above all – definitional concerns makes live music census-taking something of a differential equation, with co-dependent parameters often in flux. Logistical considerations mix with political considerations both internal to the sector (the live music industry) and related to its context (local councils or national cultural policy, for example). It is, however, this last aspect that, while in some respects the most potentially fraught, offers a key incentive. Few, if any, researchers want their work to take place in a vacuum. And while there are potential qualms about the plethora of live music censuses constituting a trend or fashion, there is a concomitant potential illustrated, for example, in Melbourne and Edinburgh – and, we hope, by the UK-wide census – for these exercises to make a real difference to the material conditions of producing live music.

Fashion or not, policy-makers are familiar with – reliant on, even – the language of censuses. They therefore provide a useful way for researchers to insert themselves into the policy process. This inevitably means 'getting one's hands dirty' and potentially fingers burnt. But it also affords the chance to marry qualitative and quantitative data in a way that aligns industry and policy engagement with primary research. Like the census reports it describes, our account is replete with caveats and cautionary notes. Bearing these in mind, though, we would still affirm the overall value – as researchers and supporters of live music – of standing up and being counted.

NOTES

1. The Agent of Change principle is that the person or business responsible for any change (the 'agent') is responsible for managing its impact. Thus, for example, a developer building housing next to an existing venue becomes responsible for ensuring that the dwellings have sufficient soundproofing, whereas if a venue opens next to existing dwellings then the onus is on the venue to ensure the soundproofing. The growing body of evidence – including censuses – and sustained campaigning both locally and by industry bodies like UK Music and the Music Venue Trust has seen Agent of Change become a political concern, and moves to place it into planning policy and legislation either adopted or planned in London and by the UK and devolved Parliaments (for a summary, see Music Venue Trust 2018).
2. The choice of a Thursday was partly informed by the Bristol Live Music Census and followed a series of focus groups with our project partners (UK Music, the Music Venue Trust and the Musicians' Union) and other concerned parties, from industry bodies to music-related charities.
3. The presence of non-academic partners is, anyway and increasingly, a key assessment criterion for research funders in the United Kingdom.

4. See, for example, the announcement of UK Music's 2018 *Measuring Music* report (UK Music 2018b), where the headline figure for the value of the 'UK music industry' is displayed much more prominently than the link to the report on which this is based.
5. The list of 'cultural activities' was adapted from work on small venues by the Music Venue Trust (2014: 21–25).
6. We note, however, that using similar sets of survey questions allows for more substantive comparisons across censuses.
7. Indeed, while our venue surveys were still open, another survey was sent to venues by one of our project partners, and researchers at one of the affiliate census institutions conducted a survey around audiences' musical participation around the same time as the city's own live music census.

REFERENCES

Becker, Howard (1982), *Art Worlds*, Berkeley: University of California Press.

Behr, Adam, Brennan, Matt and Cloonan, Martin (2014), *The Cultural Value of Live Music from the Pub to the Stadium*, Edinburgh: Live Music Exchange, http://livemusicexchange.org/wp-content/uploads/The-Cultural-Value-of-Live-Music-Pub-to-Stadium-report.pdf. Accessed 31 October 2018.

———, (2016a), 'Cultural value and cultural policy: Some evidence from the world of live music', *International Journal of Cultural Policy*, 22:3, pp. 403–18.

Behr, Adam, Brennan, Matt, Cloonan, Martin, Frith, Simon and Webster, Emma (2016b), 'Live concert performance: An ecological approach', *Rock Music Studies*, 3:1, pp. 5–23.

——— (2019), *Live Music Exchange*, http://livemusicexchange.org/about/. Accessed 5 April 2019.

Behr, Adam, Webster, Emma, and Brennan, Matt (2015), *Edinburgh Live Music Census 2015: Pilot Study*, Edinburgh: Live Music Exchange, http://livemusicexchange.org/wp-content/uploads/Edinburgh-Live-Music-Census-Report.pdf. Accessed 31 October 2018.

Belfiore, Eleanora and Bennett, Oliver (2010), 'Beyond the "Toolkit Approach": Arts impact evaluation research and the realities of cultural policy-making', *Journal for Cultural Research*, 14:2, pp. 121–42.

Bucks New University/UK Music (2016), *Bristol Live Music Census*, London: UK Music, www.ukmusic.org/assets/general/Bristol_Live_Music_Report.pdf. Accessed 31 October 2018.

City of Adelaide (2014), *Live Music Action Plan 2014–2016*, Adelaide: City of Adelaide.

——— (2017), *Live Music Action Plan 2014–2016 Final Report*, Adelaide: City of Adelaide, https://livemusicoffice.com.au/policies/adelaide-city-council-live-music-action-plan-20142016/

City of Melbourne (2014), *Music Strategy: Supporting and Growing the City's Music industry*, Melbourne: City of Melbourne.

City of Sydney (2014), *Live Music and Performance Action Plan,* Sydney: City of Sydney.

Davyd, Mark (2016), 'We need to protect the UK's music venues before it's too late', *Metro*, 10 November, http://metro.co.uk/2016/11/10/we-need-to-protect-the-uks-music-venues-before-its-too-late-6249168/. Accessed 31 October 2018.

Frith, Simon, Brennan, Matt, Cloonan, Martin and Webster, Emma (2010), 'Analysing live music in the UK: Findings one year into a three-year research project', https://iaspmjournal.net/index.php/IASPM_Journal/article/view/335. Accessed 31 October 2018.

——— (2013), *The History of Live Music in Britain, Volume 1: 1950–1967: From The Dance Hall to the 100 Club*, Farnham: Ashgate.

Frith, Simon and Cloonan, Martin (2019), 'Live Music Project', University of Glasgow, https://www.gla.ac.uk/schools/cca/research/music/projectsandnetworks/livemusicproject/. Accessed 5 April 2019.

Homan, Shane (2014), 'Livability and creativity: The case for Melbourne music precincts', *City Culture and Society*, 5:3, pp. 149–55.

Live Music Office (2014), *The Economic and Cultural Value of Live Music in Australia 2014*, Sydney: Live Music Office, http://livemusicoffice.com.au/wp-content/uploads/2015/08/LiveMusic-report-FINAL.pdf. Accessed 31 October 2018.

——— (2015), 'Hosting live music in South Australia', 26 June, http://livemusicoffice.com.au/hosting-live-music-in-south-australia/. Accessed 31 October 2018.

Mayor of London's Music Venues Taskforce (2015), *London's Grassroots Music Venues Rescue Plan,* London: Greater London Authority, https://www.london.gov.uk/sites/default/files/londons_grassroots_music_venues_-_rescue_plan_-_october_2015.pdf. Accessed 31 October 2018.

Music SA/Live Music Office (2015), *Adelaide Live Music Census 2015*, http://www.livemusicoffice.com.au/wp-content/uploads/2015/08/Adelaide-Live-Music-Census-2015.pdf. Accessed 31 October 2018.

——— (2016), *Adelaide Live Music Census 2016*, http://livemusicoffice.com.au/wp-content/uploads/2016/07/2016-Adelaide-Live-Music-Census.pdf. Accessed 31 October 2018.

Music Venue Trust (2014), *Understanding Small Music Venues: A Report by the Music Venue Trust,* London: Music Venue Trust, http://musicvenuetrust.com/2015/03/understanding-small-music-venues-a-report-by-the-music-venue-trust/. Accessed 31 October 2018.

——— (2019), 'After 4-year campaign agent of change is here', http://musicvenuetrust.com/2018/08/4-year-campaign-agent-change/. Accessed 5 April 2019.

Music Victoria/City of Melbourne (2012), *Victorian Live Music Census 2012,* Melbourne: Music Victoria/City of Melbourne, http://www.musicvictoria.com.au/assets/Documents/Victorian_Live_Music_Census_2012.pdf. Accessed 31 October 2018.

Page, Will and Carey, Chris (2010), *Adding Up the UK Music Industry for 2009*, London: PRS for Music.

——— (2011), *Adding Up the Music Industry for 2010*, London: PRS for Music.

Titan Music Group (2015), *The Austin Music Census,* Austin: City of Austin Development Department, https://www.austintexas.gov/department/music-census-reports. Accessed 31 October 2018.

UK Music (2015), *Measuring Music: 2015 Report,* https://www.ukmusic.org/research/report-archive/measuring-music-2015. Accessed 4 June 2019.

——— (2016), *Measuring Music: 2016 Report,* https://www.ukmusic.org/research/report-archive/measuring-music-2016. Accessed 4 June 2019.

——— (2017a), *Measuring Music: 2017 Report,* https://www.ukmusic.org/research/report-archive/measuring-music-2017. Accessed 26 January 2019.

——— (2017b), *Wish You Were Here 2017: Music Tourism's Contribution to the UK Economy,* London: UK Music.

——— (2018a), *Measuring Music: 2018 Report,* https://www.ukmusic.org/research/report-archive/measuring-music-2018. Accessed 26 January 2019.

——— (2018b), 'News: Measuring music 2018', https://www.ukmusic.org/news/measuring-music-2018. Accessed 5 April 2019.

——— (2019), 'Music academic partnership: MAP', https://www.ukmusic.org/skills-academy/music-academic-partnership/. Accessed 5 April 2019.

Webster, Emma, Brennan, Matt, Behr, Adam and Cloonan Martin (2018a), 'Glossary', *UK Live Music Census,* http://uklivemusiccensus.org/#glossary. Accessed 5 April 2019.

——— (2018b), 'Toolkit', *UK Live Music Census,* http://uklivemusiccensus.org/#toolkit. Accessed 5 April 2019.

Webster, Emma, Brennan, Matt, Behr, Adam, Cloonan Martin, with Ansell, Jake (2018c), *Valuing Live Music: The UK Live Music Census 2017 Report,* Live Music Exchange/University of Edinburgh/Newcastle University/University of Turku, http://uklivemusiccensus.org/#report. Accessed 31 October 2018.

Williamson, John, Cloonan, Martin and Frith, Simon (2003), *The Music Industry in Scotland,* Glasgow: Scottish Enterprise.

——— (2011), 'Having an impact? Academics, the music industries and the problem of knowledge', *International Journal of Cultural Policy,* 15:5, pp. 459–47.

7

What's It Worth? Calculating the Economic Value of Live Music[1]

Dave Laing

Out of the three primary sectors of the music industry, two offer more or less official statistics about their annual performance. For the record company sector, a series of national trade organizations publish unit and value sales data, while the International Federation of the Phonographic Industry (IFPI) uses these to create global figures. For the music publishing sector, national authors' collection societies (sometimes known as copyright agencies) provide details of their revenues and costs. At the international level, these are aggregated by the International Confederation of Societies of Authors and Composers (CISAC).

When we come to the other sector, live music, there are no comparable comprehensive statistics, no comparable international trade associations and few comparable national ones. Nevertheless, some data exists and this chapter surveys efforts to state the financial size and economic value of the live music industry in several countries and globally. It presents basic data from Australia, Germany, Italy, Great Britain and North America (that is, Canada plus the United States), plus my own estimate of the turnover of the global industry. Table 7.1 shows the national data: the size of the live music market, the year surveyed, the percentage changes compared with the previous year, and the source of the research.

The research has a wide range of sources. In Australia, the data was collected by an industry body, the Live Performance Association (LPA), and analysed by one of the 'Big Four' accountancy firms, Ernst & Young (E&Y). In France, the source was the Centre National de la Chanson, des Variétés et du Jazz (CNV), one of the numerous corporatist organizations there, which collects a 3.5 per cent levy on concert ticket prices and distributes it as a subsidy for small venues and tours. Germany's data was collected by market researchers GfK for the BDV, the trade organization of promoters and agents. In Italy, the work was done by a Milan university on behalf of the authors' collection society and other industry bodies.

	Source	Year	Value (millions)	Value (US$m)	Per cent change
Australia	LPA/E&Y	2010	A$1187	1176.7	+20
France	CNV	2011	€671	886.6	+7
Germany	GfK/BDV	2009	€2270	2999.4	–12
Italy	IULM	2009	€781	1031.9	+3
United Kingdom	PRS	2010	€1480	2175.6	–7
United States/ Canada	*Pollstar*	2011	US$2870	2870	+4

TABLE 7.1: National data on the live music industry.

In Britain, the research department of authors' society PRS for Music produced the data. In North America, it was collected by the trade magazine *Pollstar*.

Definitions of live music

Each of the national financial totals is qualified by the definition of 'live music' in use by each researcher and the extent to which they include revenue sources in addition to the primary or face value of ticket sales.

The French statistics are limited to the pop and jazz sectors since the ticket levy is also restricted to these genres, and the North America data published by *Pollstar* covers only the Top 200 tours (and excludes festivals and clubs), which is the largest part of the live music business in terms of revenues from sales of tickets. The French Society of Authors, Composers and Publishers of Music (SACEM) produced a report in 2011 that showed that the top twenty national tours in France generated 25 per cent of SACEM's royalties from the sector as a whole, and therefore a similar proportion of ticket sales revenue.

Other national research includes some or all of classical music concerts, opera and stage musicals. The data for Australia and Italy provide further detail, in the form of comparative financial numbers for different genres. The Australian figures show that pop concert revenues are about 55 per cent of the total, while in Italy pop events had 34 per cent. In both Italy and Australia, classical music accounts for about a quarter of ticket sales by value.

Table 7.2 shows which genres and types of event are included in the various national data sets.

	A	F	G	I	UK	NA
Pop tours and concerts	X	X	X	X	X	X
Pop festivals	X	X	X	X	X	
Classical concerts	X		X	X	X	
Opera	X		X	X		
Stage musicals	X	X	X	X		
Free events	X	X		X		

TABLE 7.2: Breakdown by genre of 'primary ticket sales'.

Components of the live industry's turnover

With the exception of Australia and the United Kingdom, the statistics already quoted cover only the retail value of primary ticket sales. This however, is only one segment, although the largest, of the revenues received by the live music industry. Below I discuss each of the segments that go to make up the industry's turnover.

Primary ticket sales

First, of course, is the face value of tickets sold for events. This is the only category common to all the national data. In the statistics, some researchers provide an average price per ticket sold, for example in North America, where the price fell by two per cent in 2010, while in Australia it rose by twelve per cent in 2008. In 2011, the value of ticket sales of Live Nation Entertainment (LNE), one of only two global companies in the industry, fell by seven per cent, although the *Pollstar* data for North America, LNE's largest market, shows growth of four per cent.

Ticketing fees

In recent years, 'ticketing' has become a specialist sector of the industry, as companies such as LNE are granted exclusive rights by promoters and add a service charge fee to the ticket price set by the promoter. An analysis of ticket pricing by LNE in 2010 showed that on average ticketing fees accounted for 26 per cent of the retail price excluding tax. Put another way, the ticketing fee was on average one-third of the price of the ticket itself.

Secondary ticket sales

The next category denotes additional or 'secondary' spending by consumers when tickets are re-sold. Much has been written about the pros and cons of this activity. Here, it should be noted that it has become a thriving sub-industry through such online companies as StubHub and Viagogo. The estimate of the relative value of secondary sales in the United Kingdom is GB£192 million, equivalent to 23 per cent of primary spending on tickets.

Sponsorship

In addition to the direct consumer-to-business transactions of ticket purchase, there are several other sources of revenue. Corporate sponsorship and public subsidy form an important component of the live music economy. Commercial sponsors may provide funds to specific tours, or buy what are called 'naming rights' to venues. For the biggest tours and the biggest stadia, these may run into millions of dollars. One published figure is the GB£4.5 million a year paid by the O2 telecoms company for naming rights to the Academy chain of rock clubs in the United Kingdom. The term 'public subsidy' denotes grants by the various levels of government from national ministries of culture (or in Europe, certain departments of the European Commission), through regional to local councils or legislatures. In recent years such subsidy has spread outwards in Europe from classical music to various types of festival, though more usually jazz or world music rather than rock and pop.

Detailed figures for sponsorship are extremely difficult to find, but as some kind of guide, the US-based company IEG reckoned that commercial sponsorship of music in the United States in 2008 amounted to just over US$1 billion. For 2010, the UK figure was GB£33 million.

Media licensing

This category refers to the fees paid by broadcasters and webcasters for the right to simulcast a concert or festival, or to record it for later broadcast. In Britain, it has become a regular feature of the budget of major festivals to sell broadcast rights to either the BBC or Channel 4 television. The BBC, for example, provides blanket coverage (typically 70 hours) of the Glastonbury festival.

Ancillary spending at venues

This category includes the sales of merchandise such as programmes, t-shirts and compact discs as well as food and drink bought by audience members. There are also parking fees at stadia with car parks.

The merchandise sector of the music industry is relatively important, as is shown by the fact that several major record companies and concert promoters have their own merchandise divisions, to which artists may licence the right to create 'official' products. Occasionally figures of average audience spending on shirts, programmes etc. are made public: on a major tour by a so-called heritage act these may be as high as a figure equal to 20 per cent of ticket sales. In Germany, each attendee spent on average €4.30 on merchandise in addition to the average ticket price of €34. In their report on the Australian industry in 2008, E&Y aggregated merchandise with sponsorship and catering as 'other' funding. For large pop performances, this category was worth an average of AU$501,000 compared with box office revenue of AU$746,000. Overall, E&Y found that these other sources added almost 80 per cent to the ticket sales that were the sole source of revenues included in LPA's own survey. A report by E&Y on 30,000 small venues in Australia with live music (bars, restaurants, etc.) found that only 16 per cent of consumer spend was on tickets to hear music.

The ancillary items mentioned here may seem to take us away from the music industry as strictly defined, but it is worth noting that not only do many large venues and festivals appoint official suppliers (in the drinks business, cola and beer companies compete to buy exclusive 'pourage' rights) but the money from parking charges is a vital part of the revenues of a company such as LNE, which both manages venues and promotes concert tours.

A recent innovation is the sale to concert-goers of a recording of the event itself. In some cases, this recording is made available as a physical compact disc minutes after the end of the event. Alternatively, concert-goers can pay to have an online version a day or two after the performance.

Using these categories of industry revenue segments, Table 7.3 offers a rough estimate of the live industry's global revenue from popular music performances in 2010, in US dollars.

	US$ billion	Per cent of total	Per cent change
Ticket sales	10.0	40	-8
Ticketing fees	4.1	16	-5
Venue ancillary	4.1	16	-8
Sponsorship	3.3	13	-3
Re-sold tickets	1.4	7	+20
Media licensing	2.1	8	-5
Total	25.0	100	-6

TABLE 7.3: Global turnover of the live music industry 2010.

Live music vs. recorded music

One frequently raised question in recent years is that of the relative size of the live music and recorded music businesses. Which has the highest turnover?

Both the Italian and British research can be used to make a direct comparison. In Italy, live music was reported to be worth €781 million in 2009 and recorded music €419 million. The UK research for 2010 states that 'business to consumer' totals were GB£1.24 billion (recorded music) and GB£1.48 billion (live music). In its own comparative study, published in 2010, IFPI, perhaps predictably, found that global 'recorded music retail sales', at US$25.8 billion, remained greater than the value of the live sector, which it estimated to be US$21.6 billion. And even with my higher estimate of US$25 million for live music, spending on recorded music remained slightly higher in 2010. The first indications of the market in 2011 (such as *Pollstar*'s four per cent increase in North American ticket sales) suggest that the live business worldwide may have returned to growth and may have definitively overtaken the recording industry in revenue terms.

NOTE

1. This chapter was first published on the *Live Music Exchange Blog*, 11 June 2012: http://livemusicexchange.org/blog/whats-it-worth-calculating-the-economic-value-of-live-music-dave-laing/. It is included in this collection as a representation of Dave Laing's writing about statistics in the music industries.

8

Live Music vs. Recorded Music

Richard Osborne

Britain's gone plural. UK scholars have led an academic turn away from the conception of a singular music *industry* towards thinking more expansively about music *industries*. In their pioneering article of 2007, John Williamson and Martin Cloonan outlined the importance of assessing each of the sectors that make up these industries. They wished to bring an end to the practice, fostered by record companies themselves, of equating the record business with the music business as a whole (2007: 307). They maintained that this practice was fallacious and anachronistic. In particular, it provided a disservice to live music, which was underappreciated economically (2007: 314–15) and under-explored academically (2007: 313).

This corrective manoeuvre was necessary. The twenty-first century has witnessed a rise in live music's fortunes while those of recorded music have declined. In the United Kingdom, the British Phonographic Industry (BPI) has reported a fall in revenue from £1.17 billion in 2000 to £866 million in 2018 (with inflation the 2000 figure would be worth £1.93 billion in 2018) (Green 2019: 9). Compact discs are selling in fewer numbers and they cost less to buy. Piracy, downloading and streaming have each had impact on the price of recorded music. Meanwhile, the cost of attending live performances has gone up. According to one report, ticket prices rose by 400 per cent between 1982 and 2016 (Curran 2016). In addition, there has been a rise in the amount of music festivals and events taking place. The years 2003–07 witnessed a 71 per cent increase in the number of outdoor music festivals in the United Kingdom (Anderton 2008: 39–40). Live music companies are heading the music industries. The UK Live Music Census notes that 'the largest entertainment company in the world, Live Nation Entertainment, owns both the largest live music promoter in the world, Live Nation Concerts, and the biggest ticketing company in the world, Ticketmaster' (Webster et al. 2018: 26). Live Nation's CEO, Michael Rapino, was number one in *Billboard*'s 'Power 100' list for 2018 (Billboard Staff 2018). On receiving this accolade, he boasted that

Spotify 'spends a fortune trying to figure out how to get you spend $9.99 a month. I'm trying to get you to spend $190 for a ticket' (Billboard Staff 2018). It is claimed that, while 'streaming has revived the recorded-music industry, touring [has] put far more money in artists' pockets' (Billboard Staff 2018).

The corrective manoeuvre has also had results. It has led to some excellent studies of live music in Britain, which have helped to inform legislation and policy in this field (Webster and McKay 2016; Webster et al. 2018). These studies have not been restricted to economics; they have also explored the aura of live performance in the age of digital reproduction. Cloonan has documented 'live music as ideology', charting the belief 'that in an age where everything was reproducible live music remained the ultimate un-reproducible experience' (2013: 83). Respondents to the UK Live Music Census argued that live music is 'better' than recorded music because 'the experience is authentic' and is 'different each time' (Webster et al. 2018: 29). Performance has been placed first; recorded product is secondary.

To a certain extent, this academic turn has been mirrored within the UK music industries. Prior to 2007, the general health of these industries was measured by the wellbeing of the record business. There was little reporting of live music figures; it was record company statistics that dominated. This situation began to change at the end of the noughties, when PRS for Music (the UK collection society for the performing rights of composers and publishers) first began to enumerate the different music industry sectors in Britain. They originally presented their findings in their 2008 report *The 'R' Words* (Page 2008), which was followed by annual *Adding Up the Music Industry* reports from 2009 to 2012. Since then it has been UK Music, the 'campaigning and lobbying group, which represents every part of the UK recorded and live music industry' that has compiled these figures (UK Music 2018a). They first totalized business sectors in *The Economic Contribution of the Core Music Industry* in 2013, which was succeeded by their yearly *Measuring Music* reports (2014–18).[1]

The PRS for Music and UK Music statistics appear to back up the suggestions of British academics. They have indicated that live music is ahead of recorded music. The first *Adding Up the Music Industry* report demonstrated that recorded music was worth £1.309 billion in 2008, declining six per cent year-on-year, and that live music had advanced past it to £1.39 billion, enjoying thirteen per cent annual growth (Page and Carey 2009: 7). By the time of the final PRS for Music report, the fortunes of recorded music had increased slightly, reaching a figure of £1.112 billion, but live music was now far ahead: it was evaluated at £1.624 billion in 2011 (Brookes 2012: 2). Curiously, the first UK Music report placed live music behind recorded music.[2] Using a different methodology to PRS for Music they arrived at totals for 2012 of £662 million and £714 million respectively (UK Music 2013: 34). Nevertheless, by the following year, live music was again triumphant: it had reached

£789 million via a 26 per cent increase in box office takings, while over the same twelve months recorded music had fallen to £618 million (UK Music 2014b: 10). Although streaming has subsequently aided record music, increasing its total to £700 million by 2017, this still represents only two-thirds of the value of live music, which was worth £991 million in the same year (UK Music 2018b: 11).

Academics have, in turn, used these statistics for their own ends. They have been employed, albeit cautiously, as evidence of the primacy of live performance (Anderton et al. 2013: 125–26; Webster et al. 2018: 17; Wikström 2013: 58; Williamson and Cloonan 2013: 13, 21). The statistics have also been seized upon by journalists. The detail that live music is worth more than recorded music has been repeated by numerous media institutions, among them the *Guardian* (Topping 2009: 9), *The Times* (Foster 2009: 15), the *Financial Times* (Bintliff 2010), *Billboard* (Smirke 2014), *Music Week* (Jones 2014: 7) and the BBC (Savage 2017). It is through such repetition that partial analyses become 'truth'.

There are further reasons why we should pause for thought. Overlaps between academic and organizational thinking have occurred. PRS for Music and UK Music have opened up their statistical reporting to a wider notion of the music industries, while academics have drawn upon the data of these organizations in support of their own prognoses. Yet academia and industry have divergent aims. Where Williamson and Cloonan had argued that 'the reality is of disparate industries with some common interests' (2007: 305), PRS for Music and UK Music, in their different manners, have sought to emphasize the inter-connectedness between industry sectors. UK Music, for example, have argued that the 'inter-dependency between sectors is what gives the UK music industry its diversity and economic success, fostering a unique eco-system' (UK Music 2019: 9). In doing so, the organizations have been just as tactical as the record companies had been when they sought to portray their own interests as being indicative of the music business as a whole. We therefore need to inquire about the motivations that lie behind their presentation of the statistics. In addition, there has been scant analysis of whether the figures are correct. Therefore, we must ask whether PRS for Music and UK Music provide firm evidence that live music has advanced past recorded music. Moreover, there has been little consideration of whether it is appropriate for these institutions to bring together the differing economies of these sectors. Williamson and Cloonan had stressed that we should address 'diversity of interests and scale of activities' (2007: 305, 319). How does this square with reports that list the monetary endeavours of live and recorded music side by side? There is also a need to urge caution in respect of how the statistics are applied. They have been utilized in support an argument that performers will earn more from live music than they will from recorded music (Bintliff 2010; Foster 2009: 15). Is there anything in the numbers that supports this case?

In the following I will take a closer look at the statistics of PRS for Music and UK Music by addressing four questions: (1) What is the purpose of their reports? (2) What do they include in their totals for 'recording' and 'live'? (3) How is the statistical information categorized? (4) Are performers able to assess their share of the money? I will conclude by contemplating further research in this field.

PRS for Music

What is the purpose of their reports?

PRS for Music's reports were initiated in 2007 in response to an emerging global financial crisis. In *The 'R' Words: Recession and Royalties*, the organization asked '[i]f the UK economy is about to enter a downturn what does this mean for music?' (Page and Carey 2009: 1). This document was aimed at the 'music industry's various stakeholders who find themselves in an unprecedented state of transition' (Page and Carey 2009: 1). In order to counter '[a]rmageddon-style hysteria', it chose to depict the musical world as an ecosystem in which 'value doesn't just disappear; rather some will be lost, some will be displaced and some new revenues will enter the industry' (Page and Carey 2009: 1). Its message is the old saw, 'don't put all your eggs in one basket' (Page and Carey 2009: 5).

This statistical reporting was also an advert for the virtues of PRS for Music, an organization that is adaptable to diverse revenue streams. During this period, the collection society administered performing and mechanical rights revenue for UK songwriters. It gained royalties from the multiple copyright uses that could be made of songs: live performance, record sales, broadcast, public performance, sync rights and so on. Thus, it benefitted from presenting the UK music industry as an inter-related system in which there will always be revenue for composers. This ethos informed the subsequent *Adding Up the Music Industry* reports.

PRS for Music did not expect live revenue to advance past recording revenue, however. One reason for tabulating the two fields was to test an assumption that a recession would result in 'less demand for expensive concert tickets, and relatively more demand for CDs' (Page 2008: 2). The initial analysis in *The 'R' words* placed recording music ahead of live music. In 2007 the former was worth £1392 million and the latter £1,078 million (Page 2008: 2). In the first *Adding Up the Music Industry* document these positions were reversed. Although this result challenged their initial thesis, it was regarded by PRS for Music as evidence of the virtues of their methodology. Their tallies could demonstrate a 'changing of the guard', as well as the continued need that songwriters would have for PRS for Music (Page and Carey 2009: 1).

What do they include in the totals for 'recording' and 'live'?

The PRS for Music recorded music figures are derived from BPI statistics representing 'revenues generated across all formats' (Brookes 2012: 3 note). Their live music figures also concern revenues, but are derived from estimates (Brookes 2012: 3 note).[3] PRS for Music focused on turnover so that they could identify markets that were 'growing, stagnating or shrinking' (Page and Carey 2011: 1). As a result, the recorded music figures include the share of revenue that goes to the retailer, as well as the mechanical rights share (the royalties that are due to the composers and publishers of the song). Similarly, the figure for live music includes the share of ticket sales that will go to the ticket agent and also the performing rights royalties for composers and publishers. In this respect, the focus on retail provides for some equivalence in the live and recorded music figures.

There are also some correspondences regarding what is being sold. The recorded music figures document acquisitions of a product that has been created by music makers: the recording itself. The totals are comprised of sales of physical recordings and digital downloads, as well as revenue from streaming subscription services. The live music figures illustrate consumers' spending on events. Here too they are buying something that is created by music makers: PRS for Music add up the sales of tickets for performances. Their live music figures expand beyond this, however, incorporating 'on the night' spending (Page and Carey 2009: 3). This ancillary revenue includes expenditure on food, drink and merchandise. By the conclusion of the series, the money spent on public transport and parking is being tallied as well.

It is difficult to calculate how much ancillary spend is worth, as PRS for Music do not provide precise figures. There are some clues, though. The final report notes that festivals and arenas each accounted for 'around 25 percent of the market' and that ancillary spend at these events was equal to '95 percent of the average face value ticket per person' (Brookes 2012: 3). Spend at other venues was equivalent to 'between 35 and 50 percent' of the ticket price (Brookes 2012: 3). It would therefore appear that ancillary revenue was worth at least a third of the money spent on tickets. The value of original ticket sales can be calculated at £1045 million for 2011, meaning that at a conservative estimate ancillary spend was £348 million.[4]

The PRS for Music live music figures also include secondary ticketing, enumerating the resale of tickets for profit. In 2011 this trade was worth £208 million, representing thirteen per cent of the total live music figure (Brookes 2012: 3). Although the report notes that secondary ticketing is 'legitimate under UK law and is an established practice' (Brookes 2012: 3), it is nevertheless contentious. There has been a professional trade in block buying tickets and selling them at inflated prices. PRS for Music included these figures in the belief they would offer a 'smoke signal' regarding economic downturn (Page 2008: 3). If live music was a luxury good, secondary tickets were even more so; this 'ultra-sensitive market' would indicate 'movements in consumer confidence and demand' (Page 2008: 3). In the event, the secondary market prospered in the period 2007–11.

Although the inclusion of secondary ticket sales and ancillary spend might be useful in identifying economic trends, it is not helpful when it comes to drawing comparisons between live and recorded revenues. The live figures expand beyond the purchase of items that have been generated by music makers, but the record figures do not. Recorded music does, nevertheless, generate ancillary spend of its own. The retail trade in physical recordings prompts parking and public transport expenditure; it also encourages sales of merchandise, food and drink. There is in addition a second-hand trade in records that has some parallels with the secondary reselling of tickets. Figures are not available to illustrate how much the recorded music figures would rise if this revenue were included, but it is possible to calculate the decrease in live music figures if ancillary spend and secondary ticketing were removed. In 2011, for example, PRS for Music's live music total would dip below £10.7 billion, putting it behind the £1.1 billion generated by recording.

How is the statistical information categorized?

At the highest level, the PRS for Music reports are split between business-to-consumer (B2C) revenue (the music that fans pay for) and business-to-business (B2B) revenue (the music that fans may well receive, but which is paid for via transactions between businesses) (see Table 8.1). PRS for Music wished to illustrate how the economic downturn 'might affect consumers and businesses differently' (2010: 2).

Category	**Year £ million**				
	2007	**2008**	**2009**	**2010**	**2011**
Business-to-Consumer					
Recorded music	£1392	£1309	£1356	£1237	£1112
Live music	£1078	£1391	£1537	£1480	£1624
Business-to-Consumer total	£2470	£2701	£2892	£2717	£2736
Business-to-Business					
PRS for Music gross collections	*£562*	*£608*	*£623*	*£611*	*£631*
*Adjustment for mechanical revenues**	*-£92*	*-£95*	*-£89*	*-£81*	*-£65*

(*continued*)

Category	**Year £ million**				
	2007	**2008**	**2009**	**2010**	**2011**
*Adjustment for live revenues***	*-£17*	*-£22*	*-£23*	*-£20*	*-£23*
*Adjustment for overseas payments*****				*-£85*	*-£95*
PRS for Music adjusted total	£453	£491	£511	£425	£448
PPL/VPL gross collections	*£115*	*£140*	*£141*	*£154*	*£164*
*Adjustment for record label direct revenues****	*-£57*	*-£79*	*-£72*	*-£72*	*-£83*
*Adjustment for international payments*****				*-£3*	*-£1*
PPL/VPL – adjusted total	£58	£61	£69	£79	£80
Record label direct revenues	£122	£195	£194	£218	£220
Publisher direct revenues	£80	£90	£103	£242	£210
Advertising and sponsorship revenues		£89	£90	£94	£99
Business-to-Business total	£713	£926	£967	£1058	£1057
UK music industry total	£3183	£3627	£3859	£3775	£3793

TABLE 8.1: UK music industry figures calculated by PRS for Music.

Figures are derived from Page (2008), Page and Carey (2009, 2010, 2011), Brookes (2012).
To avoid 'double counting' of revenue, the PRS for Music and PPL/VPL gross collection figures were adjusted by their compilers as follows:
* The mechanical licensing revenue derived from each sale or use of a recording forms part of the recorded music total. Consequently, it is taken away from the PRS for Music gross collection total.
** The performing rights revenue for the use of songwriters' works in venues forms part of the live music total. Consequently, it is taken away from PRS for Music gross collection total.
*** The broadcast and public performance revenue for the use of sound recordings is collected by Phonographic Performance Ltd (PPL)/Video Performance Ltd (VPL). It is divided between the performers on the sound recordings and the owners of the sound recording copyright (commonly the record companies). Rather than represent the record company share under the PPL/VPL heading, it is instead incorporated within record label direct revenues. The PPL/VPL figure is adjusted accordingly.
**** In 2010 and 2011, the money that PRS for Music and PPL/VPL distributed to their foreign affiliates for the use of 'overseas' repertoire and 'international' sound recordings was subtracted from their gross collection figures to better represent 'the contribution of UK collecting societies into GDP' (Page and Carey 2011: 2).

It was felt that a lack of financial confidence and job insecurity would negatively affect consumer spending but B2B revenue would be less exposed to recession (Page 2008: 2). This appeared to be borne out in the results. B2C revenue rose by 10.7 per cent between 2007 and 2011; the increase in B2B revenue was 48 per cent.

One consequence of reporting revenue in this manner is that, while live and recorded revenue is outlined, the third major stand of the music industries – music publishing – is not given a total of its own. This could be considered odd, given that PRS for Music looks after the rights in compositions. Yet there was method here. PRS for Music were able to demonstrate the variety of their revenue streams, as music publishing revenue is spread across their various B2C and B2B categories. The members of the society could, in theory, locate the best baskets for their eggs.

Although the PRS for Music reports proclaimed that live music had risen above recording, they reached this conclusion using B2C figures alone. Nevertheless, as they were keen to point out, an increasing amount of live and recording revenue was being derived from B2B activities (Page and Carey 2011: 2). Moreover, their decision to split revenue into B2C and B2B had more impact on recorded music than it did on live. As the collection society noted, record labels were 'reallocating their resources into B2B markets' (Page and Carey 2011: 7).

If we look again at the 2011 figures, the B2B category includes at least £300 million that could be reattributed if a broader definition of 'recording' were employed. This is made up of the £80 million that was earned by UK recording artists for the broadcast and public performance of sound recordings (the 'adjusted total' for PPL/VPL) and the £220 million attributed to 'record label direct revenues' (this includes the record companies' share of PPL/VPL revenue; synchronization fees for the use of recordings in films, television programmes, games and advertising; multiple rights income from 360° deals; and revenue from ad-supported streaming services). The figure for live music, meanwhile, is deprived of approximately £43 million, as the B2B figures include £35.1 million that businesses spent on sponsoring live music events and £8.4 million that they spent on event creation (Brookes 2012: 6).

If we further reconfigure the figures for 2011, so that the totals for recorded and live music include this B2B revenue,[5] while ancillary spend and secondary ticketing are removed, we end up with figures of approximately £1.1 billion for live music and approximately £1.4 billion for recording. From this it could be argued that throughout the 2007–11 period, recorded music was more prosperous than live music.

This result is, of course, as questionable as the totals provided by PRS for Music. The live music industry and recorded music industry are dissimilar entities; thus, there is no correct way in which their revenues can be compared. It should be noted too that PRS for Music betrayed doubts about splitting revenue along B2C and B2B lines (2010: 2; 2011: 2). Furthermore, it is unlikely that anyone would employ this means of adding up the music industries today. Ironically, this is because PRS for Music were correct in their predictions that increasing amounts of revenue would be derived from B2B sources. Their reports coincided with the first impact of streaming services on recording industry revenues. Streaming is mentioned briefly in the first two reports, but greater note of it is made by 2012. The B2C/B2B reporting method employed by PRS for Music allows the money from streaming subscription services to be captured as part of the B2C recorded music figure, but the money from ad-supported streaming services is obscured under the B2B heading. As streaming has subsequently become the most important source of revenue for record companies, it would now be untenable to exclude any of it from a recorded music total.

Are performers able to assess their share of the money?

PRS for Music embodies the close links between composition and performance. Its members derive income from 'performing' rights. In addition, many of its composer members are performers. The organization targets its literature accordingly; it is addressed at musicians as much as it is at songwriters. The *Adding Up the Music Industry* reports, for example, give guidance to performers about their economic strategy. They are informed that they should no longer 'tour at a loss to sell CDs', but instead consider live music as the 'main breadwinner' (Page and Carey 2009: 1). Nevertheless, PRS for Music's totalizing industry figures do not facilitate individual economic decisions. As we have seen, the results are skewed. The live music tallies incorporate revenue streams that are missing from the recorded music figures. Moreover, several of these revenue streams do not result in revenue for performers. This includes the money from secondary ticket sales and (for the majority of artists) ancillary spend on food, drink, transport and parking.

In addition, there is difference when it comes to the division of live and recorded music revenue. Within the recording industry there are common prices for many the goods (in particular, the B2C products). Moreover, while there are variants between different types of contract, there are also some common practices regarding what percentage of the revenue musicians will receive. Thus, it is just about possible for musicians to use the recorded music figures as a barometer of their own 'fortunes' in this area. This measure does, however, only apply to the ten per cent of artists who are not in debt to their record companies (see Chapter 3 in this collection). For the remainder, the only money they will see from their recording deals is their personal and recording advances; they will not be receiving a share of royalty revenue. These non-recouped advances are not factored into the PRS for Music figures, raising further questions about their ability to indicate the economy of performers.

The live music figures provide difficulties of their own. Although it is possible to construct a grand total in relation to ticket sales and ancillary spend, there is no commonality in the cost of events or in the artists' share of the revenue. In addition, the distance between the rich and the poor is wider in live music than in recording (Wikström 2013: 59). This is illustrated in the reports themselves. According to the 2009 figures 'the gap between the grass roots acts and superstars is widening' (Page and Carey 2010: 5). In the following year the overall total for live music went down, principally because there were fewer stadium- and arena-filling bands on tour (Page and Carey 2011: 4). The year after there was a fifteen per cent increase in live music revenues, attributed to a 'dramatic increase in stadium concerts', including a major tour by the group Take That (Brookes 2012: 3). Performers operating further down the economic scale could not have used the live music totals as an indication of their own economic wellbeing.

UK Music

What is the purpose of their reports?

In chronological terms, UK Music's reports picked up where the PRS for Music reports left off. They also have some similar aims: the PRS for Music reports chart the shifting ecosystem of the music industries; the UK Music reports seek to understand 'the economy and its constituent parts' so that they can '[t]rack trends' (UK Music 2013: 7). The principal motivation is different, however. The PRS statistics were the product of a recessionary era. By the time of the first UK Music reports, there were signs of economic recovery in both the general and music markets (UK Music 2014b: 1). Their main purpose, as a result, has been to inform the British government how well the music industries are doing.

UK Music have been motivated by what they view as an under-reporting of music industry income, exports and jobs by the Office of National Statistics (ONS). In order to assess economic contribution, the ONS allocates Standard Industrial Classification (SIC) codes to different trades and professions. UK Music has found this problematic for a number of reasons. In the first instance, music is grouped with the 'visual and performing arts'; thus, its individual contribution is obfuscated. Second, many music industry occupations are not listed under visual and performing arts; thus, their contribution is lost. Third, many music occupations are incorrectly coded and so their contribution is missing too. The great fear of UK Music is that this 'imperfect data is used for policy purposes by the Government' (2013: 1).

They have therefore sought to rectify these problems. The organization has provided its own classification of music industry trades and developed its own metrics for calculating music's contribution to the economy. UK Music wants the government to notice the successes of the music industries. They also want to work in partnership with the government to '[d]esign public policy best able to secure desired outcomes' (2013: 1). It should be noted, therefore, that the rival economies of the live and recorded industries are not the organization's focus.

UK Music was set up to portray the opposite of rivalry. In the same period as Williamson and Cloonan were pointing out the diversity of music industry sectors and how this belied the tendency of record companies to 'mask their concerns and vested interests as being those of "the music industry" as a whole' (2007: 307), the record companies were themselves realizing the limitations of their practice. The British government had become disoriented by the diverse lobbying campaigns of record companies, music publishers and recording artists. UK Music was set up in 2008 to present a united front. Feargal Sharkey, its original chief executive, explained its formation, pointedly using the singular:

> The Government has been telling the industry for 10 years, 'You are impossible to deal with, we don't know who to talk to, we don't know who does what bit' [...]. We've gone and formed UK Music and we are pushing it back on Government saying, 'We've done our part of the bargain, now it is time to deliver yours'.
>
> (Ashton 2014: 14)

The live music industry was not originally part of Sharkey's organization, which was centred instead on the copyright-holding recorded and music publishing industries. By 2011, however, they had come into its fold, enabling UK Music to proclaim that '*for the first time*, the UK's entire commercial music industry will be represented by one umbrella body' (Williamson and Cloonan 2013: 21, original emphasis). This grouping has also enabled UK Music to calculate the combined economic value of the music industries in its *Measuring Music* reports. When these reports have been issued, the number emphasized is the Total Gross Value Added contribution of the UK Music 'industry'. They do not promote comparisons between different industry sectors (UK Music 2018b).

What do they include in the totals for 'recording' and 'live'?

The UK Music reports, like the PRS for Music reports before them, view recorded music in terms of singular products and live music as more expansive events. Thus, their live music figures include ancillary spend, but their recorded music figures do not. Beyond this there is a series of differences that reflect the different aims of the two organizations. Where PRS for Music chose to exclude B2B revenue from their live and recorded totals, UK Music wish to provide overall economic profiles for their music industry sectors. This means that their recorded music figures include record company income from ad-supported streaming services, plus all other forms of direct label revenue. Live music, in turn, includes a share of sponsorship revenue. It also means that new revenue streams are considered that are not featured in the PRS reports: recorded music houses online aggregators and the design and production of physical product and packaging; live music includes production services for live music. The figures for UK Music remain lower than those of PRS for Music, nonetheless. This is because they set their own categorical boundaries and employ a different financial methodology.

There have been many attempts to define the component parts of Britain's musical industries (Cloonan 2007: 67–102; UK Music 2013: 13). These all differ and they each have their biases. In the case of UK Music, their definitions of a 'core' and 'wider' music industry are reflective of their membership. As of 2019, the organization consists of the Association of Independent Music; the Ivors Academy (formerly the British Academy of Songwriters, Composers and Authors); the Featured Artists Coalition; the Music Managers Forum; the Music Publishers Association; the Music Producers Guild; the Musicians' Union; Phonographic Performance Ltd; PRS for Music; and the UK Live Music Group. It is the activities covered by UK Music's members that provide the 'core' of their music industries, and it is this core that has been documented in their *Measuring Music* reports.

This has an effect on their recorded and live music figures. In its own mapping of the core music industries, the British government has sometimes included the retail of recordings (Cloonan 2007: 80). This sector is also factored into the PRS for Music analyses. However, the retailers of recorded music are not members of UK Music and nor are streaming companies. Correspondingly, the proceeds of these businesses do not form part of their statistical reckoning.[6] Conversely, ticketing agencies are represented in UK Music (Paul Latham of Live Nation served as chair of UK Live Music until September 2018) and therefore the retailers' share of ticket sales is included in their reports. Secondary ticketing is out, however. The profiteers in this field are not considered to be part of the music industries.

As well as defining the music industries differently to PRS for Music, UK Music have a different financial rationale. The *Adding Up the Music Industry* reports outline the total revenues of the industries. UK Music, in contrast, uses Gross Value Added (GVA) figures. This methodology is in keeping with their governmental target audience, as it is the means by which the economic contributions of different industry sectors are assessed. UK Music takes the revenue figures of live and recorded music, and subtracts 'the cost of bought in goods and services used up in the production process' (UK Music 2013: 9). What remains is the GVA contribution, which consists of the wages and salaries given to employees plus any 'operating surplus' (ONS n.d.: 6). This surplus includes financial charges, dividends to shareholders and capital investment.

The choice of GVA reporting means that UK Music's figures are approximate. GVA contributions are not calculated by analysing the accounts of individual companies. Instead a ratio is developed, which is then applied to all companies operating within a business sector. In line with their distrust of ONS accounting, UK Music have created a bespoke ratio for their reports. It nevertheless 'averages across firms known to be in the music industry' (UK Music 2013: 12). Consequently, UK Music advise against using their results to compare different industry sectors, such as recording and live. Their ratio is 'bespoke to the core as a whole, not to the component parts of the core'; therefore the results 'may vary between the different elements' (UK Music 2013: 12).

How is the statistical information categorized?

As well as influencing UK Music's definition of the 'core' music industry, the membership of the organization shapes the way that it categorizes its *Measuring Music* reports. This categorization, in turn, has an effect on their live and recorded totals. Live music includes the contributions of music festival organizers, music promoters, music agents, production services for live music, ticket agents and concert venues and arenas. The live music industry operates under the umbrella body of UK Live Music and so its GVA contribution is combined. In contrast, the recorded music figures do not include the contribution of music producers, recording studios and staff, even though they are a feature of the report. They have their own trade organization, the Music Producers Guild, and so are provided with a separate GVA contribution, which was worth £122 million in 2017 (UK Music 2018b: 8). This method of categorization diminishes the share accorded to recorded music whilst bolstering the share given to live.

There are further categorical decisions that affect the tallies of both industries. In the first instance, the copyright fees that they pay to publishers are removed from their totals. This is in contradistinction to the reporting practice of PRS for Music, but is reflective of the fact that UK Music includes the Music Publishers Association amongst its members. In 2017 the GVA contribution for publishing was calculated as being worth £505 million (UK Music 2018b: 8). Secondly, UK Music includes organizations that represent performers and songwriters. As a result, these artists are also provided with a statistical field of their own. The money that they make from gigs and records is subtracted from the live and recording totals (UK Music regard it as a 'bought in' service for these industries).[7] In turn, the payments that artists make to managers and music agents are subtracted from their own GVA figures (and are placed instead under the heading of 'music representatives'), as are the fees they pay to producers. The end result is that neither live nor recorded music is shown to have the largest GVA contribution. This honour is instead bestowed upon 'musicians, composers, songwriters and lyricists'. With a total of £2 billion in 2017 they are shown to have generated twice as much as the live music industry and three times the amount of recording (UK Music 2018b: 8) (see Table 8.2).

Category	**Year £ million**					
	2012	**2013**	**2014**	**2015**	**2016**	**2017**
Musicians, composers, songwriters and lyricists	£1547	£1700	£1900	£2000	£2000	£2000
Recorded music	£714	£618	£615	£610	£640	£700
Live music	£662	£789	£924	£904	£1000	£991
Music publishing	£402	£436	£410	£412	£473	£505
Music representatives	£151	£80	£89	£92	£96	£99
Music producers, recording studios and staff	£80	£102	£116	£119	£121	£122
GVA Total	**£3477***	**£3800**	**£4100**	**£4100**	**£4400**	**£4500**

TABLE 8.2: UK music industry figures calculated by UK Music.

Figures are derived from UK Music (2013, 2014b, 2015, 2016, 2017, 2018b).
* This is the total given by UK Music (2013: 34). The figures add up to £3356 million, however.

Are performers able to assess their share of the money?

Although musicians, composers, songwriters and lyricists have their own field in the UK Music reports, there is no detail about the revenue streams that make up their GVA contribution. Therefore, there is no way of determining how much the live and recorded music figures would increase if they were to incorporate the artists' share.[8] Moreover, this lack of detail means that these music makers are not in a position to compare their earnings with the GVA of record companies and live music organizations. Ultimately, UK Music's figures are of little help for assessing the relative levels of income that can be derived from recorded music and live.

They also make it hard for music makers to question the justice of their pay. At first glance, it looks as though they are prospering ahead of recorded companies and live music organizations, as they have the largest GVA contribution. The *Measuring Music* totals can be reversed, however, if we divide the contribution of each sector by its number of employees. For example, in 2017 record businesses generated £72,614 per capita, live businesses generated £34,579 per capita and music makers earned £21,941 each (UK Music 2018b: 8–9). Moreover, it should be noted that the GVA figures for musicians, composers, songwriters and lyricists are calculated differently to those for live and recorded music. The former are compiled on an 'income' basis and address take home pay alone; the latter work on a 'production' basis and consider both wages and operating surplus (UK Music 2013: 10).

UK Music has wished to present a unified front amongst its constituent parts. Its *Measuring Music* reports do not display or document any monetary issues amongst its members. Instead, when the organization outlines its policy issues, these are usually located beyond the core, amongst their 'wider' music industry. In the 2017 report, for example, the main issue of concern was the 'value gap'; the low royalty rates that record companies and publishers had been receiving from companies such as YouTube and Facebook. Michael Dugher, the CEO of UK Music, stressed that 'these platforms offer little adequate reward to the investors and creators of the "content"' (UK Music 2017: 6).

It is notable that UK Music depicted the plugging of this value gap within the recording and publishing industries as aiding live music as well. Dugher argued, '[t]o reach the big stage you need to have a hit record and you need to be able to pay the bills' (UK Music 2017: 6). More generally, UK Music's reports have outlined a connected system in which success in recorded music precedes success in live music. Within this 'sequential' process '[m]usicians will typically be performing compositions that either they or another artist have recorded' (UK Music 2013: 16). UK Music's ultimate endpoint, nevertheless, is a source of income that abandons the boundaries of composition, recording and performance. They believe that the most successful music makers are the ones that have become commodities. They will no longer be concentrating on sales of music, but rather on selling themselves 'as a brand, reputation or image' (UK Music 2013: 16).

Conclusion

It would be wrong to reject out of hand the findings of PRS for Music and UK Music. Their statistical data is useful and their reports identify some individual economic trends. They are also revealing of the organizations' own tactical biases, most notably their separate needs to present an inter-related music 'industry' (still using the singular): PRS for Music have wished to illustrate the diverse revenue streams that their members can draw upon; UK Music have sought to demonstrate the combined economic clout of their lobbying members. Yet herein lies a danger. The side-by-side tabulation of revenue streams has engendered a compulsion amongst readers to contrast the respective fortunes of industry sectors. This compulsion has been stronger still for those who have a vested interest in either highlighting the successes of live music or pointing towards the failings of the recorded music business. This temptation should be resisted. PRS for Music and UK Music have not compared like with like.

It is arguable, on the one hand, that the sheer *difference* between live and recorded music should lead us to resist such side-by-side by comparisons. There is no possible way of rejigging the criteria that would enable us to present a true picture of relative prosperity. The two sectors are not only ontologically distinct, they also have industries within industries that do not move in unison. It could also be argued that the *inter-connectedness* of live and recorded music is served poorly by this method of statistical reporting. Williamson and Cloonan are correct when urging us to bear diversity in mind, but UK Music are also correct when they argue that the wealth in these industries can be jointly derived. Live music drives the sales and use of recordings, just as recorded music prompts ticket sales for gigs. It could even be argued that the twenty-first century has witnessed the two sectors becoming more monetarily entwined. Although the amounts have been reduced, record companies still provide funds for tour support (IFPI 2016: 6). Mirroring this, many artists have been subject to 360° deals, whereby the record company is granted a share of live performance revenue. The distinct tabulation of sectorial revenue does a disservice to the symbiotic aspects of this relationship.

And what about the music makers? It would be wrong to gainsay the suggestion that for many artists live performance now generates more money than recording. The increased number of tours, festivals and band reformations is indicative of this trend. There is also plenty of anecdotal evidence from artists that says as much. Nevertheless, the PRS for Music and UK Music reports are not the place to turn for evidence. Their macroeconomic analyses do not satisfy the microeconomic arguments. Instead, we must turn to surveys that have tackled this subject from the artists' perspective. In 2014, UK Music accompanied their *Measuring Music* report with an *Additional Analysis of Earnings by Music Professionals*. It found that musicians gained 26 per cent of their income from ticketed gigs, 25 per cent from non-ticketed corporate gigs, two per cent from public performance payments for recordings and two per cent from royalties from record companies

(2014a: n.pag.). Singers gained 49 per cent of their income from non-ticketed corporate gigs, ten per cent from ticketed gigs, four per cent from record company royalties and two per cent from public performance payments for recordings (2014a: n.pag.). The UK Live Music Census of 2017 included a similar investigation (Webster et al. 2018). Its results showed that professional musicians earned, on average, 49 per cent of their income from performing and three per cent from recording; semi-professionals earned 23 per cent from performing and two per cent from recording; and amateurs earned 23 per cent from performing and one per cent from recording (Webster et al. 2018: 20).

These results would appear to be damning for the recording industry. In all categories in both surveys it was responsible for less than five per cent of music makers' pay. The results may have been different, however, if respondents had been asked to consider record company advances as a revenue stream.[9] In addition, it should be noted that UK Music's figures were derived from a different source to their revenue data in *Measuring Music*. The *Additional Analysis* survey was undertaken with 900 music professionals, representing just 1.3 per cent of the total number of musicians, composers, songwriters and lyricists enumerated in their main report. The UK Live Music Census drew on a wider pool of musicians and singers, collating the feedback from 1,598 respondents. It did take place at performance venues, though. What would the answers have been like if it had been compiled at record company offices or within recording studios?

More information is required. It would be good to have work that outlines the revenues or GVA contributions of each sector of the music industries *and* provides details of the share that is going to music makers. As well as aiding performers in their career choices, this information would help them to address the equitability of their pay. It would also be valuable to have questionnaires that address the intertwined ecosystem of the music industry. Performers should be quizzed about their different revenue streams, but they should also be asked how their recording careers have boosted their live music revenues and how their live music work has boosted their recording income. They could also be quizzed about the extent to which their income has been derived from self-commoditization. Which comes first, the basket or the egg?

NOTES

1. In 2019, UK Music replaced its *Measuring Music* reports with a new report titled *Music by Numbers 2019*. This report used a revised methodology, which means that 'like-for-like comparisons with the data [...] collected in previous years are not possible to make' (UK Music 2019: 7).

2. A later *Measuring Music* report attributed this downturn to the London Olympics and Paralympics, which meant that several 'large venues were put beyond live music for a long period' of the year (UK Music 2014b: 18). This analysis supports the suggestion that the health of live music revenues is dependent on a limited number of major events.
3. PRS for Music refined their methodology as their reports progressed. The estimates for live music revenue were improved; new categories were added (advertising and sponsorship revenues from 2008 onwards); and some revenues were discontinued (overseas/international payments made from the UK collection societies to foreign affiliates was discarded in 2010 and 2011) (see Table 10.1). The figures in the reports were not updated to factor in inflation, however, which problematizes any year-on-year increase/decrease calculations derived from the figures.
4. This is arrived at by taking the total live music revenue figure, taking away the PRS adjustment for live music revenues and the £208 million for secondary ticketing, and dividing the result by four to discover the total for spend on original ticket sales and the third of that money that goes on ancillary spend.
5. The B2B figures include further revenues that could be reconfigured under the headings of 'recording' and 'live'. Regarding the 2011 figures, this would include a substantial amount of the £448 million that is attributed to PRS for Music. The report details £101.6 million that the society accumulated because of 'recorded music' (Brookes 2012: 5). £65 million of this is incorporated within the B2C 'recorded music' figures in respect of mechanical licensing, but the remaining £36.6 million is hidden within the B2B PRS adjusted total. Recordings also contributed to some of PRS for Music's other revenue streams: broadcast & online, public performance and international. It should be noted that live music also generates some of the broadcast & online income for composers and publishers, albeit that it is recorded music that dominates when it comes to the income generated by radio, television and the Internet. Recorded music also makes up a significant proportion of the music publishers' direct revenue. Out of the £210 million that is allocated to them in the 2011 report, £48 million comes from sync rights (Brookes 2012: 5).
6. This has changed with the *Music by Numbers 2019* report, which, rather than focusing on the activities of UK Music members, has as an ambition to provide a 'definitive insight into the health of the British music industry' and issue the UK government with an even greater figure for the music industry contribution to the UK economy (UK Music 2019: 5). To that end the 2019 report includes 'music retail', which covers the retail of musical instruments, manufacture of musical instruments, digital music retail and physical music retail (the retail of tickets for concerts is, however, included in the live music total). It also includes the economic contribution of music lawyers and accountants. As a result the total economic contribution of the music industry for 2018 is calculated at £5.2 billion, up from £4.5 billion in 2017.
7. This figure does not appear to include non-recouped record company or publisher advances. They are instead regarded as part of the companies' capital investment, alongside money

spent on invisible imports and exports, marketing and promotion, and other aspects of A&R.

8. The exception is the *Measuring Music* report for 2014, which includes some data from 'Additional Analysis of Earnings by Music Professionals' (UK Music 2014b: 24).
9. The other categories in the UK Music questionnaire were: payments for music tuition; session fees for TV, film, computer games; commissioning fees for composition (live and media); royalties and rights payments from PRS; royalties from music publishers; sponsorship/brand endorsements. The remaining categories in the UK Live Music census were: teaching; other music-related activity; other non-music-related activity; session musician/singer; composing/writing.

REFERENCES

Anderton, Chris (2008), 'Commercializing the carnivalesque: The V festival and image/risk management', *Event Magazine*, 12:1, pp. 39–51.

Anderton, Chris, Dubber, Andrew and James, Martin (2013), *Understanding the Music Industries*, London: Sage.

Ashton, Robert (2014), 'A giant leap for music kind', *Music Week*, 3 April, pp. 14–15.

Billboard Staff (2018), 'Billboard's 2018 power 100 list revealed', *Billboard.com*, 25 January, https://www.billboard.com/articles/business/8096144/billboard-2018-power-100-list. Accessed 26 January 2019.

Bintliff, Esther (2010), 'Live music boom drives off recording blues', FT.com, 20 August, https://www.ft.com/content/c8ff8d50-ac85-11df-8582-00144feabdc0. Accessed 26 January 2019.

Brookes, Nicholas (2012), *Adding Up the Music Industry 2011*, PRS for Music, https://www.prsformusic.com/what-we-do/influencing-policy/research. Accessed 26 January 2019.

Cloonan, Martin (2007), *Popular Music and the State in the UK: Culture, Trade or Industry?*, Aldershot: Ashgate.

——— (2013), 'Live music as ideology', *Situating Popular Musics: IASPM 16th International Conference*, Grahamstown, South Africa, 27 June–1 July 2011, pp. 77–88.

Curran, Shaun (2016), 'Are gigs getting too expensive?', *Independent*, 27 July, https://www.independent.co.uk/arts-entertainment/music/are-gigs-getting-too-expensive-radiohead-bjork-beyonc-pet-shop-boys-a7158706.html. Accessed 26 January 2019.

Foster, Patrick (2009), 'Forget the new album, rock fans want the real thing', *The Times*, 14 April, p. 15.

Green, Chris (ed.) (2019), *All About the Music: Recorded Music in the UK: Facts, Figures and Analysis*, London: BPI.

International Federation of the Phonographic Industry (IFPI) (2016), 'Investing in music: The value of record companies', http://www.ifpi.org/content/library/Investing_In_Music.pdf. Accessed 26 January 2017 [no longer available].

Jones, Rhian (2014), 'UK music market's worth revealed', *Music Week*, 19 September, p. 7.

Laing, Dave (2012), 'What's it worth? Calculating the economic value of live music', Live Music Exchange Blog, 11 June, http://livemusicexchange.org/blog/whats-it-worth-calculating-the-economic-value-of-live-music-dave-laing/. Accessed 26 January 2019.

ONS (Office for National Statistics) (n.d.), *Annual Business Survey Background Information 2008 and Later,* Newport: Office for National Statistics.

Page, Will (2008), *The 'R' Words: Recession and Royalties*, PRS for Music, 16 September, https://www.prsformusic.com/what-we-do/influencing-policy/research. Accessed 26 January 2019.

Page, Will and Carey, Chris (2009), *Adding Up the Music Industry for 2008*, PRS for Music, 20 July, https://www.prsformusic.com/what-we-do/influencing-policy/research. Accessed 26 January 2019.

——— (2010), *Adding Up the Music Industry for 2009*, PRS for Music, 4 August, https://www.prsformusic.com/what-we-do/influencing-policy/research. Accessed 26 January 2019.

——— (2011), *Adding Up the Music Industry for 2010*, PRS for Music, 4 August, https://www.prsformusic.com/what-we-do/influencing-policy/research. Accessed 26 January 2019.

Savage, Mark (2017), 'Seen a gig recently? You're not the only one', *BBC News*, 20 September, http://www.bbc.co.uk/news/entertainment-arts-41331692. Accessed 26 January 2019.

Smirke, Richard (2014), 'Value of UK music industry grows to £3.8 billion', *Billboard*, 16 September, https://www.billboard.com/articles/news/6251648/uk-music-industry-grows-value. Accessed 26 January 2019.

Topping, Alexandra (2009), 'Music industry back on right track, says report', *Guardian*, 20 July, p. 9.

UK Music (2013), *The Economic Contribution of the Core UK Music Industry*, London: UK Music.

——— (2014a), *Additional Analysis of Earnings by Music Professionals*, https://www.ukmusic.org/assets/general/UK_MUSIC_Additional_Earnings.pdf. Accessed 26 January 2015.

——— (2014b), *Measuring Music: September 2014,* https://www.ukmusic.org/research/report-archive/measuring-music-2014. Accessed 26 January 2019.

——— (2015), *Measuring Music: 2015 Report*, https://www.ukmusic.org/research/report-archive/measuring-music-2015. Accessed 4 June 2019.

——— (2016), *Measuring Music: 2016 Report*, https://www.ukmusic.org/research/report-archive/measuring-music-2016. Accessed 4 June 2019.

——— (2017), *Measuring Music: 2017 Report*, https://www.ukmusic.org/research/report-archive/measuring-music-2017. Accessed 26 January 2019.

——— (2018a), 'About', *UK Music*, https://www.ukmusic.org. Accessed 26 January 2018.

——— (2018b), *Measuring Music: 2018 Report*, https://www.ukmusic.org/research/report-archive/measuring-music-2018. Accessed 26 January 2019.

——— (2019), *Music by Numbers 2019*, https://www.ukmusic.org/research/music-by-numbers. Accessed 21 November 2019.

Webster, Emma, Brennan, Matt, Behr, Adam and Cloonan, Martin (2018), *Valuing Live Music: The UK Live Music 2017 Census Report*, Live Music Exchange/University of Edinburgh/Newcastle University/University of Turku, http://uklivemusiccensus.org/#report. Accessed 26 January 2019.

Webster, Emma and McKay, George (2016), *From Glyndebourne to Glastonbury: The Impact of British Music Festivals*, Norwich: Arts and Humanities Research Council/University of East Anglia.

Wikström, Patrik (2013), *The Music Industry: Music in the Cloud*, 2nd ed., Cambridge: Polity.

Williamson, John and Cloonan, Martin (2007), 'Rethinking the music industry', *Popular Music*, 26:2, pp. 305–22.

——— (2013), 'Contextualising the contemporary recording industry', in L. Marshall (ed.), *The International Recording Industries*, London and New York: Routledge, pp. 11–29.

PART IV

PIRACY

9

Selling the Numbers on Music Piracy to Burn Down the Digital Library

Lucas Logan

On 17 November 2016, thousands of users of the private music sharing website What.CD discovered that it was inaccessible. French news sites and pro-file-sharing blog *Torrent Freak* soon after revealed that a militarized French cybercrime unit had raided multiple What.CD servers. The site's operators announced online that the site would not return and that all data was destroyed (Van der Saar 2016a). The French Society of Authors, Composers and Publishers of Music (SACEM) verified the raid the next day and stated that What had caused €41 million in damages to the music industries in its near-decade tenure (Van der Saar 2016b). There was some truth to their claims. What.CD did house infringing content (Welch 2016). Particularly significant was the inclusion of pre-releases, which made up a sizable amount of the damages that SACEM was claiming (Van der Saar 2016b). The making available of these releases has been considered harmful by the recording industry because they hurt sales upon release (Harvey 2015). SACEM's figures can nevertheless also be called into question. As with most piracy calculations, the valuation of losses is speculative and arguably inflated. The founders of What.CD and many of its 144,000 users countered SACEM's claim with the argument that the site was non-profit and operated on donations. In addition, the supporters held that What was a 'modern Library of Alexandria' for music that carefully curated and catalogued its database of 2,675,120 files, featuring 885,556 artists (Harvey 2015). The files included orphaned works and high-quality copies of music that could not be found anywhere else. SACEM's accusation of damages, users contended, was contra to the intent and use of What.

What.CD was the descendant of OiNK.CD, a similar website that is the focus of this chapter. New sites have appeared to replace What, just as What and others replaced OiNK (Van der Saar 2016b). The conflict between users, the music industries and police displayed in the What raid is typical of digital copyright disputes in the twenty-first century. Media industries have been able to successfully lobby for criminal enforcement of digital piracy, and cybercrime police units are now commonly directed at copyright violating websites (Leman-Langlois 2012). At the high end of estimates, the music industries have claimed that over €11 billion has been lost annually due to piratical activity (Horner 2019). Utilizing such figures, they have lobbied for the criminal prosecution of digital piracy, and have directed crime units at violating websites (Leman-Langlois 2012).

Illegal downloading is no longer perceived by the music industry to be their primary threat due to the ascendance of streaming, but pirate sites still exist in droves and are frequent targets of international policing. The central social and cultural problems posed by sites like OiNK and What still exist as well. For collectors and audiophiles who want to own digital files in a high-quality audio format, streaming services are not adequate, and formats such as iTunes often do not sell those file types (Gartenberg 2017). Downloading sites function as boutique centres for people to get a higher quality product than they can from streaming. Additionally, the policies and laws that shut down pirate sites and users are still in place. The history of anti-piracy efforts by the recording industry is important to evaluate because while the industry is recovering from its economic downturn, the structures that target digital piracy still exist.

This chapter explores that history and those structures through the lens of OiNK's Pink Palace. The history of digital piracy and its impact on the recording industry are also observed. Although this industry is recovering, the total global music revenue in 2018 was still only 68 per cent of its peak in 1999 (IFPI 2018: 10). I argue that streaming services have reduced piracy more than lawsuits and criminal enforcement, and focus on Spotify as an effective but imperfect tool against piracy. Spotify and its chief competitor, Apple Music, have libraries of over 30 million and 40 million songs respectively (Hall 2018). These are far larger catalogues than are held by the pirate sites discussed here. Streaming services do not offer some of the features desired by downloaders, though, such as the ability to find orphaned and unavailable works, the ability to own copies of the music, the want for higher resolution audio and the excitement of pre-releases.

The music industries base losses on a file-sharing site's advertising revenue, user visits and number of files. Lawmakers, police and courts adhere to industry numbers. The OiNK case showcases how these numbers do not reflect the actual use of the site. OiNK operated a complex sharing economy that provided a service – a well-curated digital library of high-quality audio files in multiple formats for downloading – that did not exist in the legal, legitimate economic sphere.

In this chapter, I provide an overview of relevant conflicts between the music industries and Internet users. I discuss the recording industry's history and reaction to digital piracy, and evaluate the industry's approximate 50 per cent loss in revenue in the period from 1999 to 2014. I overview larger, open pirate websites like The Pirate Bay and MegaUpload, and note similarities and differences they have with a private outlet like OiNK. I give a description of OiNK, from its rise as an elite, difficult to access private file-sharing site to its legal demise and the aftermath. I conclude that conflict between industry and pirate sites will continue, if not worsen, under current policy models. OiNK was a problematic solution to a market failure, and the market problem was never fully addressed. The study is conducted through a critical legal approach and an application of approaches that describe how policy-makers are continually attempting to expand copyright law.

The critical legal approach and the upward ratchet of copyright law

The critical legal perspective is rooted in the political economic scholarship of authors including Vincent Mosco (2009) and Allan Hutchinson (1989). This approach views the law as a political construct that reflects the interests of the most powerful stakeholders in a given society (Hutchinson 1989: 4). Mosco describes the political economy of communication as the 'study of social power relations that mutually constitute the production, distribution and consumption of communication, or the social process of exchange of social relationships' (2009: 67–68). Social power relations in the case of digital music constitute how the recording industry attempts to control music through regulatory technological and legal regulation. An examination of power relations also demonstrates how file-sharing websites have historically resisted control from the industry. In this approach, the problem is not that the owners of OiNK were violating copyright law, but that policy was constructed so as to leave no place for a cultural outlet like OiNK to exist.

It is indisputable there were hundreds of thousands of copyright infringing materials on OiNK. However, the site also offered music that was unavailable in the marketplace or in audio formats that could not be purchased. It is impossible to validate claims about losses, because OiNK was situated as a space for serious music collection and not the casual listenership associated with legal alternatives. It becomes difficult, then, to quantify losses from a private torrent website. Indeed, current legal models of streaming may now operate as places for music collectors to sample music before investing storage space in downloading superior versions of the audio files.

Related to the critical legal approach, I incorporate Susan Sell's (2010) concept of the 'upward ratchet' of copyright law, which historically allows the music industries to inflate claims of damages, increase police enforcement and create new laws and trade agreements governing digital music. Sell describes the upward ratchet – that is the incremental, unidirectional movement – of intellectual property (IP) law stemming from the United States and including the US government, trade organizations, intergovernmental organizations and international police organizations (Sell 2010: 10). Policy-makers have a tendency when regulating intellectual property to ratchet up IP law through systems of international governance. The upward ratchet leads to an energetic focus by policy-makers on combating both counterfeiting and piracy (Sell 2010: 3).

The music industry's tactics toward fighting piracy throughout the 2000s exemplify this process. In the United States and the European Union, policies were implemented to promote and enforce digital rights management (DRM), which restricts how users can copy and share media content. DRM has been criticized as limiting ownership and control of content to its users, and a rejection of DRM-fuelled traffic to file-sharing sites (Burkart and McCourt 2006: 23). Although the industry as a whole eventually removed DRM restrictions from CDs and digital files, a form of digital rights management underpins the streaming economy. The International Federation of the Phonographic Industry (IFPI) reported in 2018 that copyright infringement through stream ripping – using illicit software to download streaming music – was its primary concern in terms of piracy (2018: 42). Consequently, websites that offer stream ripping services have been taken down with lawsuits.

The music industry was caught somewhat unawares by the transition to digital networks, and spent the first decade of the twenty-first century working to toughen copyright laws and hold websites and individuals accountable for violation of IP laws. In the years leading up to the launch of Napster in 1999, the music industry in the United States ceased sales of singles and overlooked the oncoming threat of digital piracy (Burkart and McCourt 2006: 32). Napster was shut down and forced to pay $130 million in damages to the music industry. The piracy genie was not to return to the bottle, though, and the industry's efforts to work with services such as iTunes did not stem the rise of pirate sites such as Kazaa and Grokster (Burkart and McCourt 2006: 34).

Digital copyright infringement can lead to industrial-scale punishments for small-scale file-sharing, and infamously did so in the United States through dozens of lawsuits from the Recording Industry Association of America (RIAA) against individuals in the 2000s (Miller 2005: 313). The lawsuits were popularly viewed as disproportionate to the copyright infringements (Miller 2005: 314). Most notoriously, Jammie Thomas, a single mother from Utah, was charged with $9250 per song for downloading 24 songs from a file-sharing service (Kravets 2013). The logic behind the fees was that the peer-to-peer (P2P) service Thomas was using allowed other users to download the songs from her computer. Therefore, the court charged her under the assumption that every copy of every song downloaded from her computer was the equivalent of stealing an entire physical compact disc. RIAA abandoned this lawsuit model due to the bad public relations stemming from cases like Thomas's and began working with service providers for more direct ways of terminating the Internet connections of alleged pirates (Sarikakis 2012: 149).

The argument that file-sharing is a direct reflection of sales loss is prevalent in industry and governmental discussion of digital piracy policy, but various studies find the relationship between piracy and album sales to be less pronounced (Hong 2013; Lee 2016; Oberholzer-Gee and Strumpf 2016). There is little consensus in the literature on losses from piracy (Lee 2016: 4). The most generous estimates of losses from outside of the recording industry put digital piracy losses around 30 per cent of total sales (Oberholzer-Gee and Strumpf 2016: 65). Studies that conclude that piracy negatively affects album sales typically claim losses of around twenty per cent of total sales (Oberholzer-Gee and Strumpf 2016: 65). Even at these levels, file-sharing is not enough to account for the near 50 per cent loss in record sales from 1998 to 2014 that has been reported by the recording industry (RIAA 2015). Certainly, the 20–30 per cent loss is a significant hurdle for the recording industry to contend with, but its speculative piracy reporting is of concern because of the manner in which it is employed to shape copyright policy.

RIAA produces annual recommendations for the US Trade Representative's (USTR) 'Notorious Markets' list. The list is used by the United States to recommend trade policy and sanctions for nations that are accused of not protecting US copyrights. The recommendations reflect RIAA's methodology for assessing the amount of damages from file-sharing sites. Damages are assessed based on combinations of advertising revenue, user visits and the number of files hosted by the sites (RIAA 2015). The list also details each file-sharing site's registrars and alleged revenue sources. These typically consist of advertising revenue and malware-installing programs (RIAA 2015).

The websites on the USTR list consist of large, well-trafficked sites. Perhaps the most famous website on the list is The Pirate Bay, which has been repeatedly raided and had charges filed against all of its founders (Andersson 2014: 117). Another example of what happens when the sites are shut down is made clear through the raid of the popular cyberlocker site MegaUpload. The New Zealand-based website was on the Notorious Markets list and was pursued internationally by police (RIAA 2015). The FBI used digital surveillance to monitor the communications of MegaUpload operators, including Skype correspondence, for five years before the eventual raid (Martin and Newhall 2013: 149). A federal court in Virginia, where MegaUpload's web hosting service was located, ordered the seizure of eighteen web addresses associated with the company (Raymond 2013: 377–78). The investigation into the site culminated with a New Zealand police raid, directed by the US Department of Justice, of founder Kim Dotcom's mansion. This raid featured police with paramilitary gear, tactical firearms, dog units and a helicopter (Martin and Newhall 2013: 102). Dotcom was found in a safe room and put into a police van, where he was told that he was being arrested for copyright infringement (Martin and Newhall 2013: 102). The charges against MegaUpload's operators included copyright infringement, crimes related to aiding and abetting copyright infringement, criminal conspiracy and fraud (Martin and Newhall 2013: 116). RIAA sued MegaUpload in 2014 for $500 million in damages, issuing the following explanation:

> Megaupload Limited played an active role in ensuring that it had the most popular content on its servers, that the URL links to those infringing content files were widely disseminated on the Internet, and that the links were advertised and promoted by pirate linking sites, so that the maximum number of Megaupload users would access the infringing content.
>
> (Hogan 2014)

The MegaUpload case is indicative, not only of the damages pursued by the recording industry, but also of the manner by which the upward ratchet of copyright law extends to police force and criminalization. The paramilitary raid of Dotcom's mansion is an extreme example of how cybercrime and anti-terrorist police units continually extend their reach into copyright infringement. The OiNK case detailed below also includes international raids and specialized police forces raiding servers and arresting site operators. The similarities in coordination from police make the comparisons of OiNK and MegaUpload relevant to this discussion, but the similarities end there. OiNK was an invitation-only, non-profit service that operated differently from MegaUpload and similar sites. I argue that these differences are important because OiNK developed cultural structures and practices and built a community around curating and sharing. It was difficult to access, had strict rules and was difficult for many without the technological know-how to negotiate (Sockanathan 2011: 54).

The standardization of police action towards copyright infringement is particularly problematic in cases such as OiNK because it neglects the underlying culture of the communities and fails to address the market failures that cause OiNK and other private file-sharing sites to exist.

OiNK's Pink Palace

The case of OiNK's Pink Palace is utilized in this chapter because it highlights the disparity between industry and policy-makers with life and culture as experienced online. Where users of OiNK saw it as a pristinely curated music library, the recording industry was convinced that the site was a for-profit pirate operation and that its main intention was to deprive them of revenue. The dispute over the nature of the site is better understood in the context of how and for whom the site operated. OiNK was an invitation-only music-oriented BitTorrent tracker, or search index, that specialized in high-quality audio formats and required users to share in order to download. BitTorrent is a type of file-sharing protocol that allows users to download files, or torrents, from multiple other downloaders at the same time, enabling a quick, efficient method of sending and receiving data (Choi and Perez 2007).

OiNK contained a vibrant community of music fanatics, industry insiders and musicians (Sockanathan 2011: 23). One famous user, Trent Reznor of the band Nine Inch Nails, hailed OiNK's massive music selection, quality audio formats, DRM-free files and pre-releases as being superior to anything he had encountered in retail or legal digital stores like iTunes or Amazon (Westhoff 2007). When OiNK was shut down by IFPI, the British Phonographic Industry (BPI) and Interpol in October of 2007, the site's users and owners were branded as criminals and pirates, news outlets were reminded of the toll that file-sharing takes on the music industry, and criminal charges were pressed against users and administrators (O'Connell 2007). In the wake of the OiNK raids, copycat websites emerged and criticisms of the takedown were made online from former users, digital rights groups and activists (Jones 2007). The following case analysis of OiNK summarizes the infrastructure and culture of the site, details the takedown and the legal actions taken against it, and evaluates the conflict between file-sharers, law enforcement and the music industry.

OiNK's emergence and closure: The Pink Palace under siege

British programmer Alan Ellis launched OiNK's Pink Palace in 2004 (Carraway 2012: 576–77). The site relied on the BitTorrent file-sharing protocol for users to upload and download music, software applications, e-books and comics (Sockanathan 2011: 18–19). Movies, games and pornography were banned from OiNK (Phan 2007). At its peak, OiNK had 180,000 members (Phan 2007). OiNK was a private BitTorrent tracker, meaning that users had to register with the site after accepting an invitation (Carraway 2012: 577). Keeping a tracker private is done in part to help sites avoid anti-piracy crackdowns, but also to help maintain a high quality of content that is devoid of spamming and computer viruses (Andersson 2014: 103). Invitations to OiNK were heavily sought after in online message forums and chatrooms around the Web, and selling invites was strictly forbidden by administrators (Sockanathan 2011: 18–19). Invites could only be given out by OiNK users who had accrued a high ratio of materials downloaded to materials uploaded (Sockanathan 2011: 19). OiNK's entire system of rules and sharing practices was based on ratio requirements. If users did not maintain a high enough ratio, they were banned from the site (Phan 2007). If a user invited someone to OiNK and the new member abused the ratio system, both the inviter and the invitee were banned (Phan 2007). Ratio could not be bought or sold with money, and could only be accrued through sharing (Phan 2007). The Pink Palace's ratio system was notoriously particular, and many users were banned for not meeting requirements (Phan 2007). Ratio was the currency that users employed to 'purchase' music on the site. The music indexed on OiNK was considered by users to be a premium product, and users who wanted to own that product had to work to keep up their ratio. Ratio and invitation policies could also be envisioned as forms of DRM, in that they limited user access to files. Unlike the larger, open platforms of noteworthy file-sharing sites like The Pirate Bay and MegaUpload, OiNK and similar private trackers were only open to those who were granted access and spent time managing their accounts.

However particular the site was about cultivating users, the underlying construction of OiNK's sharing economy was not abnormal for a file-sharing site. Communication research has recognized the sharing economies of file-sharing websites and software (Lessig 2008; Carraway 2012; Andersson 2014), and while OiNK's requirements were stricter than other sites, it was not particularly different from sharing systems researched elsewhere. Lawrence Lessig, for instance, has defined sharing economies as environments where 'access to culture is regulated not by price, but by a complex set of social relations' that are 'insulted by the simplicity of price' (2008: 145). Indeed, the social relations required to access culture on OiNK were bizarrely complex. OiNK took donations for server maintenance and rental space, but giving money gave donors no special privileges (Phan 2007). Requesting privileges in return for donations would result in a user being banned (Phan 2007).

OiNK's administrators went to great lengths to keep the site discreet, going so far as to remove attempts to create a Wikipedia page and avoiding talking to the press (Kravets 2010). Users were required to have 'cute' avatars such as an image of a stuffed animal or pet, and civility was strictly enforced in the site's message boards and chatrooms (Sockanathan 2011: 336, 340). The site was reputed for the depth and variety of its music selection and had very strict rules regarding audio quality (Sockanathan 2011: 20). Administrators would not allow any music files to be uploaded that were not of a higher quality than those found in Apple's iTunes store or any other legal music store at the time, and there were strict rules regarding file labelling and presentation (Phan 2007). OiNK's audio quality standards led one *Wired* journalist to liken them to a 'persnickety record store clerk' (Phan 2007), and users were frequently kicked out for violations. A *New York Magazine* feature on OiNK echoed the sentiments of many users with the statement that OiNK was 'the greatest record store of all time, filled with not-yet-released albums, obscure live performances, the rarest of B-sides, and a fabulous bonus – everything was free' (Day 2007). The music was free in the monetary sense, but users were not allowed to download anything if they did not spend weeks or sometimes months cultivating their ratios (Day 2007). The early releases were largely provided by industry insiders, meaning that journalists, studio employees and musicians were uploading pre-released albums on the Internet and linking them directly to OiNK (Day 2007). This was an illegal process and leaked releases are considered to be more damaging by the recording industry than post-release uploads, which was a major reason why IFPI and BPI pressed for criminal and not merely civil charges against OiNK (Day 2007).

Leaked releases were promoted on the site in the comments sections and forums of OiNK (Lightfoot 2010). The leaks were part of what made OiNK's Pink Palace an enormous, meticulously managed digital music *bibliothèque* with an infrastructure and catalogue depth that rivalled any legal services available at the time (Sockanathan 2011: 24). The site was rooted in the users' propensity for sharing, systematizing and classifying files, filling holes in the library, reporting violations and other efforts at infrastructure maintenance (Sockanathan 2011: 25).

The site was monetarily free, but extremely labour intensive and users had to earn continued membership through their own shared work. OiNK ran on social capital and relied on the sharing and reciprocity of its users. It was a user-driven service that was only sustainable because of the demand for an extensive digital music catalogue that was not being offered by other P2P and retail sites. Andrew Sockanathan, assessing OiNK from a cultural perspective, surveyed various users and found a collection of fans and musicians that turned to the invite-only torrent site because they were tired of the recording industry's price fixing, iTunes' relatively poor quality, lack of depth and disrespect for musicians (Sockanathan 2011: 35–37). This is not to say that torrent sites were more beneficial to musicians than iTunes, but rather the perception that if the artist was not going to be supported by the source, it was better to go to a community like OiNK for free than to pay a multinational like Apple. OiNK's Pink Palace was an online forum where communal labour was used to create a commons for file-sharing and communication about culture, fandom and a massive digital library project.

OiNK's contribution to the digital commons was not acknowledged by record companies, who saw music, software and literature that they owned openly traded amongst 180,000 users. For the recording industry, OiNK was, in the words of an IFPI official, 'central to the illegal distribution of prerelease music online [...] this was not a case of friends sharing music for pleasure. This was a worldwide network that got hold of music they did not own the rights to and posted it online' (O'Connell 2007). IFPI's statement is a condemnation of OiNK's sharing economy as a criminal enterprise whose purpose was to steal cultural commodities.

After a two-year investigation by IFPI and BPI, OiNK's servers were raided in the Netherlands, while the site's founder, Alan Ellis, and six British OiNK users were arrested in the United Kingdom (O'Connell 2007). The raid was named Operation Ark Royal – a nod to British warships – and included cooperation with British and Dutch police and Interpol (O'Connell 2007). Visitors to the site after the raid were greeted with a graphic from IFPI and BPI warning of a criminal investigation into user identities (O'Connell 2007). Ellis's home, place of employment and father's home were all raided by police, along with several buildings in Amsterdam over the period of a week (O'Connell 2007). The Dutch police unit responsible for the raid was the Fiscal Investigation Unit of the Dutch Police (FIOD ECD) (Day 2007). FIOD ECD is an elite Dutch task force that primarily focuses on financing, money laundering and fraud associated with organized crime and terrorism (International Monetary Fund 2011: 34). This task force seized OiNK's servers and $300,000 in donations, which British police claimed made the site 'highly lucrative' (O'Connell 2007).

The use of FIOD ECD is significant because it signifies that Dutch police, in cooperation with British enforcement agencies, were using resources developed for high financial and violent crime to focus on enforcing IP prohibitions. The sweeps on OiNK's servers mirrored The Pirate Bay raid by dozens of Swedish police and the paramilitary raid of Kim Dotcom's mansion, in that enforcement was carried out with large quantities of police resources. The police were also acting at the insistence of IFPI and BPI (O'Connell 2007). The phenomena of media industry discourse on copyright infringement being passed along to police organizations is evident in the police insistence after the raid that OiNK was a for-profit enterprise, in spite of there being no evidence that the seized donations were used for anything but site maintenance (Sockanathan 2011: 38). The accusations of piracy and theft from IFPI, BPI and police agencies presumes that the possibility of OiNK's proprietors running a file-sharing site for the purpose of non-commodified cultural exchange is preposterous. A prosecutor representing the British government in the case claimed that OiNK was a 'cash cow' and that it was 'common sense' that Ellis was engaging in criminal activity (Lightfoot 2010). The assumption of criminal infringement was the undoing of the OiNK prosecutions, as there was not enough evidence of criminal wrongdoing to result in convictions (Lightfoot 2010).

Resolution: OiNK and its aftermath

Ellis was charged with conspiracy to defraud the recording industry but was found not guilty after a ten-day trial in 2010 (Wray 2010). The court agreed with his defence that he was simply trying to further his skills as a programmer through OiNK and had never profited directly from donations to the website (Wray 2010). The court also found evidence that IFPI members used OiNK to promote their own releases (Lightfoot 2010). Although the practice of pre-releasing is clearly not fully endorsed by record companies and is damaging to many artists, pre-releases and demos were sometimes being used to build anticipation for larger projects or tours (Horner 2019).

The OiNK users that were arrested were cleared of all or most charges as well, and found to have no link to or relationship with Ellis (Cheng 2008). The users were arrested for uploading pre-release music to the site, and one 17-year-old uploader was arrested for sharing three albums that he downloaded from other websites (Kravets 2010). His parents' house was raided and their computers seized (Kravets 2010). The charge included 'distributing copyrighted material so as to prejudicially affect the copyright holder' (Kravets 2010), which was punishable by up to ten years imprisonment. The teenager's case was dismissed after IFPI failed to provide evidence that the music was copyrighted (Kravets 2010). The user's lawyer complained that the case should have been civil and not criminal and that IFPI was setting out to make an example out of file-sharers (Kravets 2010). The overzealousness in not filing a civil suit, where OiNK would have been more vulnerable, likely sank the case against OiNK's creators. The lawyer also accused the Crown Prosecution Service of acting as a proxy for IFPI and BPI (Kravets 2010). The other OiNK uploaders were sentenced to 50 to 180 hours of community service or given £500 fines (Breihan 2010).

The recording industry bemoaned the failure of the prosecutions, and used the inability to file criminal charges as a rallying call for an upward ratchet to copyright laws and greater policing of digital copyrights. The *Guardian*, in an article dubbing OiNK the 'British Pirate Bay' despite its much smaller reach, quoted a BPI representative as saying the verdict was 'hugely disappointing' (Wray 2010). The representative pointed to the allegation that over twenty million files were shared on OiNK, the claim that copyright infringement was costing thousands of British jobs, and the estimated £414 million that file-sharing cost the UK music industry in 2006 alone (Wray 2010). IFPI and BPI also used the failure to prosecute the OiNK arrestees as evidence that copyright law in the United Kingdom needed to be strengthened (Wray 2010).

While media industries perceived OiNK as a threat and responded with force, users of the Pink Palace provided counterarguments and protests on blogs and social media. Two memorial blogs were set up for OiNK's supporters and former users, and were used to raise funds for Ellis's legal defence (Sockanathan 2011: 4). These blogs also hosted a large volume of fan-created art in support of OiNK and were home to dozens of articles defending the site and waxing nostalgic about its past (Sockanathan 2011: 34). *TorrentFreak*, a popular pro-file-sharing and digital privacy site, reported that The Pirate Bay was to launch a replacement for OiNK called BOiNK (Van der Saar 2007). The Pirate Bay soon cancelled its plans when two other OiNK replacements, What.CD and Waffles.fm, were launched as nearly identical substitutes (Jones 2007). These 'piglets' were born just days after OiNK was shut down and nearly two-and-a-half years before the OiNK case was resolved. Waffles is still active at the time of writing, and although What was shut down, two more private torrent trackers immediately emerged to take its place (Van der Saar 2016b).

The launch of Waffles and What are indicative of what *TorrentFreak* refers to as the media industry's 'hydra' problem of growth and replication (Jones 2007), and what commentary on other technology sites like *Ars Technica* refer to as part of a futile game of 'whac-a-mole' (Anderson 2007). Sockanathan's analysis of OiNK argues that it is the organizational infrastructure of its users and curators, not the site itself or its programmers, that are disruptive to media industries (2011: 35). These users appreciate the potential of organizing and sharing media online and bypass laws that forbid such activity. Jonas Andersson warns researchers not to look at private trackers such as OiNK as unified communities or activist collectives (2014: 77). Rather, the users utilize the trackers and obey the rules because it offers them access to media that they could otherwise not access due to price, availability or the quality of marketed versions (Andersson 2014: 76–77, 103). He found that users are content to utilize file-sharing sites until legal alternatives arise that can match the depth of content available in the private trackers (Andersson 2014: 76).

Andersson's research notes how Spotify, the advertising- and subscription-supported streaming music service, is an example of a practical alternative to file-sharing that could stem illegal activity (2014: 45). A European Commission (2015) report found that Spotify does significantly displace piracy, but streaming services are DRM-based and do not allow ownership and control of music. The industry's current emphasis on stream ripping and lawsuits that successfully shut down stream ripping web services demonstrate how DRM is still crucial to the music industry (IFPI 2018: 42). No piracy-killing legal alternative exists that can accommodate the desire of private tracker users for high-quality, meticulously catalogued audio collections.

The rush to establish copycat sites immediately after the international efforts to shut down OiNK demonstrates a potential weakness of using law enforcement to eliminate file-sharing sites, while the failure to successfully prosecute any of the parties involved shows the limitations on the recording industry's ability to criminalize file-sharing in the United Kingdom. In the months after OiNK, the British industry did attempt to increase its IP prohibitions through the Digital Economy Act, which would criminalize file-sharing (Giblin 2014: 166). The Act was passed in 2010, but was never fully implemented due to wide protests from civil society groups and the public (Giblin 2014). This failure to implement the Digital Economy Act also hints at the political economic limitations of European Union member states to implement draconian digital copyright laws. However, the transnational coordination of police organizations in shutting down the physical means for operating an individual website was demonstrated fully through the British and Dutch raids on OiNK and affiliated parties. Additionally, the United Kingdom did establish a permanent IP task force in 2012 – the Police Intellectual Property Crime Unit – that has cracked down on websites allegedly hosting copyrighted materials (Solon 2013).

Conclusion: Exiting the Pink Palace

The OiNK case presents problems for approaches to law and policy governing digital copyrights. At the heart of the dispute is the commodification of music and how the ownership of music should be managed. Trade groups representing the music industry are correct to point to the harmful effects of piracy, but inflated claims of monetary damages and the upward ratchet of copyright law are inadequate measures for eliminating sites like OiNK. The assumption that a file-sharing site must be for profit and that administrators and users would not voluntarily offer their labour to curate OiNK's digital shelves is emblematic of a misunderstanding by the recording industry of a niche of online fandom and culture. OiNK existed only for users who could get an invitation, its market involved ratio management and it provided goods and services unavailable in legitimated markets.

The calculations of losses based on numbers of files, website hits and the number of users are also inadequate in estimating the impact of specialized torrent trackers on music sales. BPI can point to OiNK as a factor in the alleged £414 million lost to piracy in the United Kingdom annually, but those losses are difficult to reconcile considering that many of OiNK's features were not available outside of the site's particular services. The failure to replicate OiNK's services in the way that Spotify replicated other outlets for streaming and file-sharing represents a market failure on the part of the recording industry. From a political economy perspective, OiNK existed as a cultural outlier in social relations, where users were distributing and downloading media through transactional processes that existed outside of the marketplace and in opposition to intellectual property policy.

Spotify and other streaming services are demonstrative of a corrective market measure that can reduce piracy more efficiently than stronger copyright policy. File-sharing sites are distributed globally, so uniform law enforcement to stop them is difficult to manage. The international police raids and policy pressures that attack piracy simply led to a service like OiNK splitting into What and Waffles. Enforcing harsh prohibitions on digital piracy ignores the networked structures in place that govern its operation. The upward ratchet faces continual challenges in the face of technological innovation and digital culture, but its mechanisms operate across an elaborate range of trade agreements, national and international law, regional policies and police units that rely on cybercrime enforcement. A legal equivalent to the curated music archives of private torrent trackers where users download and own digital music is still an uphill climb in this system but, as OiNK and What prove, private music downloading websites can be taken out by law enforcement. The international, decades-long game of whac-a-mole against file-sharing services is likely to persist, even as the industry as a whole recovers from fifteen years of decline.

REFERENCES

Anderson, Nathan (2007), 'Police, IFPI make bacon of OiNK BitTorrent tracker', *Ars Technica*, 7 October, http://arstechnica.com/tech-policy/2007/10/police-ifpi-make-bacon-of-OiNK-bittorrent-tracker/. Accessed 29 July 2019.

Andersson, Jonas (2014), *Online File Sharing: Innovations in Media Consumption*, New York: Routledge.

Breihan, Tom (2010), 'OiNK operator found not guilty', *Pitchfork*, 18 January, https://pitchfork.com/news/37608-oink-operator-found-not-guilty/. Accessed 3 March 2019.

Burkart, Patrick and McCourt, Tom (2006), *Digital Music Wars: Ownership and Control of the Celestial Jukebox*, Lanham: Rowan & Littlefield.

Carraway, Brett (2012), 'Survey of file sharing cultures', *International Journal of Communication* 6, pp. 564–84.

Cheng, Jacqui (2008), 'UK police herd up erstwhile OiNK users on conspiracy charges', *Ars Technica*, 2 June, http://arstechnica.com/tech-policy/2008/06/uk-police-herd-up-erstwhile-OiNK-users-on-conspiracy-charges/. Accessed 5 September 2018.

Choi, David and Perez, Arturo (2007), 'Online piracy, innovation, and legitimate business models', *Technovation,* 27:4, pp. 168–78.

Day, Adrienne (2007), 'Ripped to shreds', *New York Magazine*, 30 December, http://nymag.com/news/features/42391/. Accessed 5 September 2018.

European Commission (2015), *Streaming Reaches Flood Stage: Does Spotify Stimulate or Depress Music Sales?*, Seville: Joint Research Centre of the European Commission, https://ec.europa.eu/jrc/en/publication/eur-scientific-and-technical-research-reports/streaming-reaches-flood-stage-does-spotify-stimulate-or-depress-music-sales. Accessed 29 January 2019.

Gartenberg, Chaim (2017), 'Apple reportedly adds support for FLAC lossless audio in iOS 11', *The Verge*, 6 June, https://www.theverge.com/2017/6/6/15747518/apple-flac-lossless-audio-compressed-alac-ios-11/. Accessed 5 September 2018.

Giblin, Rebecca (2014), 'Evaluating gradual response', *Columbia Journal of Law & the Arts*, 37, pp. 147–209.

Hall, Parker (2018), 'Apple Music vs. Spotify: Which service is the streaming king?', *Digital Trends*, 3 January, https://www.digitaltrends.com/music/apple-music-vs-spotify/. Accessed 5 September 2018.

Harvey, Eric (2015), 'A history of digital album leaks, 1993–2015', *Pitchfork*, 28 January, https://pitchfork.com/thepitch/652-a-history-of-digital-album-leaks-1993-2015/. Accessed 8 November 2019.

Hogan, Marc (2014), 'Record Labels sue Megaupload and founder Kim Dotcom', *Spin*, 4 April, https://www.spin.com/2014/04/record-labels-sue-megaupload-kim-dotcom-riaa/. Accessed 5 September 2018.

Hong, Seung-Hyun (2013), 'Measuring the effect of Napster on recorded music sales: Difference-in-differences estimates under compositional changes', *Journal of Applied Economics* 28:2, pp. 297–324.

Horner, Al (2019), 'Not okay, computer: How it feels to have your music leaked', *The Guardian,* 4 June, https://www.theguardian.com/music/2019/jun/17/hackers-music-industry-leaks-radiohead/. Accessed 8 November 2019.

Hutchinson, Allan (1989), *Critical Legal Studies,* New York: Rowan & Littlefield Publishing.

International Federation of the Phonographic Industry (IFPI) (2018), *Global Music Report 2018: Annual State of the Industry*, https://www.ifpi.org/downloads/GMR2018.pdf. Accessed 29 January 2019 [no longer available].

International Monetary Fund (2011), *Kingdom of the Netherlands—Netherlands: Detailed Assessment Report on Anti-money Laundering and Combating the Financing of Terrorism*, https://www.elibrary.imf.org/view/IMF002/11776-9781455230082/11776-9781455230082/11776-9781455230082.xml?redirect=true. Accessed 20 February 2020.

Jones, Ben (2007), 'What Waffles? The Hydra lives on', *TorrentFreak*, 30 October, https://torrentfreak.com/what-waffles-hydra-071030/. Accessed 19 November 2020.

Kravets, David (2010), 'OiNK admin beats file sharing charges', *Wired,* 15 January, http://www.wired.com/2010/01/OiNK-admin-beats-file-sharing-charges/. Accessed 29 January 2019.

——— (2013), 'Supreme Court OKs $222K verdict for sharing 24 songs', *Wired*, 18 March, https://www.wired.com/2013/03/scotus-jammie-thomas-rasset/. Accessed 5 September 2018.

Lee, Jonathan. (2016), 'Purchase, pirate, publicize: Private-network music sharing and market album sales', *Information Economics and Policy*, 42, pp. 35–55.

Leman-Langlois, Stephane (2012), 'Introduction', in S. Leman-Langlois (ed.), *Technocrime: Policing and Surveillance*, New York: Routledge, pp. 1–12.

Lessig, Lawrence (2008), *Free Culture: The Nature and Future of Creativity*, New York: Penguin Books.

Lightfoot, Gareth (2010), 'IT expert awaiting OiNK web trial verdict', *Gazette Live*, 14 May, https://www.gazettelive.co.uk/news/local-news/expert-awaiting-oink-web-trial-3710489. Accessed 29 January 2019.

Martin, Benton, and Newhall, Jeremiah (2013), 'Criminal copyright enforcement against file sharing services', *North Carolina Journal of Law and Technology*, 15:1, pp. 101–51.

Miller, Brett (2005), 'The war against free music: How the RIAA should stop worrying and learn to love the MP3', *University of Detroit Mercy Law Review,* 303, pp. 303–29.

Mosco, Vincent (2009), *Political Economy of Communication*, 2nd ed., Los Angeles: Sage Publications.

Oberholzer-Gee, Felix and Strumpf, Koleman (2016), 'The effect of file-sharing on record sales, revisited', *Information Economics & Policy*, 37, pp. 61–66.

Open Rights Group (2019), *Police Intellectual Property Crime Unit*. https://wiki.openrightsgroup.org/wiki/Police_Intellectual_Property_Crime_Unit/. Accessed 16 September 2020.

Phan, Monty (2007), 'OiNK users recall defunct swap site's strange, stringent rules', *Wired*, 26 October, http://archive.today/0Nd87/. Accessed 5 September 2018.

Raymond, Anjanette (2013), 'Intermediaries precarious balance within Europe: Oddly placed cooperative burdens in the online world', *Northwestern Journal of Technology and Intellectual Property*, 11:5, pp. 361–84.

Recording Industry Association of America (RIAA) (2015), *Notorious Markets 2015*, https://www.riaa.com/wp-content/uploads/2015/10/Notorious-Markets-Report-2015-FINAL-4.pdf. Accessed 5 September 2018.

Sarikakis, Katherine (2012), 'Securitization and legitimacy in global media governance spaces, jurisdictions, and tensions', in I. Volkmer (ed.), *The Handbook of Global Media Research*, Malden: Wiley-Blackwell, pp. 143–54.

Sell, Susan (2010), 'The global IP upward ratchet, anti-counterfeiting and piracy enforcement efforts: The state of play', *PIJIP Research Paper Series*, http://digitalcommons.wcl.american.edu/research/15/. Accessed 5 September 2018.

Sockanathan, Andrew (2011), 'Digital desire and recorded music: OiNK, mnemotechnics and the private BitTorrent architecture', *Research Online: Goldsmiths, University of London*, http://research.gold.ac.uk/6569/. Accessed 5 September 2018.

Van der Saar, Ernest (2007), 'The Pirate Bay cancels OiNK replacement', *Torrentfreak*, 24 November, http://torrentfreak.com/the-pirate-bay-cancels-OiNK-replacement-071124/. Accessed 29 January 2019.

——— (2016a), 'Music Group confirms What.CD raid, claims millions in losses', *Torrentfreak*, 16 November, https://torrentfreak.com/music-group-confirms-what-cd-raid-claims-millions-in-losses-161118/. Accessed 5 September 2018.

——— (2016b), 'What.CD is dead, but the Torrent Hydra lives on', *Torrentfreak*, 2 December, https://torrentfreak.com/what-cd-is-dead-but-the-torrent-hydra-lives-on-161202/. Accessed 5 September 2018.

Welch, Chris (2016), 'Music Torrent site What.CD has been shut down', *The Verge*, 17 November, https://www.theverge.com/2016/11/17/13669832/what-cd-music-torrent-website-shut-down/. Accessed 5 September 2018.

Westhoff, Brent (2007), 'Trent Reznor and Saul Williams discuss their new collaboration, mourn OiNK', *Vulture*, 30 October, https://www.vulture.com/2007/10/trent_reznor_and_saul_williams.html. Accessed 5 September 2018.

Witt, Stephen (2015). 'Going for a song: the hidden history of music piracy', *Guardian*, 7 June 2015, https://www.theguardian.com/books/2015/jun/07/stephen-witt-how-music-got-free-music-piracy-filesharing/. Accessed 16 September 2020.

Wray, Richard (2010), 'Jury clears British "Pirate Bay" operator of fraud charge', *The Guardian*, 15 January, https://www.theguardian.com/technology/2010/jan/15/file-sharing-oink-website-acquittal. Accessed 5 September 2018.

10

Educar Para Crear: The Use of Statistics and Surveys in Spanish Music Anti-Piracy Policies

Lola Costa Gálvez

Spain has a market for recorded music that comprises a high concentration of international labels as well as a high presence of local companies (Gallego Pérez 2016). In 2018, it was listed as having the fourteenth largest music economy in the world (SGAE 2018). Its status in terms of piracy is higher still. According to International Federation of the Phonographic Industry (IFPI) figures for 2005, Spain was among the ten countries most in danger from piracy (IFPI 2006). Piracy has remained prevalent: in 2016, pirate-copying activities were valued as causing a loss to the recording industry of €60 million (European Union Intellectual Property Office 2016).

The statistics for piracy are debatable, however. From a historical perspective, Spanish governmental efforts in this area focused on individual rights to private copying. This was particularly the case between 2006 and 2012, when the 'digital canon', a tax on electronic devices, was established to counteract possible copyright offences (Jefatura del Estado 2011, 2012). Spanish music associations launched a series of public campaigns to advance their point of view, with the composers' and publishers' collection society Sociedad General de Autores y Editores (SGAE) being the most persistent about this topic (La Coalición 2014, 2016, 2017). This resulted in the production of data that has been utilized to justify policies (Calvi 2006). This data is hard to quantify, and the lack of strong governmental sources has put the anti-piracy campaigns under suspicion. Even the European Commission has been accused of 'burying' an unpublished report commissioned in 2014 by a consultancy that was not able to show any evidence of the negative impact of piracy on the music industries (Woollacott 2017). In Spain, according to SGAE, 88 per cent of music downloads in 2011 were illegal (SGAE 2013: 36) whereas CEDRO, a governmental source, contrastingly said that the total amount of pirate actions accounted for only 28 per cent of the music downloaded (CEDRO 2014: 4–17). There is a sense in which these arguments might continue ad infinitum, due to the fact 'the concrete quantitative data of illegal downloads cannot be obtained', as the Spanish culture minister admitted in 2016 (Koch 2016).

To address the situation in Spain, this chapter will take a three-pronged approach: addressing the recording industry, which has repeatedly highlighted piracy as the primary factor for decreasing sales; the State, which has employed statistics to support its policies; and, civil society, whose individuals and receivers of messages have been accused of being the main perpetrators of piracy. Resultantly, I will examine a specific issue: how statistics and surveys have been used as tools to support the Spanish music industries' anti-piracy policies.

Spanish music anti-piracy policies

One of the first digital anti-piracy measures taken by the Spanish government was to adapt the European Union Directive 2001/29/CE (European Parliament and European Council 2001) with the creation of the 'canon by private copy', defined in article 25 of the Intellectual Property Law as 'fair compensation for private copy' (Jefatura del Estado 2006). This tax was levied at the expense of consumers when buying compact discs or electronic devices as a 'compensation' for possible piracy infringements (Jefatura del Estado 2008). It was welcomed by professional music associations (SGAE et al. 2014). However, as soon as the measure was introduced, it was opposed, not only by consumers, but also by representatives of the industry, such as the Comisión Nacional de la Competencia (CNC 2009), the Spanish regulatory body of competition, as well as by Asimelec (2003), the Spanish organization for electronic and communication companies, who complained about not being involved in the tax negotiations. It was argued that these measures violated the private copying right within Spanish law (Asociación de Internautas 2012; Gay Fuentes 2010). The case raised by the electronics and digital trade associations eventually reached the European Court of Justice (Ametic 2011), which ruled against SGAE and in favour of Spanish electronic company Padawan (European Audiovisual Observatory and Council of Europe 2017). Consequently, the canon was eliminated (Consejo de Ministros 2012).

Spanish anti-piracy prosecution was ratcheted up in 2005, when a new and controversial regulatory body was created: The Intersectional commission against intellectual property infringing activities, known as the Sinde Commission (Ministerio de Cultura 2005). It emerged as a response to the music industry's demands; in the words of the lawyer of a major label, it was required because law was not 'being applied properly' (Peirano 2013). Under Spanish Intellectual Property Law, the Commission has been entitled to close illegal websites without Court authorization (del Castillo 2019). The lawyer David Bravo (2018) has argued that, in providing the Commission with this power, Spanish law 'has gone too far'.[1] He states that 'it has the paradox of having a Commission that in almost all the cases has different opinions from the justice in terms of intellectual property' (Bravo 2018). The breeding ground was the 'Soto case', in which the music majors sued individual Spanish citizen Pablo Soto for having a peer-to-peer network and 'stealing' 90 per cent of their revenue. In contrast to the Sinde Commission, the justice did not view this as a violation of the law (Romero 2014).

Alongside the Commission, the Spanish government launched an 'Anti-Piracy Plan' in 2005, which the Department of Culture devised in conjunction with a number of other governmental departments and collection societies to prosecute piracy. Its objectives have included an educational campaign to 'raise awareness' amongst companies, institutions and, more importantly, civil society. The first outcome of the Anti-piracy Plan was the *Cultura en Positivo* project, which the Spanish government left in the hands of SGAE (Ministerio de Cultura 2011). Their first campaign, *Educar para crear* (educate to create), which took place in schools in 2010, became a source of indoctrination. Following on from this, the principal role of collection societies in the project has been to lobby the Government in a call for action. As Bravo (2018) states, 'there are different points of view' on piracy, but SGAE have presented their own thoughts as the 'absolute truth'.

In 2011 and 2012, Spanish Intellectual Property Law was amended and referred to as the Sustainable Economy Laws, updated in line with the Socialist government's 'sustainability' policies, which have addressed economic, entrepreneurial and environmental issues. Known as the Sinde-Wert laws, after Ángeles González-Sinde and José Ignacio Wert, the ministers who promoted them, these regulations have been considered as the zenith of Spanish policies in terms of digital rights management, especially because they have provided the government with the power to impose penalties (Jefatura del Estado 2011, 2012). As Bravo (2018) states: 'before these regulations, Spain was lambasted by the global music industry for its rampant piracy, however, since the Sinde-Wert laws Spain has vanished from the United States' *Special 301 Report*'. Here Bravo is referring to the report compiled annually by the Office of the United States Trade Representative that identifies countries who pose trading problems for America because of their 'inadequate' intellectual property laws (USTR 2018).

After a great deal of discussion, the Spanish government passed an amendment to the intellectual property law, known as the Lassalle Law, on account of the minister José María Lassalle (Jefatura del Estado 2014). This law enables intellectual property owners to request the removal of infringing material from websites and has legitimized the collection societies' appropriation of royalties they have received for authors who are non-members (de la Cueva 2007). In 2017, the conservative Partido Popular Party utilized this law in an attempt to restart the 'digital canon' in a version that would oversee on-demand streaming music services (Asociación de Internautas 2017).

Ultimately, Spanish anti-piracy policies are based on criminalization of the users, with little understanding of how measures impact on consumers, musicians or the music industries.

Music anti-piracy statistics in Spain: Governmental sources

Created by the Spanish Department of Culture in 2005, the Intersectional Commission Against Intellectual Property Infringing Activities has been charged with leading the government's strategy on piracy, known as the 'Anti-Piracy Plan'. The commission has two main functions: mediation and arbitration (Ministerio de Cultura 2005). In addition, the commission can take punitive actions. For example, in 2018 a fine of €375,000 was imposed on x-caleta.com for hosting illegal downloading links (Castillo 2018).

The commission has seldom been keen on detailing its activities, releasing only two reports in thirteen years: one issued in 2007 (Ministerio de Cultura 2007), which addresses activity in 2005 and 2006; and one in 2018 (Ministerio de Educación, Cultura y Deporte 2018), which covers the period between 2012 and 2018 (consequently, there is no data for the years between 2007 and 2011). These reports focus on the commission's activities against pirates, rather than outlining piracy statistics.

The two reports have their differences. The 2007 report addresses the physical piracy of CDs and DVDs, alongside digital piracy. In fact, policy intervention against physical piracy is the main focus of the document. Within this context, music is not the main area of action; instead audio-visual piracy is the main concern. Music does provide the highest figures in terms of the quantity of seized material, however. It is also dominant in respect of digital piracy, particularly in relation to the number of complaints raised, which hailed from the Spanish record companies' association, Promusicae (see Table 10.1).

The report from 2018 focuses only on digital piracy. Between 2012 and 2018, 618 complaints had been filed (53 of them in 2018). 270 had not been processed due to the withdrawal of the complainant, while 348 were completed, resulting in the cancellation of 337 websites (Ministerio de Educación, Cultura y Deporte 2018).

Physical piracy						
Number of interventions	Number of seized materials	Economic value of seized materials	Territorial representation	Areas (total amount of interventions)	Areas (quantity of the seized material)	Areas (economic value of the seized material)
2927	4,305,788	€75,349,358,54	Andalusia (23.6 per cent)	Audio-visual (89.1 per cent)	Audio-visual (39.2 per cent)	Audio-visual (49.7 per cent)
			Basque Country (17 per cent)	Music (10.1 per cent)	Music (42.8 per cent)	Music (44.7 per cent)
			Madrid (10.5 per cent)	Books (0.3 per cent)	Books (2.5 per cent)	Books (0.1 per cent)
				Software (0.4 per cent)	Software (1.1 per cent)	Software (4.6 per cent)
				Others (0.1 per cent)	Others (14.4 per cent)	Others (0.9 per cent)

Digital piracy	
Number of complaints	Web domains cancelled
Audio-visual (28)	No information
Music (1037)	26
Books (57)	29

TABLE 10.1: Activities of the Intersectional Commission Against Intellectual Property Infringing Activities (2005–06). Source: Ministerio de Cultura (2007).

Looking at other governmental sources, the term 'piracy' is neither included in the Cultural Statistics Yearbook (Ministerio de Cultura 2018) nor in the survey of cultural habits and practices (Ministerio de Cultura 2015). That said, in the Cultural Strategy 2020 (Ministerio de Cultura 2017), in spite of there being no mention of the term 'piracy', several measures relating to anti-piracy are addressed. In contrast, Spanish collection societies regularly refer to piracy statistics, as will be discussed in the following section.

Music anti-piracy statistics in Spain: Private sources

SGAE began operations at the end of the nineteenth century but was only formally established in 1941, and became authorized by the Spanish Department of Culture in 1988. It has appeared to many as a force of law, participating hand-in-hand with the government in educational campaigns against piracy. Corruption has been ubiquitous and prevalent. In 2011, SGAE's general manager was arrested on charges of corruption (Lázaro 2011). He finally resigned in 2019 (Riaño 2019). In 2017, the society was placed under World Intellectual Property Organization (WIPO) arbitration; in 2018, it was placed under governmental supervision (Pardo Porto 2018); and in 2019, following several claims made against the society (Cruz 2019), SGAE was suspended from the International Confederation of Societies of Authors and Composers (CISAC) (Ingham 2019). In addition to facing criticism for its aggressive social campaigns against piracy, SGAE has been publicly denounced for authoritarian collection procedures when pursuing radio stations and record labels (Fayos Gardó 2016). It has also been accused by Spanish law of collusion with private and public television stations in respect of 'the wheel', a set of music cover versions, scheduled on television during the early morning hours, which is deliberately programmed so that authors can gain copyright royalties (Rodríguez 2017). This practice has been rejected by UFI, the Spanish independent music industry association (UFI 2017).

In 2008, the main Spanish collecting societies and trade bodies (SGAE, Promusicae (representing Spanish record companies) and EGEDA (representing audio-visual producers)) created 'The Alliance of creators and industry of contents' to research cultural piracy data and habits. It was the first cross-sectorial group to research piracy in Spain, and was supported by the Spanish minister of culture (Koch 2016). It soon began a yearly publication relating to piracy and digital content consumption habits (GFK Spain 2012, 2013, 2014, 2015, 2016, 2017, 2018; IDC Research Iberia 2009, 2010, 2011).

The compilation of these reports has been outsourced to two different consultancy firms – ID Research Iberia (from 2009 to 2011) and GFK Spain (from 2012 to 2017) – who have produced the majority of their information via surveys. These reports are not consistent. Firstly, their demographic criteria vary. In the first studies (2009–11), music consumers under 16 and over 55 years old were excluded, but in the period from 2012 to 2017 consumers up to 74 years of age were featured in the study. Nevertheless, age average seems not to be very important to these consultant firms, as it is not taken into consideration from 2011 onwards.

The reports detail a plethora of statistics, broken down into numerous categories. The first period of the study, taking place between 2009 and 2011, places a strong emphasis on showing datasets about piracy, albeit that these are only detailed in relation to economic impact, rather than in relation to content. As a methodological note, explained in the documents, the value of pirate content was based on the piracy tax of pay-per-listen contents (see Figure 10.1).

The second part of the study (2012–17), measured the impact of piracy in terms of potential earnings for the music industry. It distinguished two areas: impact of piracy and lost profit (see Figures 10.2 and 10.3).

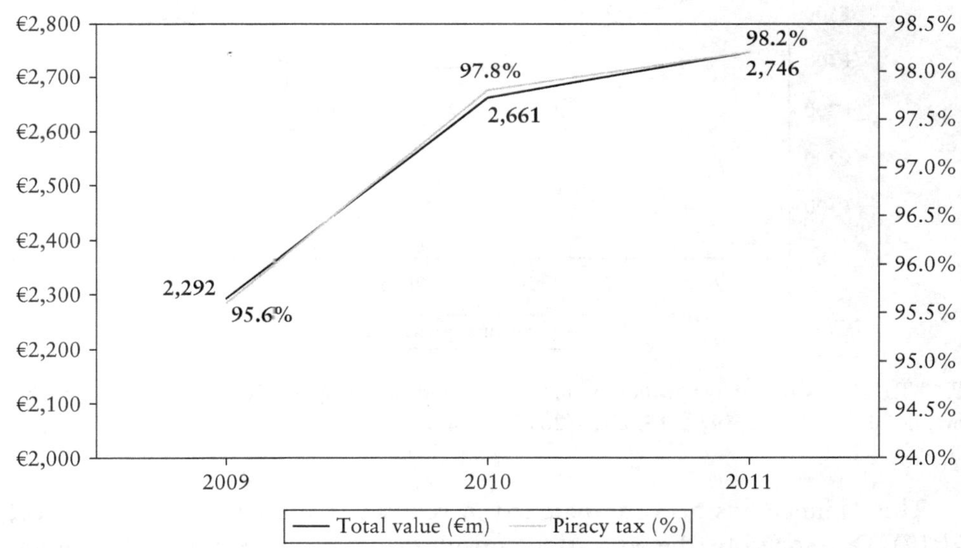

FIGURE 10.1: Piracy tax (contents per cent) and value of pirated content (€m) in the music industry in Spain (2009–11). Source: IDC Research Iberia (2009, 2010, 2011).

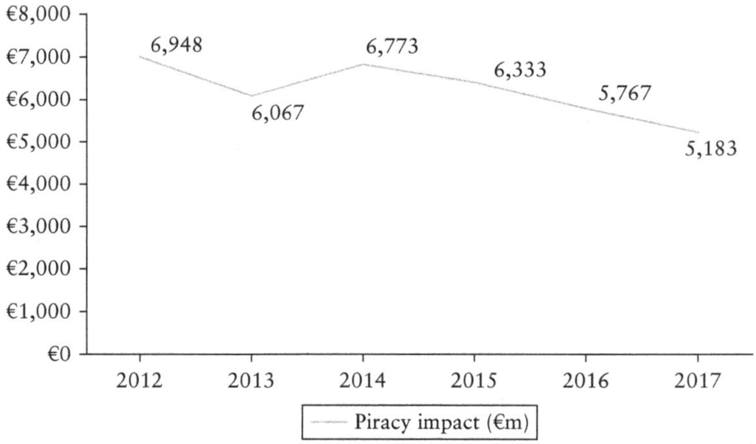

FIGURE 10.2: Piracy impact (€m) on the music industry in Spain (2012–17). Source: GFK Spain (2012, 2013, 2014, 2015, 2016, 2017, 2018).

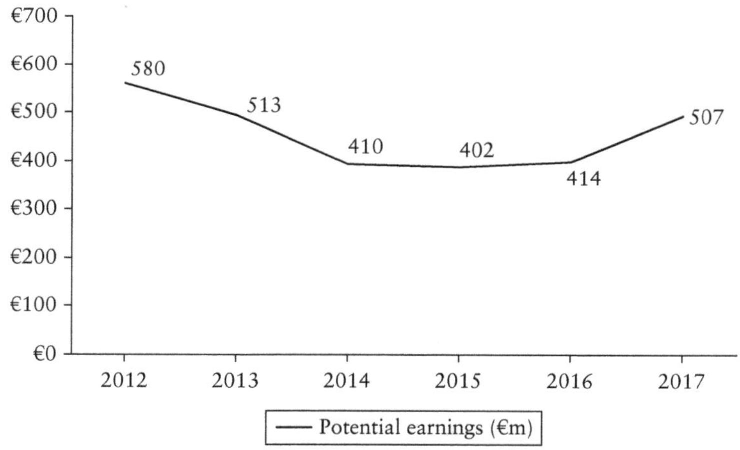

FIGURE 10.3: Value of lost profit (€m) in the music industry in Spain (2012-2017). Source: GFK Spain (2012, 2013, 2014, 2015, 2016, 2017, 2018).

The Alliance has also campaigned in schools (La Coalición 2014, 2016, 2017). Developed by the education consultancy, EducaLIKE, its Educational Workshops were launched in 2014. The first of these surveys was based on cultural habits and was titled 'Defend our culture'. It was promoted in ten elementary schools in Madrid to students aged from 8 to 11 years old. As shown in Figure 10.4, the tone of voice aimed to be plain and comprehendible.

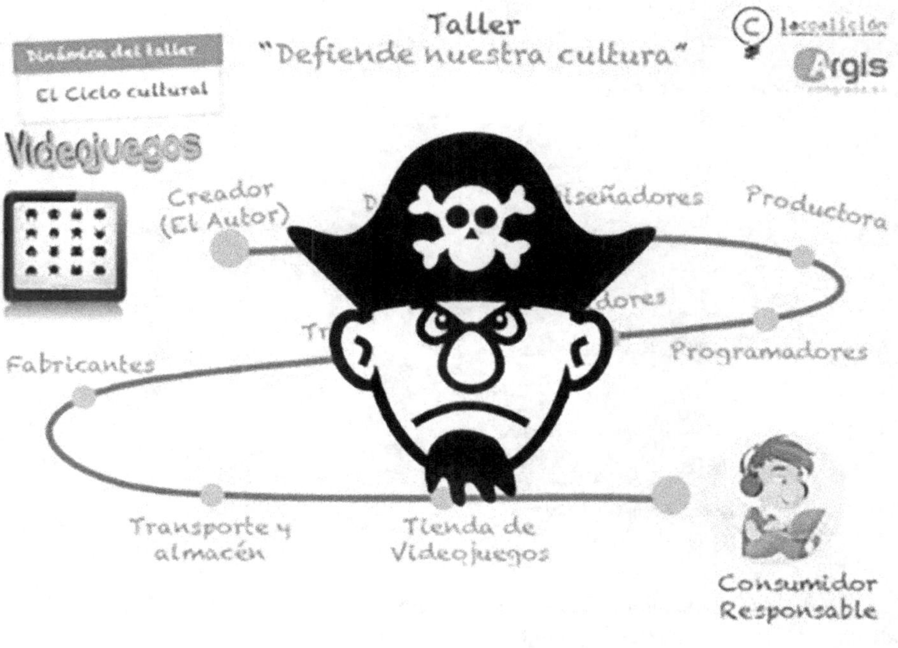

FIGURE 10.4: Educational Workshop cultural products value chain example (2014). Source: La Coalición (2014).

Nevertheless, by introducing words such as 'responsible consumer' or 'creator', rather than 'consumer' or 'author' respectively, we can witness ideology at work.

The language is loaded, encouraging students to think of certain practices as 'piracy' and others as 'defending culture' (see Figure 10.5). Particularly notable in this respect are the fourth and fifth questions: 'Did you know piracy hurts culture?' and 'Would you like to be a culture defender?'.

For the second workshop, held in 2015, the sample included 85 elementary and high school education centres in Madrid, Andalucía, Castilla-La Mancha and Castilla y León. In this case, the sample comprised of children between 10 and 14 years old. The study focused on 'raising awareness on online content piracy' (La Coalición 2015). On this occasion, students were inculcated to believe that piracy causes cultural harm: 63.2 per cent of 14-year-old students agreed that piracy 'hurts culture' (La Coalición 2015). The majority of questions encouraged a moral evaluation of piracy, utilizing words such as 'bad' or 'harm' (see Figure 10.6).

In 2016, the final workshop took place. It was undertaken in 108 elementary and high schools with students between 10 and 13 years old. It covered the majority of Spanish regions, taking place in schools in Galicia, Madrid, Andalucía, Castilla-La Mancha, Castilla y León and Aragón.

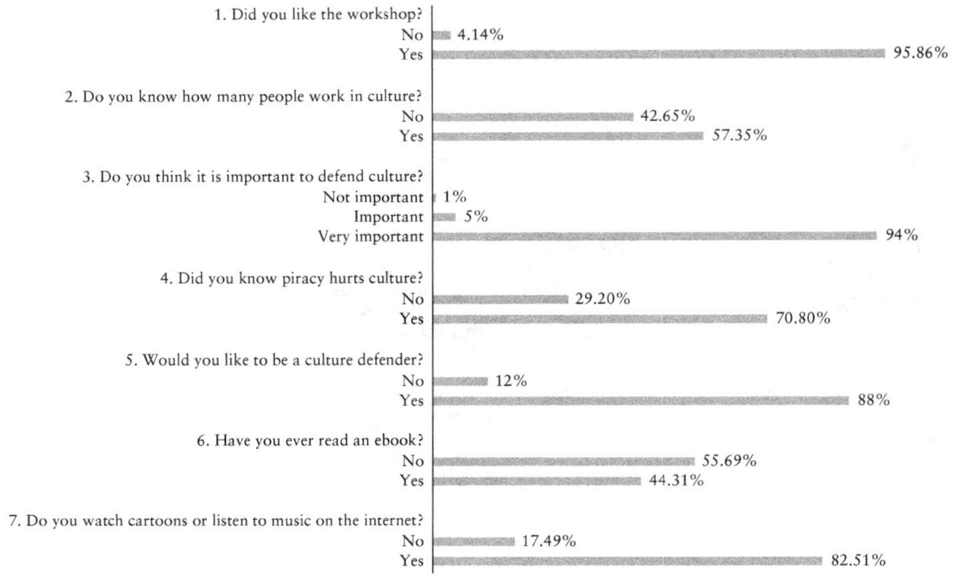

FIGURE 10.5: Survey results Educational Workshops La Coalición (2014–15). Sample: 1039 students (10 schools). Source: La Coalición (2014).

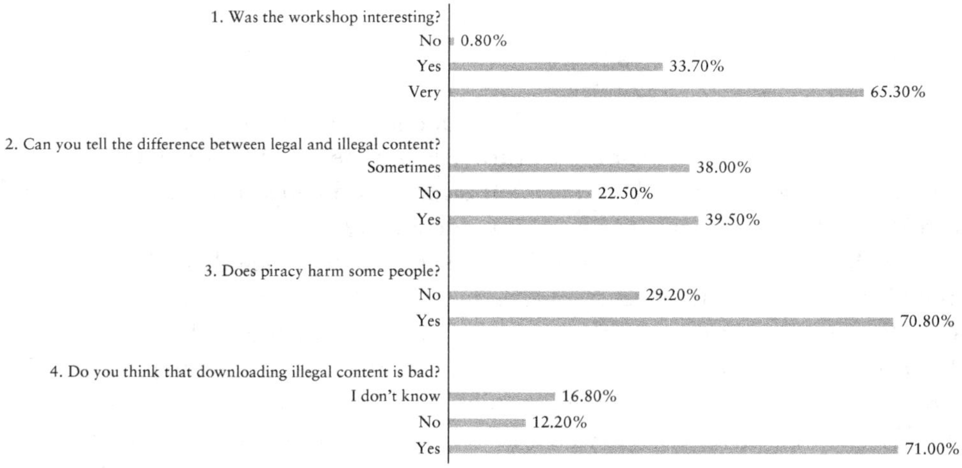

FIGURE 10.6: Survey results Educational Workshops La Coalición (2015–16). Sample: 1,200 students (85 schools). Source: La Coalición (2015).

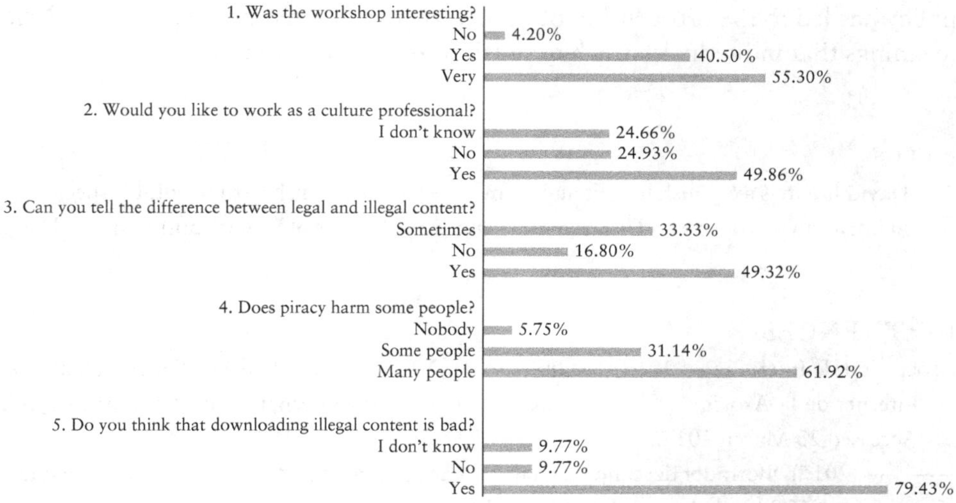

FIGURE 10.7: Survey results Educational Workshops La Coalición (2016–17). Sample: 14,000 students (108 schools). Source: La Coalición (2016).

The topics were broadly similar to the 2015 study. However, a new question asking 'Would you like to work as a culture professional?' provided a way of measuring children's cultural aspirations (see Figure 10.7).

Conclusion: Judging piracy (only) by statistics

In this chapter, I have provided an analysis of the main examples of Spanish public institutions and associations that have employed statistics and surveys to support their anti-piracy arguments. It is fair to say that governments and music companies have made numerous attempts, some of them successful (on their own terms), to respond to the digital environment. Spain has developed a legal framework based on punitive actions that strengthen the control of a system in which the majority of music production is left in a few hands. However, a broad social debate has arisen about music piracy due to the embroilment of the government with the music industry, as represented by the collection society SGAE. Understandably, industry networks need to be present as stakeholders in public consultancies, but they do not have to become central actors having the force of law institutions. In the same vein, it could be said that criminalizing users for consuming illegal music based solely on quantitative terms, rather than delving into the reasons or causes, is to deny a solution to a problem that has existed for a long time. In Spain, anti-piracy policy has led to the prosecution of users rather than attempts to understand the meanings that individuals attach to music and its consumption.

NOTE

1. David Bravo is a Spanish lawyer and ex-member of the Spanish parliament. He specializes in intellectual property and is one of the main critical voices of Spanish anti-piracy policies.

REFERENCES

Asociación de Internautas (2012), 'Manifiesto en Defensa de los Derechos Fundamentales de Internet de la Asociación de Internautas', https://www.internautas.org/html/5871.html. Accessed 23 March 2017.

——— (2017), 'Borrador del canon digital: No han aprendido nada', https://www.internautas.org/html/9578.html. Accessed 23 March 2017.

Asociación Multisectorial de Empresas de Tecnologías de la Información, Comunicaciones y Electrónica (Asimelec) (2003), 'Los Soportes Digitales y el Canon por Copia Privada. Acuerdo privado en aplicación de la ley', http://www.internautas.org/documentos/CANON-Julio_2003.pdf. Accessed 23 March 2017.

Bravo, David (2018), telephone interview with author, 12 September.

Calvi, Juan (2006), 'Plan integral de apoyo a la música y a la industria discográfica', http://especiales.elcorreo.com/pdf/estudio-pirateria.pdf. Accessed 23 March 2017.

Castillo, Toni (2018), 'El nuevo ministro de Cultura estrena las multas a webs de descargas de la Comisión Sinde-Wert con una sanción de 375.000 euros', https://www.genbeta.com/actualidad/nuevo-ministro-cultura-estrena-multas-webs-descargas-comision-sinde-wert-sancion-375-000-euros. Accessed 11 September 2018.

Centro Español de Derechos Reprográficos (CEDRO) (2014), 'Observatorio de piratería y hábitos de consumo de contenidos digitales 2013', http://www.cedro.org/docs/default-source/textos-de-inter%C3%A9s/observatorio-pirateria2013.pdf?sfvrsn=6. Accessed 23 March 2017.

Comisión Nacional de la Competencia (CNC) (2009), 'Informe sobre la Gestión Colectiva de Derechos de Propiedad Intelectual', http://estaticos.expansion.com/estaticas/documentos/2010/01/cncderechospi.pdf. Accessed 23 March 2017.

Consejo de Ministros (2012), 'Real Decreto 1657/2012, de 7 de diciembre, por el que se regula el procedimiento de pago de la compensación equitativa por copia privada con cargo a los Presupuestos Generales del Estado', http://www.boe.es/diario_boe/txt.php?id=BOE-A-2012-14904. Accessed 23 March 2017.

Cruz, Nando (2019), 'Tokio decide el futuro de la SGAE', https://www.elperiodico.com/es/ocio-y-cultura/20190529/expulsion-sgae-cisac-asamblea-tokio-7480255. Accessed 2 November 2019.

de la Cueva, Javier (2007), 'Introducción al Copyleft. Una perspectiva de su recepción en España', *Periférica. Revista para el análisis de la cultura y el territorio*, 8, pp. 113–32.

del Castillo, Carlos (2019), 'La comisión Sinde cierra webs un 70% más rápido gracias a un programa cazapiratas de La Liga de Fútbol', https://www.eldiario.es/tecnologia/comison-Sinde-acelera-cazapiratas-LaLiga_0_855314608.html. Accessed 9 February 2019.

European Audiovisual Observatory and Council of Europe (2017), 'Exceptions and limitations to copyright', https://book.coe.int/eur/en/european-audiovisual-observatory/7421-iris-plus-exceptions-and-limitations-to-copyright.html. Accessed 23 November 2017.

European Parliament and European Council (2001), 'Directiva 2001/29/CE, relativa a la armonización de determinados aspectos de los derechos de autor y derechos afines en la sociedad de la información (DSI)', https://eur-lex.europa.eu/legal-content/ES/TXT/HTML/?uri=CELEX:32001L0029&from=EN. Accessed 23 March 2017.

European Union Intellectual Property Office (2016), 'The economic cost of IPR infringement in the recorded music industry', https://euipo.europa.eu/tunnel-web/secure/webdav/guest/document_library/observatory/resources/research-and-studies/ip_infringement/study7/Music_industry_es.pdf. Accessed 20 June 2017.

Fayos Gardó, Antonio (2016), *La propiedad intelectual en la era digital,* Madrid: Dykinson.

Gallego Pérez, Ignacio J. (2016), 'Una mirada a la diversidad en las industrias radiofónica y musical en España', *CIC: Cuadernos de información y comunicación*, 21, pp. 139–55.

Gay Fuentes, Celeste (2010), 'El conflicto entre propiedad intelectual y derechos fundamentales: equilibrios difíciles entre dos mundos', *Telos: Cuadernos de comunicación e innovación*, 85, pp. 90–96.

GFK Spain (2012), 'Observatorio de piratería y hábitos de consumo de contenidos digitales 2012', http://lacoalicion.es/wp-content/uploads/observatorio_pirateria-2012_final.pdf. Accessed 23 November 2017.

——— (2013), 'Observatorio de piratería y hábitos de consumo de contenidos digitales 2013', http://lacoalicion.es/wp-content/uploads/observatorio-piratera-2013.pdf. Accessed 23 November 2017

——— (2014), 'Observatorio de piratería y hábitos de consumo de contenidos digitales 2014', http://lacoalicion.es/wp-content/uploads/resumen-ejecutivo-observatorio-2014.pdf. Accessed 23 November 2017.

——— (2015), 'Observatorio de piratería y hábitos de consumo de contenidos digitales 2015', http://lacoalicion.es/wp-content/uploads/ejecutivo-observatorio-2015-vd-es.pdf. Accessed 23 November 2017.

——— (2016), 'Observatorio de piratería y hábitos de consumo de contenidos digitales 2015', http://lacoalicion.es/observatorio-de-la-pirateria/observatorio-de-la-pirateria-2015/. Accessed 23 November 2017.

——— (2017), 'Observatorio de piratería y hábitos de consumo de contenidos digitales 2016', http://lacoalicion.es/wp-content/uploads/observatorio-pirateria-y-habitos-consumo-2016.-ejecutivo.es_.pdf. Accessed 23 November 2017.

——— (2018), 'Observatorio de piratería y hábitos de consumo de contenidos digitales 2017', http://lacoalicion.es/wp-content/uploads/ejecutivo-en.pdf. Accessed 7 September 2018.

IDC Research Iberia (2009), 'Observatorio de piratería y hábitos de consumo de contenidos digitales 2009', http://lacoalicion.es/wp-content/uploads/resumen_ejecutivo_observatorio_segundo_semestre_2009.pdf. Accessed 23 November 2017.

——— (2010), 'Observatorio de piratería y hábitos de consumo de contenidos digitales 2010', http://lacoalicion.es/wp-content/uploads/resumen_ejecutivo_estudio_pirateria_-primer_semestre-2010.pdf. Accessed 23 November 2017.

——— (2011), 'Observatorio de piratería y hábitos de consumo de contenidos digitales 2011', http://lacoalicion.es/wp-content/uploads/resumen_ejecutivo_estudio_pirateria_primer_semestre_2011.pdf. Accessed 23 November 2017.

Ingham, Tim (2019), 'Spanish collection society SGAE, plagued by corruption claims, kicked out of global pro body CISAC', *Music Business Worldwide*, 30 May, https://www.musicbusinessworldwide.com/spanish-collection-society-sgae-plagued-by-corruption-claims-kicked-out-of-global-pro-body-cisac/. Accessed 2 November 2019.

International Federation of the Phonographic Industry (IFPI) (2006), 'Informe 2006 sobre piratería de la industria discográfica', http://www.promusicae.es/estaticos/view/24-informes-ifpi. Accessed 23 November 2017.

Jefatura del Estado (2006), 'Ley 23/2006, de 7 de julio, por la que se modifica el texto refundido de la Ley de Propiedad Intelectual, aprobado por el Real Decreto Legislativo 1/1996, de 12 de abril', http://www.boe.es/boe/dias/2006/07/08/pdfs/A25561-25572.pdf. Accessed 23 March 2017.

——— (2008), 'Orden PRE/1743/2008, de 18 de junio, por la que se establece la relación de equipos, aparatos y soportes materiales sujetos al pago de la compensación equitativa por copia privada, las cantidades aplicables a cada uno de ellos y la distribución entre las diferentes modalidades de reproducción', http://www.boe.es/boe/dias/2008/06/19/pdfs/A27842-27844.pdf. Accessed 23 March 2017.

——— (2011), 'Ley 2/2011, de 4 de marzo, de Economía Sostenible', http://www.boe.es/boe/dias/2011/03/05/pdfs/BOE-A-2011-4117.pdf. Accessed 23 March 2017.

——— (2012), 'Ley N° 2/2011 de 4 de marzo de 2011 sobre Economía Sostenible (modificada por última vez por la Ley N° 2/2012 de 29 de junio de 2012)', http://www.wipo.int/wipolex/es/text.jsp?file_id=271861. Accessed 23 March 2017.

——— (2014), 'Ley 21/2014, de 4 de noviembre, por la que se modifica el texto refundido de la Ley de Propiedad Intelectual, aprobado por Real Decreto Legislativo 1/1996, de 12 de abril, y la Ley 1/2000, de 7 de enero, de Enjuiciamiento Civil', https://www.boe.es/diario_boe/txt.php?id=BOE-A-2014-11404. Accessed 23 March 2017.

Koch, Tommaso (2016), 'Guerra de cifras sobre la piratería', https://elpais.com/cultura/2016/03/31/actualidad/1459427075_663954.html. Accessed 23 March 2017.

La Coalición (2014), 'Resultados del Taller Educativo Defiende Nuestra Cultura', http://lacoalicion.es/wp-content/uploads/resultados-del-taller-centros-escolares.-20-noviembre-2014.pdf. Accessed 23 March 2017.

——— (2015), 'Concienciación y hábitos de consumo online de contenidos de alumnos de Primaria y ESO', http://lacoalicion.es/concienciacion/taller-educativo-2015/. Accessed 23 March 2017.

——— (2016), 'Concienciación y hábitos de consumo online de contenidos de alumnos de Primaria y ESO', http://lacoalicion.es/concienciacion/taller-educativo-2016/. Accessed 23 March 2017.

——— (2017), 'Concienciación y hábitos de consumo online de contenidos de alumnos de Primaria y ESO', http://lacoalicion.es/wp-content/uploads/resumen-ejecutivo-taller-2017.pdf. Accessed 23 March 2017.

Lázaro, Fernando (2011), 'Teddy Bautista y 3 miembros de la SGAE, detenidos por desviar fondos', http://www.elmundo.es/elmundo/2011/07/01/espana/1309537638.html. Accessed 8 July 2013.

Ministerio de Cultura (2005), 'Real Decreto 1228/2005, de 13 de octubre, por el que se crea y regula la Comisión intersectorial para actuar contra las actividades vulneradoras de los derechos de propiedad intelectual', https://www.boe.es/diario_boe/txt.php?id=BOE-A-2005-17765. Accessed 23 November 2017.

——— (2007), 'Memoria Anual de actividades de la comisión intersectorial para actuar contra las actividades vulneradoras de la propiedad intelectual', https://www.culturaydeporte.gob.es/dam/jcr:d7f16ccd-69c6-4332-b169-946b734dfbe0/memoriapi2006.pdf. Accessed 23 November 2017.

——— (2011), 'Cultura en Positivo', https://culturaenpositivo.culturaydeporte.gob.es/inicio.html. Accessed 23 November 2017.

——— (2015), 'Encuesta de Hábitos y Prácticas Culturales en España', http://www.culturaydeporte.gob.es/servicios-al-ciudadano/estadisticas/cultura/mc/culturabase/encuesta-de-habitos/metodologia-habitos.html. Accessed 23 November 2017.

——— (2018), 'Anuario de Estadísticas Culturales', https://sede.educacion.gob.es/publiventa/anuario-de-estadisticas-culturales-2018/cultura-sociedad-estadisticas/21521C. Accessed 23 November 2018.

Ministerio de Educación, Cultura y Deporte (2018), 'Report on the activities of section two of the Intellectual Property Commission', https://www.culturaydeporte.gob.es/dam/jcr:9db0eb08-f015-45d5-bd08-e0a801f1f6d8/2019-1q-report-secc2-cpi.pdf. Accessed 23 November 2017.

Office of the United States Trade Representative (USTR) (2018), https://ustr.gov/sites/default/files/files/Press/Reports/2018%20Special%20301.pdf. Accessed 2 April 2019.

Pardo Porto, Bruno (2018), 'El Gobierno tiene listo "un 155" para intervenir la SGAE', https://www.abc.es/cultura/abci-gobierno-tiene-listo-155-para-intervenir-sgae-201806140310_noticia.html. Accessed 7 September 2018.

Patronal española de la electrónica, las tecnologías de la información, las telecomunicaciones y los contenidos digitales (Ametic) (2011), 'Compensación por Copia Privada: Un análisis económico de modelos alternativos', http://ametic.es/es/en-que-trabajamos/regulacion/compensacion-por-copia-privada. Accessed 23 March 2017.

Peirano, Marta (2013), 'Un juzgado investiga a la Comisión Sinde por prevaricación', El Diario, http://www.eldiario.es/cultura/David_Bravo-Comision_Sinde-Propiedad_Intelectual-Descargas_ilegales_0_184082454.html. Accessed 23 March 2017.

Riaño, Peio H. (2019), 'Teddy Bautista dimite de la cúpula de la SGAE', El Pais, https://elpais.com/cultura/2019/10/10/actualidad/1570709745_036765.html. Accessed 2 November 2019.

Rodríguez, Vanesa (2017), 'La "rueda de las televisiones": un negocio de más de 50 millones al año', El Diario, https://www.eldiario.es/cultura/propiedad-intelectual/rueda-televisiones-negocio-millones_0_656535102.html. Accessed 7 September 2018.

Romero, Pablo (2014). 'Las grandes discográficas pierden definitivamente el caso contra Pablo Soto y su tecnología P2P', El Mundo, http://www.elmundo.es/tecnologia/2014/05/30/5388149f22601db2198b456c.html. Accessed 12 September 2018.

Sociedad General de Autores y Editores (SGAE) (2013), 'Anuario SGAE de las artes escénicas, musicales y audiovisuales', http://www.anuariossgae.com/anuario2013/home.html. Accessed 23 March 2017.

——— (2018), 'Anuario SGAE de las artes escénicas, musicales y audiovisuales', http://www.anuariossgae.com/anuario2018/frames.html. Accessed 23 January 2019.

Sociedad General de Autores y Editores, Artistas e Intérpretes Sociedad de Gestión, Artistas y Ejecutantes Sociedad de Gestión, Derechos de Autor de Medios Audiovisuales, Asociación de Gestión de Derechos Intelectuales and Entidad de Gestión de Derechos de los Productores Audiovisuales (SGAE et al.) (2014), '¿Por qué pedimos la retirada de la "Ley Lassalle"?', http://adepi.net/2014/09/22/los-artistas-autores-editores-y-productores-piden-la-retirada-de-la-ley-lassalle/. Accessed 23 March 2017.

Unión Fonográfica Independiente (UFI) (2017), 'Comunicado sobre la rueda de las televisiones', https://ufimusica.com/comunicado-sobre-la-rueda-de-las-televisiones/. Accessed 2 November 2019.

Woollacott, Emma (2017), 'European Commission accused of burying controversial piracy report', *Forbes*, https://www.forbes.com/sites/emmawoollacott/2017/09/21/european-commission-accused-of-burying-controversial-piracy-report/#51d153b27e1d. Accessed 23 March 2017.

11

Measuring the Immeasurable

Vanessa Bastian and Dennis Collopy

This chapter examines the challenges involved in accurately estimating the size and scale of music piracy since the turn of the millennium. The recording industry undoubtedly suffered due to this practice, yet, even as online digital piracy took root, it struggled to convince policy-makers of the significance of any resulting damage. Any claims that the industry made were countered by an abundance of often scornful academic papers, which rubbished their estimates of infringement levels. Even now, almost twenty years later, there remains wide-scale suspicion about the recording industry's numbers.

Techdirt's Mike Masnick outlined the industry's reaction to the threat of digital piracy by referring to the Kübler-Ross Grief cycle, in which shock is followed by denial, anger, guilt, despair, depression and finally acceptance (Masnick 2010). The initial stages of this grief cycle witnessed the record companies' opposition to any innovation that threatened their extant business model of selling compact discs, and led directly to ignominious campaigns to wrestle control over online distribution, as the Recording Industry Association of America (RIAA) and the major record labels vigorously prosecuted peer-to-peer file-sharing platforms such as Napster and Limewire for copyright infringement (Mitchell et al. 2018: 59). Outlining their position, RIAA estimated that over 30 billion songs had been downloaded illegally between 2004 and 2009 (Mitchell et al. 2018: 59). This campaign to reduce piracy, which lasted between 1999 and 2008, caused a public backlash. Nevertheless, even as the industry entered the acceptance stage of the grief cycle by licensing new platforms such as Spotify, it maintained its efforts to convince policy and law makers to help better defend their Intellectual Property Rights (IPR). In 2013, RIAA argued that cross-border levels of global piracy in music products represented an 'ocean of illegal downloading' and fundamentally challenged rights holders' business models (Buckles 2013).

Data and evidence were needed to demonstrate the extent of harm and damage, much of which came in the form of internal figures produced by the industry and was not suited for policy-making purposes; a point highlighted in two UK government–funded reviews of the copyright framework: Gowers (2006) and Hargreaves (2011a). The industry also faced considerable pushback on its anti-piracy lobbying efforts from the increasingly powerful tech industry who challenged the claims being made, which were referred to by some as 'lobbynomics' (Hargreaves 2011b: 18). In truth the music and other creative industries had long encountered problems in providing credible evidence to influence policy-makers, with most data produced being regarded as insufficiently rigorous.

In the highly charged and contested policy environment following the Hargreaves Review, the Intellectual Property Office (IPO) was sceptical of most research claims and sought independent research, not to counter industry or academic claims as such, but to provide a more objective and reliable set of methodologies to improve the ways in which piracy and other types of IPR infringement could be measured. The University of Hertfordshire (Herts) was commissioned in early 2013 to carry out this research. This chapter reflects our findings in the Herts study, *Measuring Infringement of Intellectual Property Rights*, which focused on music industry-specific piracy research between 2000 and 2013 (Collopy et al. 2014). The study covered a wide range of trade body-, government- and academic-generated research and focused on the methods used to estimate the levels, scale and types of music piracy, especially in the digital environment but also including offline infringement, principally involving counterfeited goods. The key challenge, as with any illicit activity hidden from plain sight, was that any attempt to accurately measure levels of music piracy was equivalent to estimating the size of an iceberg based on what is visible above the water.

Our report summarized the outcomes of a four-month review, undertaken in 2013. It had a stated aim of providing a robust overview of existing methods used to measure infringement, as well as to recommend suitable methodologies, especially those capable of being adopted across different IPR. The three main sources of information were: (1) a comprehensive and systematic review of industry and government (so-called 'grey') literature along with appropriate relevant academic literature; (2) structured interviews with music trade body representatives; and (3) a series of interviews with industry experts within the area of online IPR infringement.

The Herts review was wide-ranging in scope, covering various music industry sectors and IPR. Overall the findings evidenced a lack of appreciation among those producing research for the high-level principles of measurement and assessment of scale. Many of the approaches adopted by the music industries seemed designed for internal consumption and were usually contingent on particular technologies and/or perspectives from specific music industry sectors. Typically, there was a lack of transparency in the methodologies and data used to form the basis of claims, which made much of this an unreliable basis for policy formulation.

The research approaches found were characterized by a number of features that in summary showed a preference for reactive, often one-off investigations taking snapshots of a particular market feature. Most studies were ad hoc in nature and, on the whole, we found a lack of sustained longitudinal approaches (that is, research carried out over an extended period of time, ideally using the same respondents) that would develop the appreciation of change and meaningful behavioural as well as seasonal patterns. Typically, the studies were designed to address specific hypotheses that might serve to support the position of the particular commissioning body.

What follows is our summary assessment of the key findings in the Herts study. The first section details our review of the wide body of research into online copyright infringement. It is followed by a section outlining our coverage of a substantial range of studies into counterfeiting/physical piracy. In these sections the reviewed research is segmented into industry- and government/academic-generated research in order to highlight the source of the funding. The next section concerns our analysis of views, expressed in both interviews and the trade press, of the key trade bodies responsible for generating the bulk of the research. We then turn to the opinions of a group of research experts on the viability and robustness of the research methods employed. Finally, we summarize our recommendations, and illustrate that these now inform, indeed determine, research methods for producing IPR infringement estimates from government agencies and industry bodies.

Measuring online music copyright infringement

Industry research

The bulk of the industry research reviewed was not of a standard suitable for use in policy-making, especially within markets challenged by wide-scale infringement of IPR, such as music. The majority of the reviewed research was not accompanied by any methodology and even where one was included, it was rarely suitably in-depth or capable of meaningful scrutiny. Within other, non-music specific research, we came across a select number of outstanding pieces of research that met the IPO's evidence standard (clear, verifiable and peer-reviewed) that we believed was essential (IPO 2014). Envisional's Research for NBC-Universal (2011) (which covered film and video) and BSA's Software Analysis (2012) were felt to be methodologically sound and relevant for the music industries, the latter additionally so because it was a consistently run transparent piece of research with an evolving and improving methodology that by 2012 had become robust and was replicated globally in 2017.

Consistency of approach was an aspect of methodology that became an important part of our overall analysis and we noted that only a small number of research surveys were conducted regularly. This regularity of research was most closely associated with the larger music industry bodies that had chosen to invest significantly in large-scale surveys for their members.

We observed that the majority of music industry research was survey based and that the industry commissioned the biggest research firms to carry out annual surveys. These year-on-year surveys were 'deep dives' carried out over short time periods rather than providing longitudinal studies. We identified that the associated methodologies were often enhanced and that they changed over time, making like-for-like comparisons between individual studies more difficult. The underlying belief appeared to be that the latest survey should use the best possible and most appropriate methodology available at that time. We also saw that ad hoc research, such as a one-off project, had become a common feature, either driven by budget constraints or more likely commissioned to support specific internal company processes and strategies.

All the survey-based research showed similar characteristics. In general, the annual surveys were conducted by large, reputable research firms and the methodology was generally comparable because the surveys' methodological fundamentals remained basically the same. Even so, it was questionable whether the surveys could be replicable and verifiable since the subject matter, time frame and respondents (or their behaviour) could have changed. In addition, the circumstances, motives, timing and, most importantly, the understanding, interpretation and analysis of the data were very specific to individuals. What this meant was that the same survey could create different results if repeated at different times. What the surveys produced of value for industry were snapshots to provide insight regarding behaviours, motivations, moods and trends.

We identified six main methodologies used within industry-specific literature to identify the scale and value of infringement in different entertainment sectors. The music industry mainly relied on just two of these methods, the third and fourth in the list below:

1) Literature review and collation of secondary data sets
2) Agent-based models (simulated scenarios using computers to replicate trends and behaviours of user groups to explain industry-wide effects)
3) Online surveys
4) Bundled survey approach (involving a number of different approaches brought together in one study)

5) Mixed approach of data mining and survey-based (Ipsos) research
6) Data mining and use of various technologies to observe actual behaviour across all forms of online entertainment consumption.

Government and academic research

There was a considerable body of literature and research on the online infringement of copyright in music. However, none of the academic or government papers reviewed provided a comprehensive methodology for collecting actual input data, and the main method for measuring the level of infringement was the use of consumer surveys. Notably, many of these consumer surveys were not directed at the level of infringement but focused instead on consumer behaviour and its influence and economic impact on the industry. This was the case for most of the academic studies analysed, including many that suggested business models.

Given the difficulties of establishing comprehensive data, it was not surprising that most of the survey-based studies did not use the level of IPR infringement as their starting point. Establishing the actual level of online infringement seemed to be a by-product of the survey approach. The limitations of the survey-based methodology for estimating levels of online file-sharing were clearly described in most reviews, including those by Oberholzer-Gee and Strumpf (2010). This review highlighted the likelihood of respondents understating their participation in a 'potentially illegal activity' and of the understatement levels varying over time (2010: 11). Oberholzer-Gee and Strumpf argued for more of an observational approach, principally involving identifying the 'packets' traversing computer networks (2010: 11).

Because of the hidden nature of infringements, both online and offline, any assessments were limited by the available data, which meant assumptions played a role in attempts to measure the level of IPR infringement. Nevertheless, it was rare that these assumptions were clearly stated or outlined within the analysis. Certain commentators, such as Rob and Waldfogel (2007), argue that the findings of specific studies cannot be generalized if they are not comparable, and cannot be used for benchmarking purposes.

Whilst the survey-based approach prevailed, an online methodology could include deep-packet inspection (DPI) (which looks at data and how it is being processed across a network), despite it being very resource intensive and subject to data protection and privacy laws. Another promising approach was the use of Internet panels of users who had agreed to be subject to such DPI for the specific purpose of measuring IPR infringement levels. A hybrid approach to data collection, combining measurements of stated (survey) versus revealed (observed) preferences seemed likely to lead to the most robust results.

Counterfeiting and physical piracy research

Industry research

Overall, the bulk of industry-generated literature focused on the broader issues of counterfeiting, with little focus on music products or brands. This may be a result of much of the counterfeiting literature being commissioned by a broad coalition of intellectual property rightsholders or the adoption of the recommendation by the Centre for Economics and Business Research (CEBR) for an omnibus approach (CEBR 2000). Standard methodologies that relied on the measurement of customs seizures and some ad hoc surveys were less than ideal.

The MarkMonitor Traffic Report (2011) offered some potential for measuring online infringement of physical goods, albeit that we had significant concerns about its methodology being applied across the board. This model, while not perfect, was one we felt could be developed into the basis of a robust approach to measuring infringement. This could be important, as in the offline world it is even more difficult to establish the level of IPR infringement, given there appear to be few ways to accurately monitor or 'observe' behaviour other than using consumer surveys or mystery shoppers (Collopy et al. 2017).

Government and academic research

Some traditional methods employed frequently in the world of physical manufacture can help identify counterfeiting and piracy sources; methods that are routinely used not just by IPR enforcement agencies but also by customs officials around the world. A study by the Organisation for Economic Co-operation and Development (OECD) (2007) calculated the number of infringements on the basis of surveys of customs authorities' seizures of counterfeit and pirated goods. However, such seizures only reflect a fraction of the actual infringements taking place, so by its nature, this methodology could not take into account all infringements and any calculations were subject to assumptions based on the actual seizures. The data also did not extend to domestic counterfeiting and piracy within one territory.

Despite the limitations in its scope, the OECD approach of combining different methodologies to develop a single estimate could provide robust data. The OECD researchers correlated industry and seizure data to provide an estimate of the levels of counterfeit trade at a global level. Nonetheless, the OECD acknowledged that its methodology provided only a 'crude' indication of counterfeiting and piracy. One of the key problems was that data had not been systematically collected and evaluated by government or industry and, in many instances, the assessments made by certain parties relied excessively on fragmentary and anecdotal information. Most troubling was that, where data was absent or lacking, 'unsubstantiated opinions [were] often treated as facts' (Hargreaves 2011b: 13). A great deal of the other available literature was based on consumer surveys and, as such, focused on the demand side (such as consumer motivation). The OECD study by contrast considered only the supply side and was less influenced by any subjective assessment of behaviour.

Counterfeiting and piracy were areas widely covered by studies and surveys, but few studies contained suitably objective and robust methodologies and they all focused on particular aspects, such as specific IPR goods or certain modes of infringement (online or offline). Many snapshot-based studies (that is, studies that are not run consistently) were out of date and as such of less value due to recent rapid changes in IPR infringement and consumer behaviour. Our study recommended a hybrid approach based on hard data obtained from relevant government departments, industry and consumer surveys. As regards the latter, transparency would be key, not merely in relation to the respondents but also within the questionnaire and the assumptions applied.

According to Riccardo Sciaudone (2013) the reason why customs seizures became such an integral source of data on compliance and enforcement is that whilst customs authorities could not adjudge the actual infringement of IPR, they were nonetheless well positioned to block infringing goods from entering the internal market. The advent of the Trade Related Aspects of Intellectual Property Rights (TRIPs) agreement introduced specific international obligations on the part of individual states to enable the intervention of national customs authorities in preventing counterfeiting and piracy. This standard approach of using measurements of customs seizures, together with some ad hoc surveys in the broad-based counterfeiting and offline piracy research, was less than ideal, and we considered several methods beyond this approach.

The Office for Harmonization in the Internal Market (OHIM) European Observatory on Infringement of Intellectual Property Rights during its 2013 work programme recommended that all national approaches to counterfeiting and piracy employ a methodology compatible with their supranational approach to achieve consistency and comparability. OHIM identified the major issue for effective enforcement of IPR as the lack of knowledge of the precise scope, scale and impact of infringements. They criticized the lack of an agreed methodology for collecting and analysing data on counterfeiting and piracy, and argued that most studies were just snapshots over limited time frames, using different approaches. The task of measuring the extent of the problem was made worse by the secretive nature of counterfeiting, meaning that comprehensive data for music and other product sectors was virtually impossible to produce. Echoing the World Intellectual Property Organization's Advisory Committee on Enforcement, the Observatory called for a methodology that could work for small and medium-sized enterprises without the burden of major administration.

Despite proposing a summary framework for quantifying enforcement, the Rand Corporation report for the European Commission (2012) did not supply the kind of expected 'ideal' methodology for measuring counterfeiting levels. Its proposed economic model, based on the differences between forecast and actual sales of products, fell short of expectations and the Commission indicated it would explore alternative methodologies.

Trade body views

We interviewed a range of content industry trade bodies as part of the Herts study to try and secure a top-down as well as a bottom-up view of the way research was carried out. These interviews revealed that there were clear differences in how the various trade bodies approached research into IPR infringement. The different approaches could be assessed in relation to the allocation of resources, both financial and technical. The bulk of music industry-generated consumer research took the form of large-scale surveys, and we found that most industry research was ad hoc and rarely purpose built for policy-making and lobbying.

The bulk of music relevant research in relation to counterfeiting and piracy was based around a compilation or umbrella approach,[1] using data from different industries, which had certain advantages in terms of lobbying. However, there were also disadvantages, particularly where the data was combined with that of other industry sectors using different methodologies, as there appeared to be little effort to benchmark the different sectoral data. This may be one reason for the Hargreaves Review's dismissal of many of the claims made in an industry commissioned report, which contained data of varying provenance and quality (2011b: 7).

The overall approach to measuring counterfeiting and piracy advocated by the Anti-Counterfeiting Group involved estimating levels of infringement using different data sources, including industry (for example seizures and take-downs), government (for example customs seizures) and consumer data. This was the approach we felt should be embraced to cover this area of infringement. We also noted the availability of industry generated 'market intelligence', principally from enforcement agencies such as the Federation Against Copyright Theft (FACT), which demonstrated the widest variety of tools for dealing with infringement.

The recorded music trade bodies provided the majority of wide-scale online infringement research and, despite criticisms from many commentators, many of these reports demonstrated research quality. We identified a commitment to a wide range of research within these trade bodies and a willingness to consider using (if not already doing so) new technological solutions to assess the scale of infringements. There was a clear awareness of the need for improved quality of research after the severe criticism levelled at industry-generated data during the Hargreaves review.

Whist we did not have sight of the specific consumer research generated by RIAA or the British Phonographic Industry (BPI), RIAA were prepared to explain their approach to researching infringement. Indeed, each of their methodologies, even when less than perfect (which they acknowledged), still managed to produce data with some value for policy-making, notably because of their commitment to a consistent long-term approach to measuring online infringement to produce something akin to the longitudinal studies we recommended. RIAA argued that whatever our reservations about their methodology, the stable and consistent approach they adopted could highlight trends over time. Even so this conflicted with BPI, who chose to use different firms to conduct its infringement research. Although the RIAA steadfastly defended its claims on the level of piracy, and our findings confirmed there was value in their long-term approach to measuring the phenomenon, the International Federation of the Phonographic Industry (IFPI) conceded that no single study has achieved a precise measurement of piracy (Collopy et al. 2014: 93).

The case for long-term studies of the assessment of infringement was undermined by the need for industry research to examine issues resulting from fast-changing market conditions. This may explain why so much industry research appeared to be ad hoc rather than longitudinal, as it was born from a need to examine an issue at a particular point in time in response to changing market conditions. In its lobbying activities the recorded music industry had shifted its emphasis from claims and findings from consumer surveys to increased support for piracy-inhibiting methods such as, in the United Kingdom at least, securing court orders to block piracy-linked websites and reducing the advertising revenues that funded them.

Whilst long-term studies may have value to policy-making we questioned whether industries that are impacted by IPR infringement could ever deliver the data in the form and with the kind of precision demanded by policy-makers, notably the IPO's Evidence for Policy-Making. Indeed, our research indicates that any such studies should be conducted independently of, rather than by, industry to provide greater confidence in the findings. The Herts review concluded that the omnibus approach adopted by the Office of Communications (Ofcom) and Kantar (2012) was one to be maintained and expanded on, especially in relation to online infringement. Consistent and regular systematic research, measuring both offline and online infringement, would best be achieved by government agencies, provided it had industry's cooperation and involvement, creating an even-handed approach to measuring infringement that benefits all stakeholders.

Online infringement research experts' views

We considered various new and appropriate technologies for measuring online behaviours and interviewed several online technological experts. The interviews not only highlighted technological advances, but also provided caveats about the limits of even the most innovative solutions to measuring and observing infringement of IPR online.

Musicmetric (MM) acquired by Apple in 2015, tracked audio and audio-visual content by sound recording using different identification tags. Research commissioned by Spotify in 2012 used MM data on BitTorrent activities; however, this data was based on actual downloads (download of one file in its entirety from one source) not swarms, which is a multi-source segmented file transfer method often associated with the BitTorrent technology, the underlying assumption being that all content on BitTorrent was copyright infringing.[2] MM's 'mixed approach' used information available on social networking sites to develop a long-term view for tracking artists/sound recordings as opposed to the snapshots used by industry to issue take-downs. MM's own proprietary distributed data-collection infrastructure utilized hundreds of servers to reliably collect large quantities of data from the Internet. MM directly monitored activity in BitTorrent swarms, hour by hour, allowing the volume of activity to be measured and segmented geographically at the country and city level. The MM approach suggested real potential for smart online technologies to measure online infringement.

Nielsen, one of the most active and successful firms in the world of analytics and metrics had a tool, Nielsen Digital Media Manager (NDMM), that used 'digital watermarking and fingerprinting' to provide a more reliable way to track content' (Collopy et al. 2014: 25).

BitTorrent Inc (BTI), whose protocol had been such a significant component feature of online infringement over the previous decade, claimed to now work more closely with music creators and representatives to make their technology work as a viable legal tool for efficient distribution across online networks. The data provided by BTI for 2012 showed it was clearly able to distinguish between different types of content. However, it could not track what users of BTI did with the torrents, as there was no single server, something inherent in the architecture of its system. BTI believed that the future Internet would be asymmetric and decentralized, but with content-centric networks to allow content industries to interact with consumers. This suggested that the measurement of online infringement would become even more complex.

County Analytics (CA) segmented piracy into the different ways content was being managed and by whom: physical, home copying, hosted content (on a website's server), links/deep links (linking and redirecting users to the content), peer-to-peer (no central server required and files/content is instead linked to each other from computer to computer within the same network) and UseNet (the precursor to private and secure Internet forums). The means of identification of piracy were comprised of target identification, content verification, container labelling, manual identification, metadata, digital hash, signed metadata, fingerprinting and watermarking. Overall, CA identified that the best piracy identification approaches required a layered approach, noting that faster but less reliable techniques were generally used initially with identification, then confirmed by slower and more expensive or more inconvenient technologies.

Recommendations

While the survey approach had been the most common across online and physical piracy in both industry and government/academic research, the review's initial key recommendation was increased adoption of a hybrid or 'blended' approach. The framework for measuring music specific IPR infringement should then be implemented as follows:

- Online copyright infringement should be assessed by the blended combination of the number of 'take-down' notices and regular omnibus surveying of the level of compliant and infringed activity by consumers. It should also require a survey of trade body and enforcement organizations' infringement evidence. The use of emerging technological tools to measure observable online behaviour should be added to the blend of approaches to provide a more accurate picture;
- Offline copyright piracy and counterfeiting (i.e. trademark infringement) should include a multi-tiered but blended approach encompassing data from industry, government and consumers. This could take the form of counting industry and customs 'seizures' along with consumer, producer, distributor and retailer surveys and mystery shopping.

As in any field of official data measurement, a publicly available count of enforceable and actionable infringements would also be necessary. Such a count would acknowledge that in each area there is a highly skewed distribution, particularly of the economic impact of infringement, leading to a large proportion of the value being concentrated in a small proportion of the perpetrators. Comprehensive scoping of the infringement enforcement data could pick up on this tiny segment that escapes sampling methods. However, this could not be used in isolation, as the actual volume of enforceable infringement would be the outcome of an inevitable tension between the levels of underlying infringement by perpetrators and the expectation of enforcement by the claimant.

To address this issue, we advocated systematic, regular, ongoing survey tracking of the attitudes, perceptions and, where practical, behaviours of both perpetrators and claimants. We proposed that this regular survey tracking could take the omnibus form adopted within the Ofcom/Kantar online surveys. Even so we believed surveying should be more frequent, ideally monthly, to provide a consistent picture across each year, having noted the seasonal nature of many current surveys. In addition to sampling across the audience, there should be a comprehensive transparent count of the major infringements, which would not be sampled. This blended approach could allow for the inclusion of market intelligence data supplied regularly by industry. The entire process should be conducted or overseen by government, to ensure the methodology would be rigorous and robust and to enable measurement of the infringement of owners' rights.

Due to the difficulties in obtaining comprehensive data, the problems of assumptions and the perceived limited value to government policy of evidence presented by industry, many rightsholders in the music industry had concerned themselves with practical measures for enforcing their rights, rather than with systematic data collection. There had also been a fundamental resource issue due to the expense of systematically measuring piracy and counterfeiting, which had rendered it out of reach for all apart from well-funded industry trade bodies. We suggested that government, with the involvement and support of industry, could conduct a wide-ranging and regular survey covering all types of protected music content impacted by both offline and online infringement. We criticized the conflation of measurement of scale and the impact of IPR infringement within music industry research and also noted that the industries sometimes described the way piracy happened without focusing on measuring or estimating the scale or actual impact.

Arguably the survey model had not been used to directly assess volume, but rather to assess the plaintiff's attitude to an assessment of potential litigation for infringement, and the perpetrator's perception of the risk of detection. The modified perspective on the use of surveys could lead to a change in the design and formulation of survey content. We suggested that the survey should ideally be conducted in the context of a general monthly lifestyle omnibus survey. Survey selection methods could also be utilized in the adoption of the newly advocated assessment of infringement behaviours. Surveys, particularly of the more qualitative kind, could then be used to interpret the different types of behaviours tracked appropriately. The characteristics of each element of this method should be respected, as there could be potential to be tempted to see the opportunities of the recently developed tracking methods as a substitution of the survey methods, because considerable volumes of measurement could be obtained for the equivalent cost of a small but representative survey. It would, however, provide a better balance to keep a small panel of participants that could be surveyed and then tracked, with the surveyed volumes reduced to stay within the budget constraints prevalent at the time.

It would be essential to provide this framework in a stable format, as this very stability would allow changes in attitude, behaviour and scale to be robustly monitored. It would also be crucial that, should this process be adopted, the underlying data be made openly available, enabling different stakeholders to confirm the outcomes and utilize the same source data to investigate and demonstrate their own areas of interest while also validating their own perspective. Providing a common framework of source data would offer the opportunity for the policy debate to progress beyond the supporting evidence and to focus on the most current issues. Should the data be captured over a sustained period of time, it would further allow stakeholders to retrospectively apply new approaches and demonstrate if these illuminate new insights.

In relation to online copyright infringement, the basis of our recommended infringement-measurement methodology was a hybrid method that should include the use of consumer surveys and a more detailed inspection of consumer behaviour online. We noted one existing highly effective IPR infringement measurement tool that used voluntary 'spyware' within large-scale consumer panels on an international basis (Collopy et al. 2014: 71). Such a tool would be insightful and reliable in highlighting observed behaviour. Online measurements of IPR infringement could also include the use of web-crawling technologies to search the web, involving similar processes to those adopted by search engines.

One source of reliable objective data had been the regular reports on the volume of 'take-down' notices issued. This assessment of an overall measure could be used alongside a consumer survey similar to Ofcom/Kantar reporting to indicate the appropriate ways to weight outcomes. This framework could then be adapted to include a representatively selected longitudinal panel of participants who agree to the monitoring of their online behaviour. The primacy of selection prior to voluntary monitoring should be noted. There should be a suspicion of technologies, methods and surveys that rely on, implicitly or explicitly, self- or practitioner-selected participants.

In relation to counterfeiting/physical piracy, there would be a need to produce composite data from industry, government and consumer sources to assemble a broader picture of counterfeiting, rather than relying on a single methodology. Even though each method has weaknesses, we accepted the broad recommendations of the Rand Corporation (2009) on at least four of the five approaches to gathering enforcement information as the basis of a hybrid methodology for measuring counterfeiting (consumer surveys, producer or distributor surveys, sampling/mystery shopping and economic models).

The major issue for industry in the effective enforcement of IPR had been the lack of knowledge of the precise scope, scale and impact of IPR infringements. This gap had in part been the result of the majority of studies being conducted as snapshots, over limited time frames and using different approaches. We believed this could be addressed by adopting the CEBR 2000 proposal for omnibus surveys as well as by conducting systematic, regular, frequent and long-term studies.

A great deal of infringing behaviour would continue to remain hidden from public view and this meant different methods of weighting between survey and public data would be required, although it would be hoped that both the consumer and business research selection of survey participants could be harmonized. Continuing to anchor survey results to public records would provide a level of credibility amongst stakeholders and broaden the scope of application. Utilization of the public records would be particularly relevant when it came to assessments of economic impact. The financial value of incidents had tended to be highly skewed, with a high proportion of the overall value being focused within a small number of cases. It is this small number of high-value cases that had become part of the public record, but which had been missed by the wide-ranging sampling techniques used for surveying.

In summary, we suggested that future research into the measurement of IPR, especially copyright infringement, should be framed around the following essential criteria:

- Research funding: It would be of utmost importance that any research provide full disclosure of who commissioned it.
- Validity: To improve the general validity of the input data on the level of infringement, research should be carried out by trusted third parties who would be independent of vested interests.
- Comparability/benchmarking: In order to assess the level of counterfeiting and piracy to justify policy, it would be key to apply transparent and comparable methodologies to enable benchmarking.
- Standards: A minimum set of standards should be implemented to improve the quantitative and qualitative methods used by the music industries. Overall, any quantitative methodology must be designed to ensure validity and reliability by allowing for replicability. New quantitative surveys should be piloted and

care must be taken to ensure sample sizes involved would be large enough to provide a valid representative sample. Greater care should also be taken with constructing appropriate qualitative surveys by the use of hermeneutics.

- Repetition: Any recommended methodology must include a repetitive aspect to provide a robust and pragmatic assessment of the three core statistical characteristics of random uncertainty, likely bias and statistical independence. Any resilient statistical process should consist of repetitive, consistent and systematic elements.

Conclusion

Most of the five criteria for future research recommended in the Herts study in 2014 have since been adopted by the IPO. As a result, these criteria are much in evidence in the research relating to copyright infringement commissioned by the organization since the recommendations were first announced at an Ofcom hosted workshop on 'Good Evidence for Copyright Policy' held in September 2013 (Collopy 2013; CREATe 2013). Following this workshop, the recommended research methodology (blended surveys carried out frequently over longer periods) became the IPO's accepted standard for measuring infringement and led to them (with full disclosure) commissioning Kantar (as a trusted and independent third party) to carry out their Online Copyright Infringement (OCI) tracker.

In 2019 the OCI will be in its ninth wave and is testament to the benefits of a long-term systemic process that allows for repetition and consistency. The findings and data from the OCI tracker have been used by other researchers (for example CREATe in Glasgow) to create a long-term data set of online audience behaviours.[3] Although Kantar have been replaced in 2019 by Herts original research partner Audiencenet to continue this work, the emphasis remains a consistency of approach as well as regular and frequent surveys. What has changed in 2019 is the confidence in this methodology, which has led to it being employed to measure IPR infringement in physical goods as well.

Whilst online piracy has been widely thought to have been in decline since the advent of streaming, there remain calls from industry trade bodies for measuring the phenomena over time. This may be the result of the mutating nature of piracy, as it moves from a download-driven phenomenon towards other technologies, such as streaming. A summary analysis of stream ripping as the new form of piracy was written as part of an IPO and PRS for Music study in 2017 (PRS for Music 2017). The influence of the original Herts study guidance can be seen in the blend of results from stated preferences (Kantar surveys) and revealed preferences (Incopro data on Alexa sourced website traffic). This analysis revealed that the results of certain industry studies continue to be presented in misleading ways. For example, in one study, data from different countries had been aggregated to produce a headline figure, even though it was clearly evident that some markets, such as the United Kingdom, were at the lower end of the spectrum of piracy, whereas others, such as Brazil, encountered greater activity.

Whilst there remains an ongoing industry need to monitor levels and the effects of piracy, it is also crucial to ensure the tools and methods used to assess these levels and effects are robust, rigorous and appropriate so as to minimize and ideally avoid some of the uses and abuses of statistics we witnessed within our extensive review. Nonetheless since that review, we have witnessed continued conflicts in the data produced by government agencies, such as OECD and the European Union Intellectual Property Office, and that generated by industry, including private IPR enforcement firms. In early 2020 the IPO is expected to publish a further commissioned review of the enforcement landscape to take account of research carried out over the past five to six years and to identify future potential threats facing rights holders and content owners. This new review is needed to support ongoing policy-maker and enforcement involvement in the digital and physical goods markets at a time when it is believed that wide-scale digital copyright infringement has radically declined, yet at the same time there seems to have been a significant rise in the online availability of counterfeit goods. Regardless of which position one takes in the debate over the effects of piracy, it is beyond doubt that this war of words requires, not least within the IPR enforcement policy-based context, independently generated, mutually acceptable trusted data calculating levels of infringement.

NOTES

1. We used these terms to distinguish it from the omnibus approach. The latter indicates the measurement of infringement across different sectors and rights using a uniform methodology to accumulate data.
2. They were aware, however, that some content is distributed under Open Commons licences that are non-infringing.
3. CREATE is the UK Copyright and Creative Economy Centre, based at the University of Glasgow (see https://www.create.ac.uk/).

REFERENCES

BSA (Business Software Alliance) (2012), 'Shadow market', https://techpost.bsa.org/2012/05/15/shadow-market-global-software-piracy-study/. Accessed 29 May 2019.

Buckles, Brad (2013), 'One year, 20 million links to illegal songs sent to Google: This is how it's supposed to work?', *RIAA News*, 20 May, https://www.riaa.com/one-year-20-million-links-to-illegal-songs-sent-to-google-this-is-how-its-supposed-to-work/. Accessed 29 May 2019.

Centre for Economics and Business Research (CEBR) (2000), *Counterfeiting: Economical Impact on Four Key Sectors of EU Industry*, London: CEBR.

Collopy, Dennis (2013), 'Measuring infringement of IPR – IPO report summary findings', https://www.researchgate.net/publication/281838602_Measuring_Infringement_of_IPR_-_IPO_Report_Summary_Findings. Accessed 17 June 2019.

Collopy, Dennis, Bastian, Vanessa, Drye, Tim, Koempel, Florian, Lewis, David and Jenner, Peter (2014), *Measuring Infringement of Intellectual Property Rights*, Newport: Intellectual Property Office, https://assets.publishing.service.gov.uk/government/uploads/system/uploads/attachment_data/file/325020/IP_Measuring_Infringement.pdf. Accessed 29 May 2019.

Collopy, Dennis, Drye, Tim, Koempel, Florian, Carey, Chris and Jenner, Peter (2017), *Share and Share Alike: The Challenges from Social Media for Intellectual Property Rights*, Newport: Intellectual Property Office, https://assets.publishing.service.gov.uk/government/uploads/system/uploads/attachment_data/file/641461/Share_and_share_alike_report.pdf. Accessed 17 June 2019.

Envisional (2011), *An Estimate of Infringing Use of the Internet,* Cambridge: Envisional Limited, https://www.ics.uci.edu/~sjordan/courses/ics11/case_studies/Envisional-Internet_Usage-Jan2011-4.pdf. Accessed 29 May 2019.

Gowers, Andrew (2006), *Gowers Review of Intellectual Property*, Norwich: Her Majesty's Stationery Office, https://assets.publishing.service.gov.uk/government/uploads/system/uploads/attachment_data/file/228849/0118404830.pdf. Accessed 29 May 2019.

Hargreaves, Ian (2011a), *Digital Opportunity: A Review of Intellectual Property and Growth*, Norwich: Her Majesty's Stationery Office, https://assets.publishing.service.gov.uk/government/uploads/system/uploads/attachment_data/file/32563/ipreview-finalreport.pdf. Accessed 29 May 2019.

——— (2011b), *Supporting Document CC Data on the Prevalence and Impact of Piracy and Counterfeiting*, Norwich: Her Majesty's Stationery Office.

Intellectual Property Office (IPO) (2014), *Guide to Evidence for Policy*, Newport: Intellectual Property Office, https://assets.publishing.service.gov.uk/government/uploads/system/uploads/attachment_data/file/510985/Guide_to_evidence_for_policy.pdf. Accessed 29 May 2019.

IPO (2013) 'Standards for good evidence workshop'. Intellectual Property Office. https://www.gov.uk/government/news/standards-for-good-evidence-workshop. Accessed 16 September 2020.

MarkMonitor (2011), 'Traffic report: Online piracy and counterfeiting', https://www.markmonitor.com/download/report/MarkMonitor_-_Traffic_Report_110111.pdf. Accessed 29 May 2019.

Masnick, Mike (2010), 'Has the recording industry reached the bargaining stage of grief', *Techdirt*, 1 February, https://www.techdirt.com/articles/20100201/0126377984.shtml. Accessed 29 May 2019.

Mitchell, David M., Scott, C. Patrick and Brown, Kenneth H. (2018), 'Did the RIAA's prosecution of music piracy impact music sales?', *Atlantic Economic Journal*, 46:1, pp. 59–71.

Oberholzer-Gee, Felix and Strumpf, Koleman (2010), 'File-sharing and copyright', working paper, Boston: Harvard Business School.

Ofcom/Kantar (2012), *Online Copyright Infringement Tracker Wave 2*, https://www.ofcom.org.uk/__data/assets/pdf_file/0028/69805/report-wave-2.pdf. Accessed 29 May 2019.

Organisation for Economic Co-operation and Development (OECD) (2007), *The Economic Impact of Counterfeiting and Piracy*, Paris: OECD, https://www.oecd.org/sti/38707619.pdf. Accessed 29 May 2019.

PRS for Music (2017), 'Stream-ripping takes over as most aggressive form of music piracy increases 141%', 7 July, https://prsformusic.com/press/2017/stream-ripping-takes-over-as-most-aggressive-form-of-music-piracy. Accessed 17 June 2019.

Rand Corporation (2009), 'Film piracy, organized crime and terrorism', https://www.rand.org/content/dam/rand/pubs/monographs/2009/RAND_MG742.pdf. Accessed 29 May 2019.

——— (2012), 'Measuring IPR infringements in the internal market: Development of a new approach to estimating the impact of infringements on sales', https://www.rand.org/content/dam/rand/pubs/technical_reports/2012/RAND_TR1279.pdf. Accessed 29 May 2019.

Rob, Rafael, and Waldfogel, Joel (2007), 'Piracy on the silver screen', *The Journal of Industrial Economics*, 55:3, pp. 379–95.

Sciaudone, Riccardo (2013), 'Book review: Enforcement of Intellectual Property Rights through border measures: law and practice in the EU', *Scripted*, https://script-ed.org/article/1093/. Accessed 29 May 2019.

PART V

DIGITAL SOLUTIONS

12

One Penny from Brazil: Music Publishing, Revived but Untransformed

Michael Jones

In 2000, in a review of an extensive research programme into media economics and media culture, its leader, Simon Frith, made the simultaneously prescient and yet overdue recognition that, 'the music industry is not a manufacturing industry, it is a rights industry' (Frith 2000: 388). The recognition was overdue because, as he argues, the then dominant music industry research paradigm (which he identifies as the 'Production of Culture' approach) had become preoccupied 'with the object manufactured being [...] the record' (Frith 2000: 390). To paraphrase Frith, his argument was that, to understand music industry, we should not be distracted by the making of records but should instead follow the money. The principal beneficiaries of music sales are music rights owners.

In this discussion, I want to explore a recent phenomenon: the return to music-industrial prominence of music publishers. Publishers have long been main players in music industry (Harrison 2017; Passman 2015) but, in the 1960s, the rise of performers who were also songwriters (the Beatles and Bob Dylan as the most obvious examples) tended to draw attention away from the phenomenon of 'Tin Pan Alley' (Keightley 2010) and towards the recording industry with its value chain of A&R, marketing, promotion, sales and distribution. As I will argue, music publishers tended to become passive passengers in a music economy driven by major record companies.

As major record companies faltered in the early 2000s, and as the music economy began to change under the pressure of the take-up of digital communication, so music publishers found new ways to be active participants in that turbulent economy. Even so, the habits of passivity can still be identified. Further, these habits can be argued to be a key effect of the forms of contract that became standard to music publishing throughout the twentieth century. In more recent times, the Featured Artists Coalition (FAC) has argued that music publishers and record companies should 'use or lose' the copyrights they come to own. I hope to show the necessity for, and justice in, that demand through unpacking new approaches to accounting to signed songwriters, ones that see them re-designated as 'clients' of the music publishers with whom they have contracts, rather than the, always poorly realized, status of 'partners' that such contracts enshrine.

Uses not units

The recording industry business model was that end users bought 'units': albums or singles released in physical carriers. As the practice of illegal file-sharing showed, many music users wanted recordings more than they wanted the compact discs that held them. From the perspective of rights owners, the first decade of the twenty-first century was very much a battle to create new, law-abiding (and paying) habits among Internet-users. As memory of the recording industry's absolute dominance of 'the music industry' begins to recede, there is now a new sensibility and a new confidence exhibited especially by music industry trade bodies such as the International Federation of the Phonographic Industry (IFPI) and the Music Publishers Association (MPA); one conveyed in this observation of Leslie Meier:

> Figures compiled by the International Federation of the Phonographic Industries (IFPI) [...] suggest that in 2012, the value of global recorded music revenues grew for the first time since 1999, reaching US$16.5 billion [...]. Moreover, if music publishing revenues are added to the equation, the worldwide music copyright industry exceeded US$25 billion in 2014.
>
> (2017: 3)

What is notable here, though, is not so much the beginning of recovery of revenues from sales – and now uses – of recordings, but that Meier should include the additional revenue from music publishing to establish that recovery. Even though music publishing income was always substantial, it is a sign of changing times when books about popular music begin to consider that revenue accrues from sources beyond the sales of recordings. As the inclusion of the figures show, 'digitization' is at last coming to seem a boon to owners of music copyrights *in general* – whether as recordings or songs – rather than solely a 'bogeyman' to (major) record companies.

In a combination of ways, all 'players' in music industry – whether record companies, music publishers, live agencies and promoters or musicians themselves – are beginning to adjust to a new economic environment in which there are now multiple revenue sources. Among these, while individual payments from music streaming might be microscopic, the accumulating totals of payments can be impressive, especially when synergies can be generated by cross-promotion of recordings across all fields. Take Drake as an example; *Forbes* magazine cites him as the 'most streamed artist on the planet' (1.3 billion streams) whose 2017 earnings they estimate at $94 million (McIntyre 2017). We have no way of knowing what sources of revenue contributed what proportions of this total, but the income from streams on this scale will have been very great indeed.

When the focus of music-industrial activity switches away from selling records and towards encouraging user-generated 'plays', then rights-ownership takes on a new resonance; as an article in the UK trade paper *Music Week* put it:

> Amid all the changes in the music industry, one sector that is experiencing a resurgence is music publishing. The management of rights attached to compositions used on multiple platforms is as old as music publishing itself, and the quasi-symbiotic relationship between authors and composers and their publisher is as important, if not more, today than it ever was.
>
> (Legrand 2016: 14)

This new 'visibility' is reflected in an assertive and self-confident tone evident in interview after interview in *Music Week*. Take for example these comments, made by David Renzer, chairman of Spirit, a US 'rights management company': '[w]e're building Spirit B-Unique into a powerhouse boutique music publishing company that is already enjoying tremendous worldwide success' (Gumble 2017: 2).

What is striking about this observation is that B-Unique was formerly a UK independent record company. As Mark Lewis, co-president of the newly amalgamated company, puts it, 'we're basically a record company that's morphed into a publishing company' (Gumble 2017: 2). Their formation of a joint company, together with the industrial relocation of that company (from recording to music publishing) shows how prescient Frith's remarks were: seventeen years after he made them, a record company becomes a music publisher because it is there that 'tremendous worldwide success' is to be found.

If a 'boutique' music publisher is flourishing, then this is a reasonable indicator that the vastly larger 'major' publishers are similarly thriving. The Managing Director of one of those majors, Warner-Chappell, confirms this when commenting that 'publishing is a very creative space right now' (Sutherland 2017: 10). Even so, as someone who continues to be published by another of those majors, Universal Music Publishing Group (UMPG), I would argue that UMPG's supply of publishing figures to me, as one of its signed writers, identifies an experience far removed from this generalized euphoria.

Universal Music Publishing Group's 'Royalty Window'

In April 2015, UMPG switched to online royalty accounting. Under the title 'Royalty Window', the system replaced their former paper-based system. In and of itself there is nothing remarkable in a switch to 'paperless' accounting; it is common practice across all forms of money-transfer. In many ways, digital delivery of royalty collection information outstrips paper-based royalty accounting, both in the variety of forms of representation of the sources and the amount of royalties collected and in terms of the fine granularity of the detail digital representation affords. So it was that, in 2016, I learned, in an accounting of the second (six-monthly) period of 2016 that recently I had earned one penny in Brazil.

On encountering this fact I was simultaneously impressed and dismayed, with the questions, 'how did they find that?' and 'only a penny!?' representing the twin poles of the emotional continuum. These immediate impressions eventually gave way to a more critical reading of the entire enterprise of the Royalty Window but they did not give way immediately. There is something both dazzling and persuasive about the switch to digital: 'dazzling' because the graphical interfaces are both attractive and (superficially at least) quite useful, 'persuasive' because micro-payments take enormous amounts of paper to account.

I was one of many songwriters whose copyrights were transferred, in 2006, from the music publishing division of Bertelsmann Music Group (BMG) to UMPG following the latter's acquisition of the former. For me, a typical BMG royalty statement ran to eleven pages, but, if I downloaded the UPMG statement it would run to 107 pages, and this for someone whose songs are nowhere near as popular as they had been when those royalty statements were far shorter.

For example, in 1999 a song with the title 'Toulouse' yielded £19.74 from unit sales in two 'territories' (Germany, Austria and Switzerland, which combined represent the 'G.A.S.' territory, and Hong Kong). This was reported in a limited section of a page that accounts two other songs in full and two in part (broken across the top and bottom of the page respectively). In stark contrast, the same song, which yielded £3.09 in royalties in 2017, takes seven *pages* to account, so small are the payments generated. If we set aside, momentarily, how little the yield is from streams, the Royalty Window begins to lose its novelty when we realize that there is a sub-text to the graphical representation of royalties accrued.

The penalties of assignment

Garfield (1986) and Southall (2008) are two authors who discuss, in colloquial terms, how punitive music industry contracts were (and, by implication, can still be). Yet this 'knowledge' tends not to deter aspiring musicians and songwriters from seeking 'deals'. One such musician, and former student, once wrote to me in an email about his ongoing efforts to become successful and concluded by observing that he was 'still searching for that elusive recording and publishing deal'. The problem in this construction is that 'a deal' is conceived as a quantity, as an object, which is 'elusive' and requires a hard 'search' to secure. But a deal is not an artefact, not a quantity, and it is not something 'lost' or well-hidden; a 'deal' is a quality, it is more accurately and more productively understood as an agreement between two parties. These two parties, to cite a legal fiction, are empowered equally to agree how to trade one valuable item for another as the basis for a working agreement. The 'trade' is that, in return for his or her copyright, the musician-composer will receive 'royalty' payments for however long the agreement to assign or license such rights is in force.

In my own experience, three problems arose from signing a 'deal': first, my copyrights could not be retrieved; second, my royalty payments were fixed as a proportion of income generated by them but with no guarantee that the publishers would work to generate royalties; and third, there was no provision that I would earn from any sale of my copyrights to a third party. To consider the last of these first, the observation was made previously that my copyrights were assigned from BMG Music Publishing to UMPG in 2006. This was not the first time that this particular group of copyrights had been assigned. This first happened when I 'signed' a publishing 'deal' with Block and Gilbert Music in 1984, where this assignment was from me to the contracting company. Those copyrights were then assigned again when this company was dissolved.

BMG was formed in 1987 and its newly established London office quickly persuaded the majority partner in Block and Gilbert Music (Derek Block, still a leading music agent and artist manager in 2019) to assign his copyrights to them. Because of the nature of the publishing contract I had signed, firstly, I could not resist or prevent this sale and, secondly, I could not participate in the windfall income earned by Block and Gilbert (BG) from the sale. This same set of conditions applied when BMG sold my copyrights (along with those of thousands of other songwriters) to UMPG. What money they earned from this sale passed to the company; nothing came to the writers whose copyrights they had had assigned to them (in my own case, and likely those of others, quite indirectly) as a result of purchases of existing catalogues undertaken from 1987 onwards. No amount of pastel-shaded, three-dimensional bar charts can compensate for the reality that, once assigned, copyrights only earn to the extent that they do, individually, from sales or uses. What I mean is that songwriters 'buried' in mass catalogues do not earn from the sales of those catalogues, only their owners do (for example, what if BMG had invested, on behalf of its writers, a large percentage of UMPG's payment and paid its writers a regular dividend proportionate to their earnings?).

Further penalties of signing a deal

The page within the 'Royalty Window' graphic that identified that I had earned a penny from Brazil is headed 'Client Song Listing' and this is a cause for (great) concern: the point here is that, in agreeing the final, negotiated offer, I was not, nor did I become, a 'client' of BG, I was 'simply' a party to an agreement of assignment of copyrights. When I return to that contract, it makes for confusing reading. It reads confusingly, not simply because the language of the law is discursively so removed from everyday speech but because, beyond their payment of royalties to me, it is not clear what they are giving me (if anything) in return for my copyrights. Further, how the relationship is expressed in the original document is highly misleading; both of these dimensions of the contract warrant examination because both have a bearing on how, today, earnings from the copyrights are represented to me, digitally. The first source of confusion is in how the agreement is represented:

> Dear Sirs,
>
> We hereby engage you and you agree to enter into an agreement with us on the terms and conditions set forth below in this letter agreement (*sic*) and on the terms and conditions of the General Conditions attached hereto and made a part hereof wherein we are referred to as 'the Licensee' and you are referred to as 'the Owner'.

The essential point that needs here to be grasped is that, while I (and my songwriting partners) may accurately be described as 'the Owner' of the copyrights, BG were certainly not 'Licensee(s)'. Had they been 'licensees' we would have retained our copyrights and allowed BG to take a commission on any paying uses they generated during a limited period of time. I discussed this point with a lawyer who specializes in music industry agreements; his opinion was that the drafting was 'extremely sloppy' but not 'intentionally misleading'. The root of the 'sloppiness' reveals itself later in the document when, quite suddenly, references appear to 'CBS Songs Limited':

> Dear Sirs,
>
> In consideration of, and as an inducement to, CBS Songs (sic) Limited ('CBS') entering into an agreement dated today with ('the Owner') the undersigned acknowledges that [...]

What seems to have happened is that, in their haste to sign us as songwriters, Jeff Gilbert (Block's partner whom Block had recruited from CBS Records) had adapted an existing CBS *licensing* agreement as a full song-publishing one. Whether or not this is sufficient grounds to render the original agreement null and void is moot; for the purposes of this argument it 'muddies the water' because, in no true sense, were the original copyrights *licensed* to BG, they were assigned, and not just assigned, but assigned 'irrevocably' and 'in perpetuity':

> [*clause*] 7. In consideration of the agreement for payment of royalties hereinafter contained you as beneficial owner hereby irrevocably assign and transfer [subject to the condition of general condition 12 hereof] to us for the Territory the whole of your copyright and interest, present, future or contingent whatsoever and wheresoever, now and hereafter known, in all the work[s] TO HOLD the same unto us absolutely throughout the World for the Rights term and all possible renewals and extensions thereof wherever and to the extent the law of any country so allows and thereafter as far as possible in perpetuity.
>
> (all capitalization and punctuation as per the original)

This is the reason that UMPG continue to account royalties to me in 2019. They own the songs that became assigned to them for the life of the copyrights, and the reason why BG could assign the rights to them was because of this clause in the contract I signed. To have signed away my copyrights forever is an enormous sacrifice, and mistake, on my part. It is both mistake and sacrifice because the contract does not truly indicate what, aside from royalties, I might have expected in return for agreeing to their terms.

The collective trade body for the UK music publishing industry is the MPA. On their website they assert the following about the working relationship between publisher and writer:

> The relationship between a music publisher and a songwriter/composer is supported by a publishing contract setting out the rights and obligations of each to the other. Under these contracts songwriters and composers assign the copyright in their music to the music publisher in return for a commitment to promote, exploit and protect that music.[1]
>
> (Music Publishers Association 2019)

In the contract that has led to my using the UMPG Royalty Window, BG appear to be under no obligation other than to pay royalties. Further, the agreement contains no indication of any effort the company might make in promoting the copyrights I assigned to them and neither am I afforded any means of monitoring the company's commitment at what cannot help but seem the beginning of a (business) relationship between us. While it is clear from the contract that it does not constitute a legally recognizable 'joint venture', it is reasonable to draw the inference from their offering 'a deal' that the music publisher would want to work with me as a songwriter and would want to 'work' (in the sense of make money from) the copyrights they have been assigned. Whatever the strengths and weaknesses of the making of such an inference, and however much the contract was not the basis of a joint venture, what the assignment *did not* make me was a client of BG. It is for this reason that I am now not a client of UMPG and, for what are likely to be an identical set of reasons, neither are any of UMPG's many other writers, living or dead.

It is vital to contest this re-designation from equal party to an agreement to 'client' because what the acceptance of client status carries with it is a further dilution of the nearly non-existent obligations music publishers make to songwriters. If I accept my imputed 'clienthood' then UMPG becomes a variety of 'collection agency', which retains my custom by tracking down even the tiniest royalty payment from the most distant 'market' (as in the case of one penny from Brazil) and commissions me for its efforts. As it is, PRS for Music already plays this function for me and, in any case, UMPG have to do nothing to 'retain my loyalty' because they own my copyrights 'in perpetuity'. Bagehot and Kanaar make the point that,

> All publishers [...] offer a positive obligation that they will at least use reasonable endeavours to exploit compositions but such an obligation is very nebulous and the cynically minded might think that the words were included in a contract merely to give it the appearance of being more fair and reasonable and thus with a better prospect of enforceability by the courts in the event of a dispute.
>
> (1998: 141)

By re-positioning a 'signed writer' (an assignor of copyrights) from someone with whom they work to someone *for* whom they work to collect royalties, UMPG could be argued to be accomplishing something far more profound than simply 'future-proofing' themselves against litigation as a potential eventuality. If I accept that I am a client of UMPG then, in turn, my client-status is a *de facto* acceptance that UMPG is not to be seen as an agency working to generate revenue from copyrights, but only as one that collects revenue generated by some other party. 'Client' shifts the 'nebulous' obligation into an even more imperceptible form. Yet perhaps there is a sense and a logic to this that serves a larger purpose for them, as well as for all large-scale music publishers.

The dead letter office

Inevitably, any graphical representation of revenue distributed draws attention to its peaks rather than its troughs. In a block diagram, just like physical tower blocks, the eye engages with the tallest structures and implicitly dismisses the 'ground' on which they stand as necessary, supporting landscape; except that the 'flat land' here is, in fact, evidence of gross inactivity on the part of UMPG.

If we consider the six categories of royalty collection activity, the greatest proportion of my royalties is consistently 'mechanicals'. Although mechanical royalties can be generated by streaming (and this diagram gives no indication of their derivation), it seems likely that these continue to be generated from sales of compact discs (a brief trawl at the time of writing through Amazon turned up 'customer reviews' of recent purchases of a range of different albums containing songs I have co-written). Essentially, UMPG plays no part in the promotion of these CDs; their sales happen entirely by chance and there is therefore no indication why there was a comparative surge in sales in the first half of 2016. This in turn throws into question the comprehensiveness of the data on offer: the Royalty Window can tell me that my earnings were above average in one period but cannot tell me why.

After mechanical royalties, performance royalties are the second most lucrative source of income for me. Again, as performing rights can derive from streaming, it is not clear from what source or sources these royalties accrue, although the (depressing) truth is likely to be that, for a whole six months, hardly any radio station anywhere played one of my songs (still the most lucrative source of performing royalties). Here again though, UMPG play no part in securing radio plays for the copyrights it owns; as in the case of sales these are chance affairs and they are happy to collect their share of the royalties so generated. In turn, that 'share' is not inconsiderable. To return to the original music publishing contract:

> [*clause*] 5.01 We shall pay to you the following royalties in respect of the works:
> b. (Sixty Five percent) of gross income in respect of the mechanical reproduction of the works save that in respect of income arising from the mechanical reproduction in the United Kingdom the figure shall [*sic*] 75% (Seventy Five percent).

UMPG 'earns' 0.35 of my one penny from Brazil for very little effort. And this lack of effort is reproduced across the board. Royalty payments show no evidence that the company has secured any 'covers' of songs I have written or any 'syncs' of songs of mine that have been recorded, yet it is covers and 'syncs' that are so much part of the new found, and increasing and intensifying, industrial centrality of music publishers.

The horns of a dilemma

The synchronization of music with moving image has long been a lucrative area for music publishers, from the first 'talking picture' onwards. What has intensified and foregrounded sync is a combination of factors, driven by digitization. David Yoffie (1997) was the first to engage with the then barely emergent phenomenon and Henry Jenkins (2006) (among others) developed this exploration. Essentially, as memory capacity, processor speeds and Internet bandwidth grew and became independent from landline connections, it became increasingly easy to stream sound and moving image to smaller and smaller devices. One of the areas to exploit this phenomenon was digital gaming (Donnelly 2014; Collins 2008a, 2008b, 2013).

Alongside the rise of gaming, there has also been a proliferation in television channels. This has intensified the demand for incidental and featured music and has increased exponentially the space for advertising and branding (Jackson et al. 2013), with the latter's increasing reliance on a distinctive music soundtrack generalizable across virtual and real spaces (Meier 2017: 9). When all of this is coupled with the commonality of user-generated audio-visual (AV) content (Wyrwoll 2014), the significance of YouTube as a 'freemium' streaming service (Vernallis 2013), the economic support offered to 'bloggers' by the carrying of 'sidebar' ads (increasingly AV 'pop ups'), and the rise of online television and film providers (some of whom, Netflix as an example, now make their own content [Jenner 2014]), then there should be little wonder that, just so long as they are collectable, this is a bumper time for harvesting sync royalties. Even so, this is not a 'bumper' time for me as a songwriter; my royalty payments proceed inexorably downwards as the data (the 'numbers', courtesy of the Royalty Window) show more graphically than ever before.

The blunt truth is that no one is 'working' my copyrights, yet, when challenged on the general point of under-utilization of their massive catalogue, Guy Moot, Managing Director of Sony/ATV denied this vehemently:

> Question: Your independent competitors would say that you have too many copyrights to give them all the attention they deserve. What is your response?
>
> [W]e have a huge resource. We've got 15 people working on synchronisation [...] we're fully staffed up to deal with the amount of copyrights we've got [...]. We're very focused on the catalogues we have and we staff accordingly.
>
> (Sutherland 2016: 11–12)

There is no way of knowing how many copyrights each of these fifteen employees are responsible for and what the division of labour is between those who work new copyrights and those who work back catalogue, but there is an air of defensiveness in Moot's comment that is complemented by the hollowness in the further comment of Warner-Chappell Managing Director Mike Smith, '[t]here's a real drive to make sure you're looking after your writers 150%' (Sutherland 2017: 10). What seems apparent is that the writers who are looked after '150%' are those who have (almost literally) 'track records' of hits, whether in the form of sales of their own works, or as covers, or as syncs placed in games, television programmes, film soundtracks or in AV branding exercises.

Syncs are alluring because not only can a 'one-off' sync be lucrative, some syncs can go on earning sometimes for decades; consider 'Mad World', written by Roland Orzabal (of Tears for Fears) and sung by Gary Jules. Jules' version was used on the soundtrack of the film *Donnie Darko* in 2001. Subsequently, this version alone has appeared in five further films and in fifteen television programmes, in an unknown number of television ads (notably in the United Kingdom for Lloyd's Bank in 2016) and it also topped the iTunes chart in 2006 as a result of featuring in, as well as lending its name to, the first iteration of the video game *Mad World*. If we added in the number of times the Tears for Fears original has featured in such contexts, as well as further cover versions (including those by Tiesto and by Akon featuring Eminem), then this one song by Orzabal (written as a 19-year-old in 1982) is a 'pension' in its own right (and Tears for Fears had at least two bigger hits than this). In all of this we cannot know who was active in securing the uses of the song and/or recording, but we can be sure that the rights owner would drive the deal in each case.

The dilemma facing a songwriter such as myself is that, on the one hand, a hit song (or preferably songs) can be, exactly, a pension and in increasingly uncertain economic times a pension is an attractive 'prize'. The flip-side of such venality is that the treatment of the song (or a specific recording) can fail to respect the original, to the extent that it can be positively offensive to its integrity. Take for example the use, in October 2017, of Stephen Sondheim's 'Send in the Clowns' by the carmaker, Audi. Sondheim's original elucidates the heartbreak of the female lead, Desiree, in his musical *A Little Night Music*. In the Audi version, the plaintive even heart-rending piece becomes an aggressive assertion of 'vorsprung durch technik', one in which the steely power of the automobile reflects not just the driver's superior driving skills, as against those of other drivers represented as 'clowns' (hence the soundtrack, the 'sync'), but, by implication, his or her superior taste, sensibility and, more importantly still, income and status. Sondheim earns from this sync (as he does from over 900 cover versions of the song) but earning is surely not everything in the face of a use of a copyright that does such violence to the original. A violence, it must be remarked, that goes entirely unregistered by one of the advert's 'music supervisors', Ayla Owen (of The Most Radicalist Black Sheep Music), who commented to *Music Week* that '[t]he current Audi music vibe is all about classic songs reinterpreted with a progressive twist, and Clowns is a brilliant example of this approach' (Homewood 2017: 12).

The same old song

The key set of numbers missing from the UMPG's Royalty Window is the total of the units of energy used by the staff of UMPG in seeking covers and syncs of the songs I wrote and they own. These units of energy could be expressed both as calories (used up in searching for opportunities) and joules (generated in pushing against the competition to secure those opportunities). A persuasive counter-argument might be that, just because such 'numbers' do not appear in my statement does not mean that such energy has not been expended. All those songs may have been listened to and rejected or else they may all have been listened to and even now are 'on hold' waiting for exactly the best and most apposite opportunity to deploy them. A counter-counter-argument would be that I have no evidence that this work has taken place (in the sense there are never any meetings with, or correspondence with, my 'partners'). If, perhaps, I truly was a 'client' of theirs, this would be a very bad example indeed of customer relations.

What surprises me about this evident lack of effort and demonstrable lack of discussion is that so much energy would seem to have been expended to find a penny in Brazil. More puzzling still, the securing of covers and syncs is very much in the interest of UMPG. If we return to the originating contractual assignment we find the following:

> [*clause*] 5. 01 We shall pay to you the following royalties
> (e) 65% (Sixty Five percent) of gross income in respect of any synchronisation licences granted by us or our licensees.
> (f) [W]e shall pay you fifty percent (50%) of such sums where such income is attributable to Cover Recordings.

What this means is that UMPG earn 35 per cent of any sync they secure, and an extremely generous 50 per cent of the royalty produced by a cover version. Somehow, though, these appear to be insufficient incentives in and of themselves to work the catalogue; instead, as revenues from streaming and from AV usages of music go on increasing, there is an air of complacency about this inactivity wherein merely owning rights is enough. It is this complacency that goes to the heart of the matter.

While it is indeed the case, in Meier's quoting of IFPI figures and Sutherland quoting Renzer's anticipation of (implicitly sustainable) 'worldwide success', that music publishing is in an expansive phase, this expansiveness conceals (from a songwriter's perspective) a great deal of frustrating and familiar passivity on the part of individual music publishers.

It now seems a long time since illegal file-sharing began to disrupt the certainties of the business model of the recording industry. Why the disruption was so severe was that the three principal music industries – recording, live performance and music publishing – all had vested interests in the creation of recording stars; stars who, in turn, were then largely expected to write their own material. Because of this expectation, there had become far less for music publishers to do than they had been used to in the days of the Tin Pan Alley 'song-pluggers'. So it was they became for many decades passive owners of copyrights and passive collectors of royalty payments generated by the efforts of the promotions and sales departments of the major record companies. Now that the days of 'song-plugging' appear to have returned, a combination of ingrained passivity and deep mine-shafts full of copyrights means that, for the most part, those copyrights remain as dead as the last air on which the strains of their sounds were carried.

Conclusion

To find a penny in Brazil seems to take effort, but perhaps it does not, perhaps the money simply flowed to London from Rio or Sao Paulo by digital means, triggered by the International Standard Recording Code (ISRC) embedded in the streamed or synced track. Certainly, it is someone's job to fit the payment to the beneficiary, but as the publishers Kobalt are demonstrating, royalty distribution is likely to become a process of instant triggering and receipt. Frith was right to argue that 'the music industry is [...] a rights industry'. Despite this, as well as being overdue and prescient, there is still something misleading about his observation. 'Industry' is an active term, it is concerted effort towards the production of an outcome, and the problem with music publishing as an example of 'the music industry' at work is that the effort of the songwriter is made exchangeable in return for the promise of royalty payments but once copyrights have been assigned, the effort of the songwriter has for too long ended there. Clearly, in digital times, there are now far more ways for songwriters to be proactive in terms of garnering 'plays' for their work, but while signed to a music publisher, is the songwriter working for themselves or for the publisher?

I signed my first music publishing contract a long time ago. Perhaps the key, and fatal, clause in that contract was this one:

> [*clause*] 7 [...] Without prejudice to the generality of the foregoing, the interest present, future or contingent hereby assigned includes the following sole and exclusive rights.

This is a stark and definitive slamming of the door on cooperation. From that fateful day onwards the songs I wrote were condemned to be ignored; condemned to generate money without effort for any publisher to whom they were (and will in the future be) assigned. That signing was, in effect, the end of *my* music industry and yet, all these years later, I am willing and able to promote the songs I wrote. The stark reality is, though, that the disincentive is a profound one, because those songs are not, in fact, 'mine'; they are, as the clause indicates, (now) the 'sole and exclusive' property of UMPG.

Music publishing does not need to be this way; even the 'majors' appear to have relinquished 'in perpetuity' clauses and there are examples of new companies (such as Sentric) who offer an 'easy in, easy out' assignment of copyright (a period of notice of one month to remove copyrights from them). All of this is too late for me, although a subsequent music publishing contract I signed with EMI contained a ten-year 'reversion' clause, which shows that, even years ago, it was possible to evade a demand for 'in perpetuity' assignment if not exclusivity:

> [*clause*] 7. SPECIAL and ADDITIONAL CLAUSES
> Term of the agreement: September 1st 1993, 1993 – August 31st, 2003.

Even so, while this knowledge is comforting, it is so only to a limited extent. Whether in the UMPG case, or the case of the EMI contract, there is still no obligation on the part of the music publisher to do anything with the copyrights assigned to them, beyond the collection and transfer of royalties subject to their high levels of commission. The creation of a Royalty Window comes a long time after the event, and 'the event' has largely been a catastrophic one for me. What needed to be spelled out, not just in my publishing contracts but in all publishing contracts, is a commitment from the publisher that they will 'use or lose' the titles they are assigned. This has been one of the six key demands of FAC since its formation in 2009: '[c]opyright owners to be obliged to follow a "use it or lose it" approach to the copyrights they control' (FAC 2019).

What is interesting about FAC is that two other of its six core demands also coincide with this unpacking of my responses to having earned a penny in Brazil: 'An agreement by the music industry that artists should receive fair compensation whenever their business partners receive an economic return from the exploitation of the artists' work'; 'All transfers of copyright should be by license rather than by assignment' (FAC 2019). It is ironic that my first, hastily, and poorly drafted, music publishing contract should have referred to the assignees as 'licensees' when they were not because, if BG had been licensees, those first 50 songs would now not be in the perpetual possession of UMPG. On the other hand, if 'fair compensation' was an industry standard then I may have earned more from being 'signed' to them for so many years.

In summary, the music industry has always been a 'rights industry', it is just that this was less apparent when the recording industry dazzled us with the stars it made. The years of painful transition from a recording dominated music industry seem at last to have revealed the defining truth that the 'numbers' that count are those that flow from rights ownership. In turn, these can only be made to tell their full story when one looks beyond the view available from the Royalty Window.

NOTE

1. It is interesting and notable that even in 2019, the MPA do not identify alternatives (such as the songwriter/composer limiting by licence the use of their rights) to this 'all or nothing' practice of assignment.

REFERENCES

Bagehot, Richard and Kanaar, Nicholas (1998), *Music Business Agreements,* London: Sweet & Maxwell.

Collins, Karen (2008a), *From Pac-Man to Pop Music: Interactive Audio in Games and New Media*, Basingstoke: Ashgate.

——— (2008b), *Game Sound: An Introduction to the History, Theory, and Practice of Video Game Music and Sound Design*, Boston: MIT Press.

——— (2013), *Playing with Sound: A Theory of Interacting with Sound and Music in Video Games*, Boston: MIT Press.

Donnelly, Kevin (2014), *Music In Video Games: Studying Play*, Routledge: London.

Featured Artists Coalition (FAC) (2019), 'About', *FAC*, https://www.thefac.org/. Accessed 22 March 2019.

Frith, Simon (2000), 'Music industry research: Where now? Where next? Notes from Britain', *Popular Music,* 19:3, pp. 387–93.

Garfield, Simon (1986), *Expensive Habits: The Dark Side of the Music Industry*, London: Faber and Faber.

Gumble, Daniel (2017), 'Spirit in the sky: "Highly selective" approach delivers Storming Q1 for Spirit B-Unique', *B-Unique*, 3 April, p. 2.

Harrison, Ann (2017), *Music: The Business*, 7th ed., Virgin: London.

Homewood, Ben (2017), 'Audi/Faultline & Lisa Hannigan', *Music Week*, 13 November, p. 12.

Jackson, Daniel, Jankovich, Richard and Sheinkop, Eric (2013), *Hit Brands: How Music Builds Value for the World's Smartest Brands*, London: Palgrave-MacMillan.

Jenkins, Henry (2006), *Convergence Culture: Where Old and New Media Collide*, New York: NYU Press.

Jenner, Mareike (2014), 'Is this TVIV? On Netflix, TVIII and binge-watching', *New Media and Society,* 18:2, pp. 257–73.

Keightley, Keir (2010), 'Taking popular music (and Tin Pan Alley and jazz) seriously', *Journal of Popular Music Studies*, 22:1, pp. 90–97.

Legrand, Emmanuel (2016), 'Indie publishers find faith in the future', *Music Week*, 28 March, p. 14.

McIntyre, Hugh (2017), 'Spotify's most popular artists of 2017: Ed Sheeran beats Drake for most-streamed artist of the year', *Forbes,* 5 December, https://www.forbes.com/sites/hughmcintyre/2017/12/05/spotifys-most-popular-artists-of-2017-ed-sheeran-drake-and-rihanna-beat-them-all/#15c5b0f25db7. Accessed 22 April 2017.

Meier, Leslie (2017), *Popular Music as Promotion: Music and Branding in the Digital Age,* Polity: Cambridge & Oxford.

Music Publishers Association (2019), 'FAQs: What is music publishing?', *Music Publishers Association*, https://mpaonline.org.uk/faqs/. Accessed 3 April 2019.

Passman, Donald (2015), *All You Need to Know About the Music Business*, 9th ed., New York: Simon & Schuster.

Southall, Brian (2008), *Pop Goes to Court*, London: Omnibus.

Sutherland, Mark (2016), 'Nice guy finishes first', *Music Week,* 5 December, pp. 11–12.

——— (2017), 'The Smith's reunion', *Music Week*, 15 May, p. 10.

Vernallis, Carol (2013), *Unruly Media: YouTube, Music Video, and the New Digital Cinema*, Oxford: Oxford University Press.

Wyrwoll, Claudia (2014), *Social Media: Fundamentals, Models, and Ranking of User-Generated Content*, Wiesbaden: Springer.

Yoffie, David (1997), *Competing in the Age of Digital Convergence*, Boston: Harvard Business School Press.

13

Tokens and Techno-Economic Paradigms: On the Value of Blockchain Technology to the Music Industries

Marcus O'Dair

Blockchain technology, journalists have claimed, could 'completely transform' (Dickson 2017) and indeed 'revolutionize' (Aitken 2016) the music industries. Perhaps because such qualitative claims are easily dismissed as hype, but also due to an ongoing obsession with numbers in the music industries and in 'capitalist realism' more broadly (Fisher 2009), there has been a tendency to attempt to quantify the potential value of this emerging technology. Two trends can be identified. The first is to *underestimate* its value on the grounds that a given project is deploying a 'cryptocurrency' with a low financial value or has raised only a financially insignificant sum. The second trend is to *overestimate* the value of blockchain technology, at least in the short term, due to the rising prices of some cryptocurrencies and an explosion in token sales as a means of raising capital. In both cases, the obsessive focus on numbers has to some extent been a distraction.

It is the argument of this chapter that blockchain technology does indeed have transformative potential for the music industries – for instance by aligning the incentives of multiple stakeholders via tokens, reconciling data silos (that is, isolated islands of data) and automated licensing by means of 'smart contracts'. Yet this value is impossible to quantify at this early stage in what Carlota Perez (2002) refers to as a techno-economic paradigm. It is also suggested that, while the total cryptocurrency market cap is in many respects a distraction, more granular statistics, for instance those relating to pilot projects, *can* be of relevance; the chapter includes analysis of statistics published by Blokur, a start-up deploying blockchain technology to reconcile conflicts in music publishing data.

Cryptocurrencies, blockchains and token sales

Blockchain technology emerged with the cryptocurrency, bitcoin, 'a digital, decentralised, partially anonymous currency, not backed by any government or other legal entity' (Grindberg 2011: 160). Bitcoin is 'a peer-to-peer electronic cash system' (Nakamoto 2008): 'the world's first completely decentralised digital currency' (Brito and Castillo 2016: 1). The price of bitcoin at the time of writing in November 2017 is $7228, although that figure will be out of date the moment it is typed. Indeed, part of the reason it is unhelpful to attempt to quantify the value of blockchain technology through the price of a given cryptocurrency or the total cryptocurrency market cap is because the numbers change so frequently. Bitcoin's price volatility has earned it widespread attention as a speculative asset: original bitcoin users, primarily 'cyberlibertarians' attracted to the cryptocurrency for ideological reasons (Golumbia 2016: 3), have been joined of late by considerable numbers of risk-tolerant investors: in November 2017 it was reported that Coinbase, a cryptocurrency exchange, had just added 100,000 new bitcoin users in a single day (Cheng 2017).

Given the publicity surrounding bitcoin, and the common conflation of bitcoin and blockchain technology, it would be easy to assume that the potential value of blockchains to the music industries is directly related to bitcoin. Artists as diverse as rapper The Game and heavy rock band Mastodon have been accepting the cryptocurrency since 2014; more recently, Björk has also accepted bitcoin payments for her music. Yet bitcoin is, in fact, only of indirect relevance to the potential value of blockchain technology to the music industries. It is better understood as 'the first major blockchain innovation' (Gupta 2017). The second innovation, for Vinay Gupta, was 'the realisation that the underlying technology that operated bitcoin could be separated from the currency and used for all kinds of other interorganisational cooperation' (Gupta 2017). This marked the birth, as an entity distinct from bitcoin, of the blockchain: a particular data structure in which each 'block' not only tells us the value of the previous block but also contains a digest of that value, which allows us to verify that the value has not been changed (Narayanan et al. 2016: 11). A blockchain, then, is 'a type of distributed ledger that is composed of a chain of cryptographically linked "blocks" containing batched transactions' (Hileman and Rauchs 2017: 11).

In the wake of this second innovation, other coins have emerged on top of the bitcoin blockchain. These so-called 'metacoins' introduced the notion of tokenization: the process of digitally representing an existing, off-chain asset on a distributed ledger (Hileman and Rauchs 2017: 11). Entirely new blockchains have emerged too. For Gupta, the third blockchain innovation, primarily associated with etheruem, perhaps the most prominent of these newer blockchains, are 'smart contracts': 'little computer programs [built] directly into blockchain that allowed financial instruments, like loans or bonds, to be represented, rather than only the cash-like tokens of the bitcoin' (Gupta 2017). Rather than contracts in the legal sense, smart contracts can be understood as self-executing software programmes that automatically perform a given function, for instance making a payment when triggered by a given event (Hileman and Rauchs 2017: 11).

Presently, the application of blockchain technology that is attracting the most attention in the music industries and beyond is the token sale, known by some as the initial coin offering or ICO. As Yan Chen explains:

> In an initial coin offering (also known as a token sale), a project team sells its token to the general public for the first time. In some sense, an initial coin offering is simply a Kickstarter-style crowdfunding campaign, which allows the general public to participate in an early-stage project. However, blockchain tokens are usually tradable, while Kickstarter purchases usually are not. By selling tokens to the public across the globe, a project team can raise financial capital to support the development of its project.
>
> (Chen 2018: 7)

As of November 2017, a total of $3.2 billion has been raised via token sales (Coin Schedule 2017). Only 1.2 per cent of these token sales are for start-ups categorized as 'art and music', but that still represents an impressive $39,310,901 (Coin Schedule 2017). Even more remarkable than the sums raised, perhaps, is the speed at which money is raised through token sales: $35 million in 35 seconds, for instance, is not unheard of, even for companies yet to produce a product (Sahdev 2017).

Certainly, these are striking figures. As with the price of bitcoin, however, the headline statistics relating to the sums raised via token sales are to some extent a distraction when assessing the relevance of this technology to the music industries. Care must be taken, for instance, to design tokens that align incentives in the longer term and that have some intrinsic utility: only a quarter (24.9 per cent) of tokens offer governance powers, for instance, and about the same proportion (26.1 per cent) offer a share of profits (Adhami et al. 2017). While some may invest in token sales because they truly believe in a given project, many investors are simply speculators, purchasing tokens in the hope of quickly selling them at a profit (Chen 2018). Designing a successful token is about more than raising money fast; as John Conley (2017) argues, it requires careful consideration of monetary theory, financial economics and game theory.

Blockchain technology may well have transformative potential for the economy at large, but this value is not directly related to cryptocurrency prices or token sales; the more important numbers lie elsewhere. This is true, too, of the potential value of blockchain technology to the music industries.

The high numbers: Claims for the application of blockchain technology in the music industries

Though blockchain technology has been primarily associated with financial services, there are a number of start-ups proposing to deploy the technology in the music industries, even to the extent that there is a danger of 'blockchain fatigue', or 'getting blockchained out' (Dredge 2017a: 1). As Stuart Dredge points out, such fatigue is bizarre, given that this is a nascent technology, although it is perhaps a natural response to the sometimes overwhelming hype. In fact, blockchains cannot be so easily dismissed: use cases, even within the music industries, are already reasonably diverse. As Dredge states, 'there is no such thing as a standard "blockchain music startup" any more than there is an "internet music startup"' (Dredge 2017a: 1):

> Some of these companies are working on Bandcamp-style D2C [Direct to Consumer] platforms for artists, while others are Spotify-style streaming services. Some are trying to crack the age-old industry problem of a global database of rights, while others hope to encode those rights into the music itself, akin (although this can be a controversial point) to a DRM [Digital Rights Management] wrapper. And these are just the ones we have obvious existing non-blockchain examples to compare them to. One of the hopes for blockchain technology is that it will provide the base for a whole bunch of new startups that we can't conceive of yet. Trying to predict them in 2017 is like standing up in 1991 at the dawn of the world wide web and trying to predict Facebook.
>
> (Dredge 2017a: 1–2)

Broadly speaking, music blockchain start-ups can be divided into projects relating to live performance and ticketing (including Viberate, Hello Sugoi, Aventus and Guts) and projects addressing recordings, metadata and licensing (among them Ujo Music, Blokur, Jaak, Mycelia, Dot Blockchain Music and Singular DTV). Incumbents are experimenting with the technology too: in April 2017, it was announced that Spotify had acquired a blockchain start-up, Mediachain, while PRS for Music announced a blockchain initiative with the Society of Authors, Composers and Publishers of Music (SACEM) and the American Society of Composers, Authors and Publishers (ASCAP) in the same month (Music Business Worldwide 2017). Token sales, the most recent subject of attention, have achieved celebrity endorsement from the likes of DJ Khaled and The Game. Blockchain technology has become a standard topic at music conferences, and the subject has been covered with some excitement by online media: blockchain technology, it is claimed, could 'revolutionise music streaming' (Sharma 2017), 'completely transform the music industry' (Dickson 2017) and 'revolutionise the music industry' (Aitken 2016).

Perhaps because such qualitative claims are easily dismissed as hype, there has been a fixation, of late, on statistics. Imogen Heap's 'Tiny Human', released in collaboration with Ujo Music in 2015, the first instance of musicians receiving automatic payments for their contribution to a recording via smart contracts, has been dismissed on numerical grounds. David Gerard (2017), for instance, points out that the track sold only 222 copies, raising the equivalent, at the time, of about $133 in ether (the 'cryptofuel' used on the ethereum blockchain). In fact, the value of ether has subsequently increased dramatically: that same quantity of ether is, in November 2017, worth approximately $45,000. More importantly, the amount raised for 'Tiny Human' was never the point: the track served as a proof of concept (Heap 2017). It is precisely such pilot projects that are needed at this early stage in the deployment of blockchain technology. The sums raised are almost irrelevant. Similarly dismissive comments have been made about the decision to reward those who purchased Björk's 2017 album *Utopia* with a cryptocurrency named audiocoin. As of November 2017, one audiocoin is worth $0.002. To dismiss this project on the grounds that audiocoins have a low financial value, however, is to again miss the point. If the issuing of audiocoins is significant for Björk, it is because of the value gained over time from those fans who utilize these tokens on an ongoing basis. Like 'Tiny Human', it is best understood as an early pilot project.

The dance music artist RAC, who released a token to accompany his 2017 album, *EGO*, and the singer-songwriter Tatiana Moroz, who has issued her own coin, Tatianacoin, are both attempting similar projects. Ujo Music, who are working with RAC, have conceded that they have 'no idea' what they are going to do with the token, 'and nor does RAC himself', but they have suggested that possible options would include backstage access and advance tickets for concerts (Dredge 2017b). Meanwhile, Tatianacoins, which can be collected and sold by fans, are also intended as a means of allowing holders to access VIP experiences, for instance 'to chat directly with Tatiana and other fans, and access multimedia content, VIP experiences, recording studio sessions, private concerts and personalised fan gear' (Coleman 2017). Like 'Tiny Human' and *Utopia*, these are useful experiments, ones to which the financial value of Tatianacoins tokens, fixed at $0.05, is largely irrelevant.

Also of only indirect relevance to the potential value of blockchain technology to the music industries are statistics relating to music token sales, impressive though these undoubtedly are. Aventus apparently raised $18.7 million in ether in just seven minutes (Aventus 2017); Viberate, we are told, raised the equivalent of $10.7 million in four minutes and 42 seconds (Viberate 2017); Singular DTV raised a reported $7.5 million in 15 minutes (Meegan 2016); and Guts, who raised $2.5 million in their pre-sale, are hoping for a further $17 million in their main token sale (Dredge 2017c). It seems likely, however, that a lot of the start-ups funded by token sales will be short-lived, and not only due to regulatory challenges. Many start-ups that have raised funds via token sales have yet to develop a product or service, or even a fully articulated business model; many have also failed to design tokens with intrinsic utility. These companies might state that their tokens are not for speculation, but this is only to ignore, or to pretend to ignore, the simple truth that speculation is at the centre of the token sale explosion, which is driven by risk-tolerant investors purchasing tokens only to quickly sell them on at a profit.

The figures relating to token sales can be misleadingly high, just as the figures relating to the sums raised by Imogen Heap with 'Tiny Human', or the value of audiocoin issued by Björk, can be misleadingly low. Cryptocurrency transactions are inherently transparent, even if the identities of those making the payments may remain opaque (Meiklejohn et al. 2013). Such transparency brings a measure of reliability to the transactions themselves, although we still cannot be certain that initial investors have not purchased pre-sale tokens at a significant discount, with the intention of then selling them to make a quick profit. What are certainly open to question, however, are the additional claims made by some blockchain start-ups. For instance, Viberate state on their website that the value of 'the music industry' is $250 billion; no source or explanation is provided (Viberate 2017). Similarly, Guts, in their white paper, state that 30 per cent of all tickets 'are resold with mark-ups between 30% and 700%', yet they do not cite a source (GET Foundation Team 2017). In addition, Hello Sugoi (2017) state that the live events sector is worth $20 billion, that up to 85–90 per cent of inventory for a given event may be sold on the secondary market and that primary market ticketing is on average 49 per cent lower than secondary ticketing; again, no sources are given. The point is not that these figures are wrong, but simply that readers – and, indeed, potential investors – have no way of knowing how the figures have been calculated. As Ruth Towse states, measuring the size of a given sector of the economy involves first agreeing what constitutes that sector and even this can be controversial (2010: 39); there has, for instance, been a blurring of boundaries between music and other industries (Wikström 2013: 179). For Towse, the second stage in measuring the size of a given sector of the economy involves making calculations using one of three methods, the *income* method, the *expenditure* method or the *output* method, all of which should produce the same result (2010: 41). No start-up in this space has stated that it is using any such methods. Instead, citing figures without sources or methods only adds to the 'Wild West' quality of blockchain technology, linked to its cyberlibertarian roots.

How, then, might we explain this obsession with statistics? Blockchain start-ups might be tempted to present, and even to inflate, figures in order to increase interest in a forthcoming token sale, or to justify a token sale that has already taken place. Yet the obsession extends beyond blockchain start-ups: the music industries have always been obsessed with numbers. Historically, concern has been with chart placings and sales figures; more recently, the focus has been on streaming figures and social media metrics. Then there is the annual *Measuring Music* report issued by UK Music (UK Music 2018). Numbers that remain private, for instance those relating to the algorithms that underlie streaming platforms, are no less coveted. This interest in quantifying consumption is to an extent understandable: publicly listed companies, for instance, need to demonstrate healthy quarterly results. It could also be interpreted as evidence of post-Napster anxiety: the recorded music industry, unable to quite believe that its fortunes are once again moving in the right direction with the growth of streaming, forever seeks reassurance in the statistics. Music, like other creative industries, is also a hit-based business, in which occasional 'hits' offset the more numerous 'misses' (the proportion of hits to misses, of course, is another area of numerical obsession). Counting streams and social media numbers before signing new artists might seem to a record label A&R a sensible way to minimize this risk. Interestingly, as Shuker (2012: 307) points out, social networking sites directly parallel file-sharing: Napster and MySpace both began in June 1999.

The obsession with quantification can also be understood more broadly, however, as illustrative of the bureaucracy that characterizes what Mark Fisher calls 'capitalist realism' (Fisher 2009). This term refers to the sense 'that not only is capitalism the only viable political and economic system, but also that it is now impossible even to *imagine* a coherent alternative' (Fisher 2009: 2, original emphasis). One characteristic of post-Fordism, Fisher argues, is the proliferation of auditing culture, which can be understood as 'a fusion of PR and bureaucracy, because the bureaucratic data is usually intended to fulfill a promotional role' (Fisher 2009: 50). This is as true of blockchain start-ups funded via token sale as it is of corporates striving to satisfy their shareholders. The danger in both cases, he suggests, is that 'work becomes geared towards the generation and massaging of representations rather than to the official goals of the work itself' (Fisher 2009: 42). Symbols of achievement are more valued than the achievement; targets become ends in themselves. To reduce music to its economic value is, of course, to neglect its social and cultural value. Yet those values, harder to quantify, are neglected by the bureaucracy and metrics of capitalist realism.

Disruption: Timelines and techno-economic paradigms

Blockchain is a 'disruptive' technology, in the sense identified by Joseph Bower and Clayton Christensen (1995); that is, it can be understood as the latest wave of renewal in the sea of capitalism. The enduring contribution of Bower and

Christensen has been to show that disruptive technologies often fare worse than sustaining technologies in the short-term, at least by traditional measures, but that such apparently poor performance is misleading; what is significant is the performance trajectory of the disruptive technology compared with that of the market. This is why the technical limitations blockchain technology has at present are not a reason to write off the whole technology. Indeed, Klaus Schwab (2016) regards blockchains, alongside other technologies including artificial intelligence, as part of the 'fourth industrial revolution'. Gupta (2017), Melanie Swan (2015), William Mougayar (2016) and Phil Godsiff (2016) also portray blockchains in revolutionary terms.

There are two important caveats. The first is that blockchains are immature: significant technological barriers to adoption remain, for instance in terms of scalability. The second caveat is that there are also political, economic and legal barriers to adoption that have nothing directly to do with the technology. Even assuming that the scalability issues are overcome, the technology may never be adopted at scale. If adoption does occur, it will not occur overnight. Indeed, even some of those who see blockchain as a profoundly important – even foundational – technology also expect its adoption to be slow. Marco Iansiti and Karim Lakhani, for instance, argue that blockchains have the potential to profoundly change our economic and social system, 'but while the impact will be enormous, it will take decades for blockchain to seep into our economic and social infrastructures' (Iansiti and Lakhani 2017).

It is useful at this point to refer to the landmark work by Perez (2002) on the relationship between financial capital and new technologies. Those rushing to invest in token sales are not traditional venture capitalists, as they are in Perez's model. Nevertheless, her work provides a welcome sense of historical perspective. For Perez:

> A *technological revolution* can be defined as a powerful and highly visible cluster of new and dynamic technologies, products and industries, capable of bringing about an upheaval in the whole fabric of the economy and of propelling a long-term upsurge of development [...]. The irruption of such significant clusters of innovative industries in a short period of time would certainly be enough reason to label them 'technological revolutions'. Yet what warrants the title for the present purposes is that each of those sets of technological breakthroughs spreads far beyond the confines of the industries and sectors where they originally developed. Each provides a set of interrelated generic technologies and organizational principles that allows and fosters a quantum leap in potential productivity for practically all economic activities.
>
> (2002: 8)

Perez identifies five such technological revolutions in 200 years: the Industrial Revolution (c. 1771), the 'age of steam and railways' (c. 1829), the 'age of steel, electricity and heavy engineering' (c. 1875), the 'age of oil, the automobile and mass production' (c. 1908) and the 'age of information and telecommunications' (c. 1971). If a technological revolution occurs approximately every 50 years, the next one is about due, and blockchains, perhaps alongside artificial intelligence/machine learning and virtual/augmented reality, are one of the 'new and dynamic technologies' that could usher it in.

Viewed through Perez's framework, the period of explosive growth that blockchain technology is currently experiencing will inevitably be followed by a crash as early expectations are disappointed. We can then expect a second wave of stable, steady growth, quite different to the turbulence of the initial phase, as the new technology becomes accepted. This will be a period of prosperity and relative harmony. As the technology matures, diminishing returns will set in. Finally, as the next generation of radical technologies emerges, the cycle begins again. Such a framework provides a useful sense of perspective, and a reason for even those who consider blockchain a potentially transformative technology to be cautious of the speculative bubble of bitcoin and token sales: this is simply the tumult characteristic of what Perez calls the 'installation period', a period she divides into 'irruption' and 'frenzy' (2002: 47). In terms of blockchain technology, we may currently be in the irruption phase, characterized by 'revolutionary breakthroughs and multiple trial and error applications', as well as the co-existence of the new techno-economic paradigm with the previous one (2002: 91). We can expect a crash before we reach a period of steady growth characteristic of the 'deployment period' (2002: 36–37).

By conceptualizing blockchains as a disruptive, and potentially transformative technology, the current technological limitations – like the small amounts of money (initially) raised by Imogen Heap's 'Tiny Human' experiment and the low financial value of the audiocoin associated with Björk's *Utopia* album – seem less significant. Many previous disruptive technologies ostensibly underperformed before going on to cause creative destruction, and even to pave the way for new techno-economic paradigms. This is not to proselytize, but it is to suggest that the question we tend to ask of blockchain technology – will it be adopted in the music industries? – is wrong. The interesting question, in fact, is this: if it is adopted, will it be for good or ill?

Playing the numbers: The true value of blockchain technology to the music industries

It was suggested earlier in this chapter that some statistics relating to the value of blockchain technology to the music industries are open to question. How, then, might we understand the potential value of this technology? To begin by considering the economy as a whole, Don Tapscott and Alex Tapscott state that blockchain technology will 'upend business models and disrupt industries'; and that it 'is pushing us to challenge how we have structured society, defined value and rewarded participation' (2017: 5). Swan predicts that blockchain technology 'could become the seamless embedded economic layer the Web has never had, serving as the technological underlay for payments, decentralised exchange, token earning and spending, digital asset invocation and transfer, and smart contract issuance and execution' (2015: vii). The technology is certainly unique in giving network participants the ability to independently verify the integrity of the shared database without having to rely on a trusted third party (Hileman and Rauchs 2017: 13). As I argue above, it does seem reasonable, then, to regard blockchain technology as at least potentially transformative.

In the specific context of the music industries, I have stated elsewhere (O'Dair et al. 2016; O'Dair and Beaven 2017; O'Dair 2017) that blockchains could transform the music industries in a number of ways: speeding up royalty payments; making it easier for artists and managers to audit accounts; providing access to alternative sources of capital; replacing data silos with a networked database of music copyright information; securely linking digital works to associated metadata; and easing the process of licensing content. These are significant changes. It is not easy, however, to put a financial value on them. This is in part because the technology is still nascent: as Mougayar acknowledges, blockchains may be revolutionary but 'we are in the early stages of understanding the movement, distribution and creation of "value" outside of the traditional norms of currency, commodity and property as the main vehicles for value transfer and appreciation' (2016: 157). Similarly, Adam Greenfield argues that, while blockchain technology could allow us 'to organise ourselves in entirely new ways', thereby presenting 'profound implications for the way we assemble ourselves into groups', it is still 'far from clear' what this might mean for the political economy of everyday life (2017: 143–44). It is also difficult to quantify the potential value of blockchain technology because a number of different business models have been identified, including commercial application development, consulting, freemium, maintenance fees, network participation fees and premium support packages, and there remains a 'significant degree of uncertainty' as to which revenue models will prove most effective (Hileman and Rauchs 2017: 44–45). Within the creative industries, some are looking at the potential for limited digital editions, others at new payment models, and still others at monetizing data (O'Dwyer 2017). There is no single 'blockchain model'.

Above all, it is difficult to quantify the potential value of blockchain technology because, as Perez states, the wealth-creating potential of a given technological revolution is only realized when accompanied by an adequate socio-economic framework (2002: xviii). It is vital to resist technological determinism; what blockchains could do and what they will do are two very different conversations. As argued above, factors that are not directly related to the technology, for instance regulatory uncertainty (Hileman and Rauchs 2017: 67) and concerns with data protection laws (Hileman and Rauchs 2017: 99), present significant barriers to adoption. In terms of the application of blockchain technology in the music industries specifically, there is the 'garbage in, garbage out' problem: since music, unlike bitcoin, is not native to the blockchain, a trusted third party may still be required to determine whether or not data is accurate (Hileman and Rauchs 2017: 18). The technology itself can only ever be part of the solution and it cannot be understood in isolation. While blockchains may facilitate disintermediation, for instance, Andrew McAfee and Erik Brynjolfsson point out that there may be sound economic reasons for intermediaries to remain, relating to transaction cost economics and incomplete contracts (2017: 309–16). Whatever the most ardent blockchain technology enthusiasts might claim for so-called smart contracts, they argue that 'complete contracts', so comprehensive as to adjudicate every conceivable future decision, are simply not possible (McAfee and Brynjolfsson 2017: 315). According to Richard Caves (2000), incomplete contracts are particularly characteristic of the creative industries, given the unusual degree of uncertainty surrounding the production and consumption of creative products. Further, it should not be assumed that disintermediation is even desirable. Technological determinists opining on how blockchains can revolutionize the music industries, for instance, all too often neglect the fact that a move away from collective licensing is as likely to reduce compensation as much as it is to increase it. Collection and distribution of royalties might appear precisely the kind of 'friction' that should be removed if possible – but collective bargaining and licensing could be lost in the same process of disintermediation, and collective bargaining can lead to higher income for the majority.

Crunching numbers: Blokur case study

It is impossible to easily quantify the potential impact of blockchain technology for the music industries overall. This is not to suggest, however, that no figures are of interest. While the headline figures can be misleading, more fine-grained figures, for instance relating to pilot studies, can be illuminating. In this section, I examine one such study, conducted by a start-up named Blokur – interestingly, not one funded by token sale. Blokur was founded by Phil Barry, who, in his previous position leading the Ujo Music team, was largely responsible for Imogen Heap's 'Tiny

Human' release. Blokur are specifically concerned with music publishing data; to quote from their website, 'Blokur reduces costs and increases revenue for music publishers and CMOs [collective management organizations] through automation and better data, enabled by blockchain technology and machine learning' (Blokur 2017). Unlike a number of start-ups in this space, Blokur do make qualitative claims, and two in particular are given prominence on their site. The first is that 'our tech automatically surfaces conflicts in rights data and resolves 70% without human intervention' (Blokur 2017). The second claim on the Blokur website might sound slightly less impressive, although the financial consequences, especially for a large publisher, could be significant. It reads as follows: '[b]etter data = more revenue. Our music publisher clients experience a 4% increase in ownership shares used by CMOs to pay royalties' (Blokur 2017). There is no information on the Blokur site about how these figures have been calculated. In order to assess the company's claims, I conducted a semi-structured interview with Barry on 7 November 2017. The following information derives from that interview.

What, then, of the first figure on the Blokur website: that their technology 'automatically surfaces conflicts in rights data and resolves 70% without human intervention'? What technology do Blokur use, and how does it identify and resolve conflicts? The process, according to Barry, can be broken into two layers. The first layer concerns the creation of a publicly shared state of current ownership. This is where the (ethereum) blockchain is deployed, as it allows the synchronization point to be shared rather than centralized. As stated on the Blokur website, 'Blokur reconciles different sources of rights data to a single blockchain state' (Blokur 2017). While blockchain technology is critical to identifying conflicts in rights data, however, this is only half the process. Barry explains that there is also a second layer, which concerns reconciling data from multiple sources, for instance from Music Brainz (the so-called 'open music encyclopaedia'), songwriters, publishers and societies. Significantly, this layer utilizes an algorithm, rather than blockchain technology: to return to the Blokur mission statement, the company is 'enabled by blockchain technology and machine learning' (Blokur 2017). The Blokur website also states that their algorithm 'resolves data conflicts automatically' (Blokur 2017).

The claim that Blokur can resolve 70 per cent of conflicts without human intervention, Barry explains, derives from a pilot project. For commercial reasons, he is unable to identify the main publisher with whom Blokur worked, but he describes it as one of the five largest in the world. Reportedly, the pilot project also involved three collection societies (again unnamed). The reliability of Blokur's pilot could be called into question if the sample size was too small, but Barry states that the project focused on approximately 20,000 songs, and that, due to the involvement of the three societies as well as the publisher, those 20,000 songs constituted a total of approximately 70,000 data points. From this information, we can begin to calculate the approximate number of tracks represented by that 70 per cent figure. Strikingly, Barry states that some degree of data conflict could be identified for every single song in the pilot study, although in many cases this was simply missing data (a writer's collecting society, for instance, might not have been listed). Barry's team concentrated on what he calls 'commercially significant' conflicts: those for which either the list of stakeholders, or the allocation of shares between those stakeholders, differed between one database and another. Such conflicts, Barry states, were identified in 65 per cent of cases. (Significantly, Barry also suggests that this figure might be higher for other publishers, given the size and good reputation of the one with whom he worked, and the relatively high quality of the societies involved.) In citing a figure of 70 per cent, then, Blokur are referring to 70 per cent of the 65 per cent of songs for which a commercially significant conflict was identified. This works out at 45.5 per cent, or approximately 9100 songs out of a total of approximately 20,000. This seems a significant proportion, as well as a significant sample.

What of the second figure on the company website: that Blokur's music publisher clients experience a four per cent increase in ownership shares used by CMOs to pay royalties? According to Barry, Blokur reached this figure by assessing the publisher's total share of the 20,000 songs both before and after the reconciliation process. In carrying out this process, Blokur took account of both mechanical rights and performing rights. Across these two royalties, Barry states, the average increase in the share owned by the publisher, compared to the share allocated to the publisher by the societies, was four per cent. Again, given the size of the sample, this is a reasonably reliable figure and potentially represents a significant increase in revenue for the publisher, although not one we can quantify based on the information available.

Barry acknowledges that Blokur's solution is far from perfect: there remains the issue of the 30 per cent of catalogue for which rights conflicts are not reconciled automatically by their technology. This is Blokur's current focus. The pilot study does, however, help us to begin to understand both the potential, and possible challenges, of applying blockchain technology in the music industries, by concentrating on specific, pilot study statistics rather than broader headline figures.

Conclusion

If we accept that blockchains are a disruptive technology then the bold claims made for the technology may be justifiable in the longer term, even if such claims tend to neglect both current technological limitations and broader political, economic and legal barriers to adoption. Yet the superficially exciting headline statistics (for instance, the value of a particular cryptocurrency, or the amount raised in a token sale) are not particularly meaningful. If blockchain, along with other 'fourth industrial revolution' technologies, represents a technological revolution, we are still very early in the 'installation period'. Jeremy Silver (2016) predicts that mainstream adoption of blockchain technology by the music industries, for instance, might take ten or fifteen years. According to Perez, we can expect a crash before we reach the steady growth of the 'deployment period'; 'economic euphoria' is likely to be followed by a collapse in confidence (2002: xvii). Media pundits have made comparisons to the 'tulip mania' of the 1630s and the excitement around token sales (Innanen 2017), and the price of certain cryptocurrencies certainly has the appearance of a speculative bubble. Like all bubbles, it is in danger of bursting, not least due to regulatory uncertainty: in America, the Securities and Exchange Commission recently warned investors against investing in so-called ICOs, while China has reportedly banned them altogether (Adhami et al. 2017).

Even if and when the speculative bubble bursts it is unlikely to mark the end for blockchain technology: by applying Perez's model we can predict not only a crash but also a subsequent period of steadier growth. The fact that we are so early in the cycle does mean, however, that it is not possible to easily quantify the value of the technology at this frenzied early stage. We should not, then, dismiss Björk's issuing of audiocoins, or Imogen Heap's 'Tiny Human' experiment, simply because of the relatively small amounts of cryptocurrency involved, any more than we should celebrate the token sale as a new source of capital for artists and music start-ups simply because the sums raised in a short period have been significant. The truly important question is what value the technology can create in the longer term, and that, at present, is unquantifiable - despite the capitalist realist obsession with attempting to measure forms of labour that are inherently resistant to quantification. What we can measure are pilot studies, for instance the one carried out by Blokur. Part of the value of this chapter, it is hoped, lies in shedding light on such pilots and on the methodologies that underpin their results.

REFERENCES

Adhami, Saman, Giudici, Giancarlo and Martinazzi, Stefano (2017), 'Why do businesses go crypto? An empirical analysis of initial coin offerings', *Social Science Research Network*, 3 October, https://ssrn.com/abstract=3046209. Accessed 10 November 2017.

Aitken, Roger (2016), 'MUSE: Leveraging blockchain technology to revolutionize music industry', *Forbes*, 23 January, https://www.forbes.com/sites/rogeraitken/2016/01/23/muse-leveraging-blockchain-technology-to-revolutionize-music-industry/#75b18e012418. Accessed 10 November 2017.

Aventus (2017), 'Thanks and thoughts post token sale', 8 September, https://blog.aventus.io/thanks-and-thoughts-post-token-sale-bedee3ed847c. Accessed 3 November 2017.

Blokur (2017), 'Homepage', http://www.blokur.com. Accessed 10 November 2017.

Brito, Jerry and Castillo, Andrea (2016), *Bitcoin a Primer for Policy Makers*, 2 ed., Mercatus Center: George Mason University.

Bower, Joseph and Christensen, Clayton (1995), 'Disruptive technologies: Catching the wave', *Harvard Business Review*, January–February, https://hbr.org/1995/01/disruptive-technologies-catching-the-wave. Accessed 10 November 2017.

Caves, Richard (2000), *Creative Industries: Contracts Between Art and Commerce*, Cambridge, MA and London: Harvard University Press.

Chen, Yan (2018), 'Blockchain tokens and the potential democratization of entrepreneurship and innovation', *Business Horizons*, 61:4, pp. 267–75, Stevens Institute of Technology School of Business Research Paper, https://ssrn.com/abstract=3059150. Accessed 10 November 2017.

Cheng, Evelyn (2017), 'Largest US Bitcoin exchange added 100,000 customers in one day after Futures announcement', *CNBC*, 3 November, https://www.cnbc.com/2017/11/03/coinbase-adds-100000-users-after-cme-announces-bitcoin-futures-plans.html. Accessed 10 November 2017.

Coin Schedule (2017), 'Crypto token sales market statistics', 10 November, https://www.coinschedule.com/stats.php. Accessed 10 November 2017 [no longer available].

Coleman, Lester (2017), 'Musician & Bitcoin enthusiast Tatiana Moroz reintroduces Tatianacoin', *Cryptocoin News*, 12 February, https://www.cryptocoinsnews.com/musician-bitcoin-enthusiast-tatiana-moroz-reintroduces-tatianacoin/. Accessed 10 November 2017.

Conley, John (2017), 'Blockchain and the economics of crypto-tokens and initial coin offerings', working paper, Nashville, Vanderbilt University Department of Economics Working Paper Series, http://www.accessecon.com/Pubs/VUECON/VUECON-17-00008.pdf. Accessed 10 November 2017.

Dickson, Ben (2017), 'Blockchain could completely transform the music industry', *Venture Beat,* 7 January, https://venturebeat.com/2017/01/07/blockchain-could-completely-transform-the-music-industry/. Accessed 10 November 2017.

Dredge, Stuart (2017a), 'Block'n'roll: The new kids on the blockchain', *Music Ally*, 407, pp. 1–15.

——— (2017b), 'Ujo music on blockchain: "It's such an uphill battle with existing companies"', *Music Ally*, 4 August, http://musically.com/2017/08/04/ujo-music-blockchain-uphill-battle-existing-companies/. Accessed 10 November 2017.

——— (2017c), 'Blockchain startup Guts Tickets raises $2.5m (so far) from ICO', *Music Ally*, 31 October, http://musically.com/2017/10/31/blockchain-startup-guts-tickets-raises-2-5m-far-ico/. Accessed 10 November 2017.

Fisher, Mark (2009), *Capitalist Realism: Is There No Alternative?*, Winchester: Zero Books.

Gerard, David (2017), *Attack of the 50-Foot Blockchain: Bitcoin, Blockchain, Ethereum and Smart Contracts*, Scotts Valley: CreateSpace.

GET Foundation Team (2017), *Guaranteed Entrance Token*, white paper, GUTS Tickets, Amsterdam, https://guts.tickets/files/GET-Whitepaper-GUTS-Tickets-latest.pdf. Accessed 10 November 2017.

Godsiff, Phil (2016), 'Disruptive potential', in M. Walport (ed.), *Distributed Ledger Technology: Beyond Blockchain*, London: Government Office for Science, https://assets.publishing.service.gov.uk/government/uploads/system/uploads/attachment_data/file/492972/gs-16-1-distributed-ledger-technology.pdf. Accessed 24 October 2017.

Golumbia, David (2016), *The Politics of Bitcoin: Software as Right-wing Extremism*, Minneapolis: University of Minnesota Press.

Greenfield, Adam (2017), *Radical Technologies: The Design of Everyday Life*, London and New York: Verso.

Grindberg, Reuben (2011), 'Bitcoin: An innovative alternative digital currency', *Hastings Science & Technology Law Journal*, 4, pp. 160–211.

Gupta, Vinay (2017), 'A brief history of blockchain', *Harvard Business Review*, 28 February, https://hbr.org/2017/02/a-brief-history-of-blockchain. Accessed 10. November 2017.

Heap, Imogen (2017), 'Blockchain could help musicians make money again', *Harvard Business Review*, 5 June, https://hbr.org/2017/06/blockchain-could-help-musicians-make-money-again. Accessed 24 October 2017.

Hello Sugoi (2017), 'Homepage', https://www.hellosugoi.com. Accessed 10 November 2017 [no longer available].

Hileman, Garrick and Rauchs, Michel (2017), 'Global blockchain benchmarking study', *Social Science Research Network*, 21 September, https://papers.ssrn.com/sol3/papers.cfm?abstract_id=3040224. Accessed 10 November 2017.

Iansiti, Marco and Lakhani, Karim (2017), 'The truth about blockchain', *Harvard Business Review*, January–February, https://hbr.org/2017/01/the-truth-about-blockchain. Accessed 10 November 2017.

Innanen, Antti (2017), 'Why today's ICO craze resembles the Tulip mania of the 1630s: And how things could turn out better this time', *Business Insider*, 5 September, http://nordic.businessinsider.com/icos-and-tulips-2017-9/. Accessed 10 November 2017.

McAfee, Andrew and Brynjolfsson, Erik (2017), *Machine Platform Crowd: Harnessing Our Digital Future*, New York and London: Norton.

Meegan, Danielle (2016), 'SingularDTV reaches ICO cap in 15 minutes', *Ethnews*, 3 October, https://www.ethnews.com/singulardtv-reaches-ico-cap-in-15-minutes. Accessed 10 November 2017 [no longer available].

Meiklejohn, Sarah, Pomarole, Majori, Jordan, Grant, Levchenko, Kirill, McCoy, Damon, Voelker, Geoffrey and Savage, Stefan (2013), 'A fistful of Bitcoins: Characterizing payments among men with no names', *Proceedings of the 2013 Internet Measurement Conference*, Barcelona: ACM, pp. 127–40.

Mougayar, William (2016), *The Business Blockchain: Promise, Practice and Application of the Next Internet Technology*, Hoboken: Wiley.

Music Business Worldwide (2017), 'Spotify acquires blockchain firm to build "A more transparent music industry"', *Music Business Worldwide*, 26 April, https://www.musicbusinessworldwide.com/spotify-acquires-blockchain-firm-to-build-a-more-transparent-music-industry/. Accessed 11 November 2017.

Nakamoto, Satoshi (2008), 'Bitcoin: A peer-to-peer electronic cash system', www.bitcoin.org/bitcoin.pdf. Accessed 10 November 2017.

Narayanan, Arvind, Bonneau, Joseph, Felten, Edward, Miller, Andrew and Goldfeder, Steven (2016), *Bitcoin and Cryptocurrency Technologies*, Princeton and Oxford: Princeton University Press.

O'Dair, Marcus (2017), *How Blockchain is Transforming the Creative Industries: Copyright and Rights Management in the Second Era of the Internet*, Toronto: Blockchain Research Institute.

O'Dair, Marcus and Beaven, Zuleika (2017), 'The networked record industry: How blockchain technology could transform the record industry', *Strategic Change*, 26:5, pp. 471–80.

O'Dair, Marcus, Beaven, Zuleika, Neilson, David, Osborne, Richard and Pacifico, Paul (2016), 'Music on the blockchain', Middlesex University, July, https://www.mdx.ac.uk/__data/assets/pdf_file/0026/230696/Music-On-The-Blockchain.pdf. Accessed 10 November 2017.

O'Dwyer, Rachel (2017), 'Does digital culture want to be free? How blockchains are transforming the economy of cultural goods', in R. Catlow, M. Garrett, N. Jones and S. Skinner (eds), *Artists Rethinking the Blockchain*, Liverpool: Liverpool University Press.

Perez, Carlota (2002), *Technological Revolutions and Financial Capital*, Cheltenham: Edward Elgar.

Sahdev, Navroop (2017), 'The tokenization of the economy: ICOs and the implications for cryptoeconomics', *Social Science Research Network*, 23 October, https://ssrn.com/abstract=3057083. Accessed 10 November 2017.

Schwab, Klaus (2016), *The Fourth Industrial Revolution*, London: Portfolio Penguin.

Sharma, Rakesh (2017), 'How blockchain could revolutionise music streaming', *Investopedia*, 14 October, http://www.investopedia.com/news/how-blockchain-could-revolutionize-music-streaming/. Accessed 10 November 2017.

Shuker, Roy (2012), *Popular Music Culture: The Key Concepts*, 3rd ed., London: Routledge.

Silver, Jeremy (2016), 'Blockchain or the Chaingang? Challenges, opportunities and hype: The music industry and blockchain technologies', CREATe working paper, Centre for Copyright and New Business Models in the Creative Economy, University of Glasgow, http://www.create.ac.uk/publications/blockchain-or-the-chaingang-challenges-opportunities-and-hype-the-music-industry-and-blockchain-technologies/. Accessed 11 November 2017.

Swan, Melanie (2015), *Blockchain: Blueprint for a New Economy*, Beijing: O'Reilly.

Tapscott, Don and Tapscott, Alex (2017), *Realising the Potential of Blockchain: A Multistakeholder Approach to the Stewardship of Blockchain and Cryptocurrencies*, Geneva: World Economic Forum, http://www3.weforum.org/docs/WEF_Realizing_Potential_Blockchain.pdf. Accessed 10 November 2017.

Towse, Ruth (2010), *A Textbook of Cultural Economics*, Cambridge: Cambridge University Press.

UK Music (2018), *Measuring Music: 2018 Report*, https://www.ukmusic.org/research/measuring-music-2018/. Accessed 26 January 2019.

Viberate (2017), 'Homepage', https://www.viberate.io/en/. Accessed 03 November 2017.

Wikström, Patrik (2013), *The Music Industry: Music in the Cloud*, 2nd ed., Cambridge: Polity.

14

The Harkive Project: Computational Analyses and Popular Music Reception

Craig Hamilton

Over the past two decades digital, data and Internet technologies have emerged as important and influential factors in how popular music is produced, distributed and consumed (Leyshon 2014; Burkhart 2014; Wikström 2013). These technologies, now allied to practices of data collection and computational analysis, play a significant role in how audiences engage with cultural goods and in how those audiences are understood (Amatriain 2013; Vanderbilt 2016). Popular music audiences are now highly individualized and defined by a number of new categorical variables (Prey 2019). Concurrently, audiences are also understood through large-scale, agglomerated data points (Morris and Powers 2015), enabling service providers to derive forms of knowledge that are then deployed within Data-Derived Business Models (DDBMs), that is models where data is a key resource (Hartmann et al. 2014), leading to a form of 'curation by code' (Morris 2015).

For popular music scholars these are intriguing developments, but studying these new environments is difficult because the systems involved are technologically complex, subject to rapid change and often hidden behind commercial and legal firewalls (Ananny 2016). Simultaneously, the everyday use of online technologies by many people is providing scholars with new opportunities and methods in humanities research (Berry 2011; Kitchin 2014; Piper 2016). This in turn invites us to consider the researcher's role and how we may take into account the technologies and practices that have so changed the field.

Given the growing importance of streaming services, scholars seeking to understand the contemporary conditions of music reception face the problem of exploring socio-technical systems they presently lack sufficient access to, or the technical knowledge and/or resources required to usefully undertake such an examination (boyd and Crawford 2012). Although, in the case of streaming services, recent work by Hagen (2015), Nowak (2016), Prey (2015) and Webster et al. (2016) has made progress in developing our understanding, a wider question for popular music scholars is how such an inquiry may be usefully undertaken.

Through The Harkive Project (www.harkive.org) my aim has been to make a contribution by discovering more about the changing conditions of everyday music reception and, for the purposes of this book in particular, the manner in which statistical analyses are deployed by service providers. Harkive generates a rich resource of text-based data in which respondents describe everyday acts of music reception, including reflections on how recently emerged data-derived technologies now play a key role within that activity. By analysing that data through similar types of computational techniques to those used by key players in the digital music space my aim is twofold: to investigate how computational techniques may provide us with new means of understanding audience behaviour, and to raise questions about the potential pitfalls of using such techniques without proper engagement with the figures, rationales and processes behind the results they help to produce.

In this chapter, I first examine how one digital music service, Spotify, uses data collection and analysis in delivering the 'Discover Weekly' element of its service. I then survey how scholars from a variety of fields are exploring broader questions raised by activity of this kind, and discuss how this work can help us critically approach the new technologies of music reception. I next describe the data collection and analysis methods used by The Harkive Project and demonstrate how computational and algorithmic approaches have been applied to the data collected by this project. This allows me to show that such an approach has numerous potential benefits for researchers, but equally that it raises a number of issues around the role, approach and technical skills of the humanities researcher. Ultimately, I suggest that through further engagement with these issues, via a combination of critical, practical and collaborative work, we may move towards a greater understanding of the digital, data and Internet technologies that are increasingly influential in many everyday experiences with popular music.

'A personalized mixtape': Spotify and Discover Weekly

Spotify users can create playlists from the large catalogue of songs the service carries. Matthew Ogle, a Product Manager at the company, has described the playlist as the 'atomic unit' and the 'common currency' of Spotify (Dredge 2016). Since 2007, users have generated over two billion unique playlists, each containing digital traces of who created it, how the songs within it are ordered and how popular the playlist has been with other users. Ogle has described this data as a valuable proprietary asset (Dredge 2016). It forms a key component of the process behind the creation of Spotify's Discover Weekly playlists, which were launched by the company in July 2015.

Spotify also holds data on each song within its catalogue. Some of this relates to the value chain (publishers, rights holders and so on), genre and sub-genre, song duration and year of release. This information is augmented by Echonest, the self-defined 'music intelligence' operation Spotify acquired in 2013, which generates information about tempo, musical key and other structural elements through computational analysis. In addition, Spotify's web-crawling and natural language processing technologies analyse online conversations occurring outside the Spotify interface on blogs, social media and media outlets. Together these data generation and processing activities enable the catalogue and user base to be organized and segmented according to a large number of variables. The metadata around each song is coupled with analysis of user activity data, and helps Spotify create detailed, individualized 'taste profiles' of users and data abstractions of artists and genres (Pasnick 2015), which in turn help to identify the songs selected for inclusion in users' individual Discover Weekly playlists. The ordering of those songs is then established by further analysis of the two billion user-generated playlists, dictating what Ogle refers to as the 'flow' of Discover Weekly playlists. Ogle and his developers settled on 30 songs for each playlist, or roughly two hours' worth of music, which they felt was 'more human, approachable' and thus more like the advertised 'personalized mixtape' than a machine-derived selection (Pasnick 2015).

According to Spotify figures, users streamed five billion songs from these playlists in the first ten months of release (Swant 2016) as Discover Weekly garnered favourable press coverage, including description of its curatorial efficacy as 'magic' (Pasnick 2015; Swant 2016). The success of the rollout validated Spotify's use of data-derived approaches in creating listener experiences and Ogle, speaking in March 2016, confirmed their intention to develop further 'appointment[s] to listen' features (Dredge 2016). Indeed, the collection and use of what is often framed by businesses as 'freely' available data (Puschmann and Burgess 2014) is a key component in the leveraging of a competitive advantage for Spotify (Titlow 2015).

To present and explore some of the issues related to statistical analysis in popular music at this present time, Spotify's Discover Weekly represents an ideal starting point. Although the manner in which Spotify collects and processes data is unique to its own operational methods, these are indicative of what Hartmann et al. (2014) have described as DDBMs. Spotify's competitors each engage in similar data-derived activities and although the details vary from company to company, they each provide means of generating understanding of listener activity and inferences of taste through digital monitoring. Alongside the monitoring of listener activity taking place within service interfaces, other activities related to what Negus calls the reception of music (1997: 9) – Google searches, social media discussions, online purchases – now often occur within digital interfaces where data collection and analysis is possible (Amatriain 2013; Vanderbilt 2016). This wide-reaching data grab enables different and disparate data from numerous sources to be reciprocally contextualized, facilitating the production of a form of knowledge that is deployed via services' interfaces.

At a core practical level the socio-technical systems facilitating such activity centre on mathematical and statistical operations that reduce social actions to quantifiable metrics, generating forms of cultural knowledge that to varying degrees help to influence or guide many everyday experiences. We may think here, as Webster et al. (2016) do, of recommendation playlists, or more widely in terms of the foregrounding (or not) of certain types of content through social media interfaces, online retail spaces, or financial and governmental services (O'Neil 2017). Because of the growing centrality of such systems to many everyday activities, including popular music reception, we may wish to consider what their consequences and implications are. In the next section I survey some of the ways scholars outside of popular music studies are exploring these implications, before looking at how the questions raised may lead us towards possible solutions.

'Gatekeepers of consequence'

A useful place to begin is with Tania Bucher's concept of the 'algorithmic imaginary' (2016). This allows us to consider not only how digital monitoring and statistical processing systems impact upon experience, but equally how user action impacts upon the design and function of those systems. With automated music recommendation we can observe a cyclical process whereby data is gathered on listener activity, from which inferences of taste are derived, leading to recommendations that positively or negatively influence choices. Elsewhere in the digital space, and particularly with social media platforms, we can see where the outcomes may not necessarily be benign. Tufekci (2015), for instance, highlights the negative reaction to Facebook's emotional contagion study (investigated in Kramer et al. 2014) and argues that questions around the potential harms/benefits of similar systems have moved 'beyond hypotheticals' now that 'algorithms act as de facto gatekeepers of consequence' (Tufekci 2015: 206).

In terms of popular music this is not limited to the digital delivery of music. Bucher's algorithmic imaginary is seen also in the foregrounding of media content and advertising online, and increasingly in the promotional and A&R activities of record companies (Thompson 2014). Algorithms, fuelled by consumer data and cultural content metadata, are deployed as subjective decision makers (Zhu and Chen 2008). Tufekci defines algorithms as 'computational processes that are used to make decisions of such complexity that inputs and outputs are neither transparent nor obvious to the casual human observer' (2015: 205), a definition applicable to the work of companies offering cultural goods through digital interfaces, and to Spotify's Discover Weekly in particular.

Prey (2015), via Lefebvre (1991), takes us further, through his conceptualization of music streaming interfaces as ongoing dialogues between ideas of form, concept and practice, arguing that ideas of identity begin to shift during this constant negotiation. For Prey, algorithmic recommendation systems mean that users are effectively conceived of as more than one user, all of the time. The same happens to ideas of musical genre, which are also constantly updated by systems such as Echonest. Under such systems, what Cheney-Lippold (2017) calls 'measureable types' shift constantly according to newly available data, which decouples identities from lived experience. Prey suggests that under this systemic gaze we are therefore not individuals, but rather the result of processes of data-derived individuation. The question then necessarily changes: it is not whether the recommendation engine gets it 'right', but instead to what extent the user (or the genre) is constructed by the process. Given the close relationship between digital monitoring, dynamic interfaces and music reception, and since categories now change in computerized 'real-time' rather than in negotiated, social time, we are invited to acknowledge the connections between algorithmic systems and our experience of our place, actions and even our understanding of the world around us (Lynch 2016). The line between the virtual/abstract and the real becomes blurred, and the technologies of online music environments come to have real-world consequences.

For popular music scholars seeking to explore this subject these are intriguing but complex conditions. To consider how such an inquiry may take place we may look towards van Dijck, who suggests that we 'look into the credibility of the whole ecosystem of connective media' (2014: 298), which ultimately leads towards questions regarding the type of critical questions we should be asking. For van Dijck this means considering how we can critique ideas related to 'datafication' (Mayer-Schönberger and Cukier 2013) in ways that avoid replicating or reinforcing the assumptions, positions and beliefs that underpin it. The starting point is what van Dijck calls the 'digital transformation of sociality' (2014: 199). This means examining the commercial realization and conception of value inherent in data and also addressing the perceived value data technologies has for new types of academic inquiry. In other words, we cannot critically engage with systems like Spotify until we know *how* to critically engage with them, and to do this we must first acknowledge the starting points (the assumptions and beliefs) of our own modes of inquiry. However, this drive for objective scholarship is complicated by the growing availability and use of similar tools, techniques and datasets to those used commercially.

Consider the complex set of individual and contingent choices involved in the decision to play a song, and then the extent to which data-derived abstractions – however complex – could reliably represent those choices. Can data points alone be used to examine ideas of musical choice? As van Dijck observes, 'promoting the idea of metadata as traces of human behavior and of platforms as neutral facilitators seems squarely at odds with the well-known practices of data filtering and algorithmic manipulation for commercial or other reasons' (2014: 200). As boyd and Crawford (2012) argue, by using what is essentially corporate data as the unreflexive basis for inquiry (where Tweets are treated as true reflections of belief), such an inquiry is inherently flawed. A process that seeks to speak to power (that is, independent, critical research) instead becomes part of what van Dijck calls the 'deep government and industrial drive toward gathering and extracting maximal value from data, be it information that will lead to more targeted advertising, product design, traffic planning, or criminal policing' (2014: 14). This is what Liu (2016) calls a 'polluting proximity' between object and mode of study, which is further complicated by van Dijck's (2014) point that the trading of personal data in return for communications and other services has 'nestled into the comfort zone of most people', raising additional, ethical issues about the data we as researchers collect (Zimmer 2010, 2015).

As van Dijck observes, however, the widespread adoption of digital services by publics is also seen as a great potential benefit to academics. Despite the concerns raised above, we can simultaneously view them as revolutionary research tools for investigating human activity through the data they produce. We are thus presented with the question of what might (critically, usefully) happen if we attempt to replicate the processes that also necessitate our questions. What in other words can a research process existing in Liu's 'polluting proximity' tell us about the processes, issues and questions raised by data-derived, networked knowledge?

Through an analysis of responses gathered by The Harkive Project, which relies on similar types of data collection and machine-derived analysis to those used by companies operating DDBMs, I want to begin exploring the negotiations highlighted by Prey and Bucher, the tensions Liu and van Dijck foreground, and the technicalities and conditions those tensions and negotiations take place within. In order to describe this, it is first necessary to briefly explain what Harkive is and what the methods developed around it are.

The Harkive Project

Harkive is an online project running annually on a single day in July that invites people to provide detail and reflection on their experiences with music. Since

2013 it has gathered over 10,000 individual entries.[1] These text-based reflections come from posts made to social media platforms, or from participants who have emailed the project directly or have completed an online form. The project does not impose word limits. It simply asks potential participants to describe how, where and why they listen to music. Each entry represents a snapshot of an individual's engagement with music, and each (to varying degrees) contains a description of technology use, or the locations and everyday situations involved when engaged in music reception activities. A key consideration for the purposes of this chapter is that all information is in a digital format, and thus can be computationally processed at scale. Stripping away the individual detail within each response, the 'raw material' can be understood as data.

The volume, variety and complexity of the Harkive data presents a number of methodological and intellectual challenges, but also opportunities. How can I make sense of the data Harkive generates, and how could the method I use to do that critically engage with the role of data-derived technologies in popular music? In response, I conceived of Harkive, following De Certeau (1984), as a 'space' where people can reflect upon their engagement with music, whilst simultaneously as a 'place' replicating many of the data collection and processing practices employed by service providers such as Spotify.

Using a number of automated collection methods,[2] data is gathered into a single database according to Tidy Data principles (Wickham 2014), making it ready for computational analysis at the point it is collected. The dataset contains respondents' texts, along with metadata (time/date stamps, which platforms each story was collected from, and so on) and additional variables generated through unsupervised machine learning algorithms, including topic modelling (Blei 2012) and sentiment analysis (Jockers 2015). As such, the texts can be considered alongside not only numeric abstractions produced through computational analyses, but also in terms of the processes generating those abstractions. They can also be considered in their 'original' format of texts.

David Blei (2012) defines topic modelling as a process providing 'a suite of algorithms to discover hidden thematic structure in large collections of texts. The results [...] can be used to summarize, visualize, explore and theorize about a corpus'.[3] Topics can be understood as recurring data points (in this case, words) across a larger dataset (a corpus). The model, meanwhile, is a statistical representation of the extent to which each individual entry in a dataset (the documents within a corpus) contains data points (topics/words). In applying this to the Harkive dataset, the immediate potential is that the larger a collection of documents becomes the more difficult and labour intensive it is to manually explore, encode and reveal themes. Beyond simply saving time and effort, however, a further potential advantage lies in the possibility that themes/topics within a dataset may not be immediately apparent because they may be hidden or otherwise made 'latent' by complexity and/or scale.

I employ the most commonly used approach in topic modelling, latent dirichlet allocation (LDA) (Blei et al. 2003). Blei argues that automated modelling of this kind can help humanities scholars 'build a statistical lens that encodes [...] specific knowledge, theories, and assumptions about texts' (Blei et al. 2003). According to Blei, LDA is based on two assumptions: there are a finite number of patterns of words, or groups of terms, that occur together within a corpus; and each document within a corpus exhibits these to varying degrees. Although the documents and words are observable through a manual reading, the thematic structure may be hidden, and will be more likely to be hidden as corpus scale and/or complexity increases. LDA infers 'hidden' structures based on what can be computationally processed (by counting the frequency of words), and represents these in terms of the probabilistic likelihood that a document 'belongs' to a given topic. I applied this process and rationale to the Harkive dataset from 2013 to 2017 inclusive, and a total of 8773 texts.

Topic modelling and music reception texts: Observations and questions

Using the topicmodels package (Hornik and Grün 2011) with R software (Gandrud 2016), the LDA process revealed eight topics, as shown in Table 14.1, which displays the top twenty words associated with each topic by frequency. The LDA process had no 'knowledge' about the corpus contents, processing it only according to the statistical probability of words appearing together. Nevertheless, I was able to interpret relatively distinct themes. The appearance together, for instance, of 'morning', 'home' and 'commute' was interpreted as being related to ideas of *Time and Place*. Another topic, containing the words 'love', 'beautiful' and 'happy', was interpreted as relating to *Experience and Emotions*. Other topics were *Radio*, *Physical Formats*, *Choice* and *Context*, while another related to *Harkive* itself, with words such as 'post', 'Tweet', 'project' and 'write'.

The process also revealed a topic that appeared to relate to ideas around *Streaming*, which this discussion will now focus upon. Words such as 'stream' and 'app' appeared alongside brand names such as 'Soundcloud' and 'YouTube'. More pertinent, however, were the most frequently occurring words: 'Spotify' and 'playlist'.

To explore these results further, and to consider how data from multiple sources can be used in concert to explore how computational techniques can help produce potentially actionable insight, I want to first demonstrate that it is possible to visualize the LDA results alongside other variables, including those derived from other unsupervised analyses.

Emotions and experience	*Radio*	*Streaming*	*Physical formats*	*Time and place*	*Context*	*Choice*	*Harkive*
Song	Radio	Spotify	Album	Morning	nowplaying	Sound	It
Love	Play	Playlist	Listen	Home	Vinyl	Play	Project
Time	Tune	Office	Band	Bit	Thank	Record	I'm
Favourite	Head	Track	Record	Car	Walk	Track	Post
Follow	Live	Headphone	Boy	iPod	BBCMusic	Try	Video
Play	Hear	iPhone	Version	Time	YouTube	Actual	Story
Beautiful	Come	Stream	Nice	Start	Bus	Friend	Stuff
Make	BBC	Tweet	Play	Night	caitlinmoran	Heard	July
Hear	Whilst	Soundcloud	House	Shuffle	Sun	Phone	Day
Happy	Look	Phone	Mix	Soundtrack	Spotify	Decide	Write
Feel	Sing	YouTube	Player	Drive	Summer	Piece	I've
Call	Talk	iTunes	Set	Commute	Girl	Star	Probably
Start	Watch	Single	Recent	Train	Kid	Artist	Twitter
Amaze	Bed	Check	People	Sleep	Black	Time	Blog
Life	Breakfast	Speaker	Shop	Late	Bowl	Usual	Share
Live	Heard	Enjoy	Release	Hour	craigfots	Minute	Read
Manic	Mix	Lunch	Blue	Afternoon	Love	People	Email
Street	Garden	Wait	Even	Journey	Heart	Mean	Look
Perfect	Kitchen	App	Lot	Choice	Sunny	Loud	Pretty
Name	Station	Get	Finish	Tuesday	King	Album	Contribute

TABLE 14.1: Top twenty frequently occurring words across eight 'topics' revealed through LDA processing of 8773 Harkive texts.

To place this within the context of the technologies discussed earlier, we may recall how Spotify combines user data, analysis of recordings and analysis of online conversations from external sources to facilitate the creation of user taste profiles when producing Discover Weekly playlists. I am following a similar rationale here in my Harkive analysis.

In Figure 14.1, for instance, we see LDA topic allocation results displayed according to the various channels where Harkive texts were originally gathered. The visualization shows that many of the texts gathered from blogs were allocated to the *Harkive* topic, while texts gathered through the form on the Harkive website have been allocated only to topics interpreted as relating to *Choice*, *Streaming* and *Harkive*. Figure 14.2, meanwhile, visualizes LDA results alongside another unsupervised algorithmic analysis, sentiment analysis (Jockers 2015), suggesting that texts in the *Radio* and *Context* topics exhibit less variety in sentiment than other topics. In comparison, the *Choice*, *Harkive* and *Physical Formats* topics contain many more texts that the sentiment analysis algorithms have deemed to contain positive language.

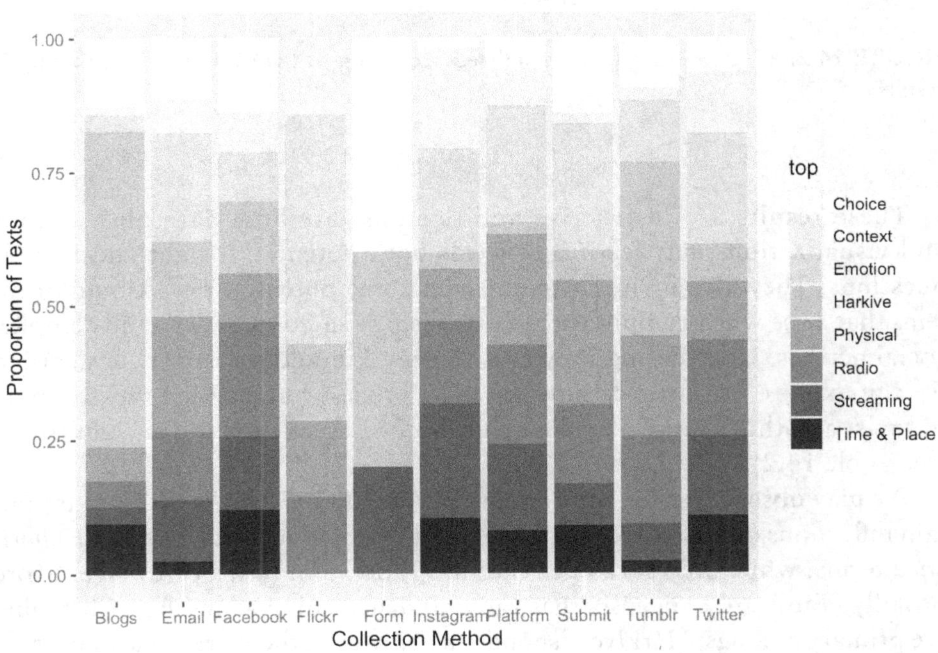

FIGURE 14.1: Harkive texts by LDA topic as a proportion of total gathered via each collection channel.

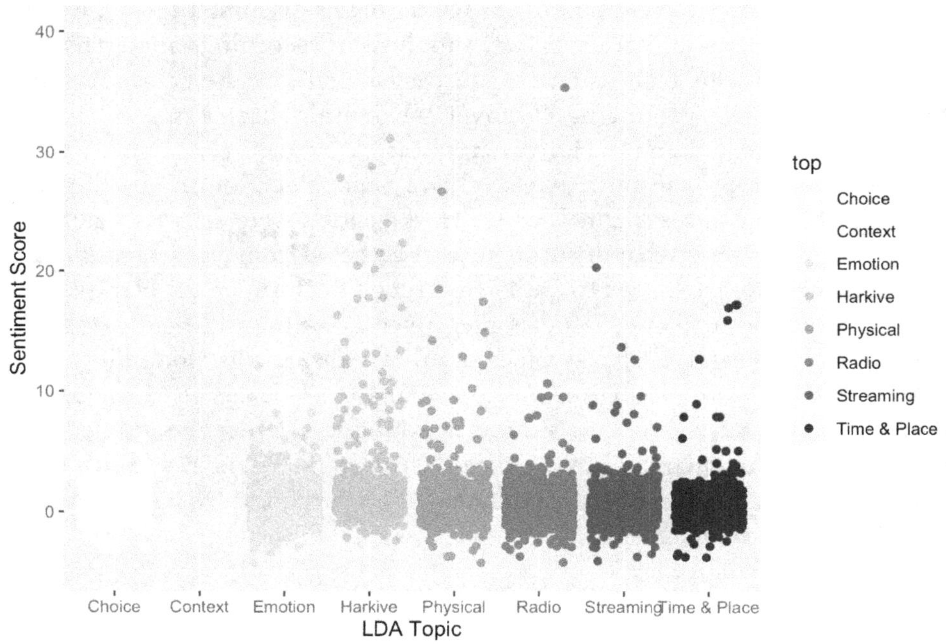

FIGURE 14.2: 8773 Harkive texts visualized according to LDA and sentiment analysis results.

These results are instructive and demonstrate how data abstractions and visualizations may lead us towards both potential insight and further questions. They also invite us to consider some potential pitfalls and problems that arise when computational processing is used to understand complex social actions. Considering Prey and Cheney-Lippold's observations earlier, we can explore for instance how the LDA process has enabled the grouping of texts, and thus Harkive respondents, according to each of the eight topics (see Table 14.2).

We may observe that around twenty per cent (1797) of the 8773 texts contain reflections on music reception that are expressed in *Emotions and Experience* terms, while only seven per cent (575) do so in terms of *Choice*. More broadly, Table 14.2 suggests that radio and streaming as modes of listening are primary amongst Harkive respondents. However, there are some important points to consider in light of these observations. The first is that the numbers behind topic allocations are less conclusive than the broad categorical allocations suggest.

LDA topic	Number of texts
Emotions and experience	1797
Radio	1526
Streaming	1287
Context	996
Physical formats	995
Time and place	934
Harkive	663
Choice	575

TABLE 14.2: 8773 Harkive texts organized according to their allocation into one of eight topics by LDA processing.

Text	Topic	LDA1	LDA2	LDA3	LDA4	LDA5	LDA6	LDA7	LDA8
4990	2	.1179	.1557	.1179	.1713	.1368	.1368	.1368	.1368
5050	4	.1157	.1157	.1157	.1713	.1343	.1343	.1343	.1343
5057	2	.1318	.1682	.1136	.1136	.1318	.1318	.1318	.1318
5099	5	.1136	.1318	.1136	.1136	.1500	.1500	.1500	.1500
5108	6	.1225	.1225	.1225	.1225	.1225	.1225	.1225	.1225
5112	7	.1250	.1078	.1250	.1250	.1078	.1078	.1078	.1078
5117	2	.1078	.1422	.1250	.1078	.1422	.1422	.1422	.1422
5148	1	.2173	.1220	.0863	.1458	.0982	.0982	.0982	.0982
5152	1	.1318	.1318	.1136	.1318	.1318	.1318	.1318	.1318
5160	3	.1179	.1179	.1368	.1368	.1368	.1368	.1386	.1386

TABLE 14.3: Random selection of ten texts, shown according to topic allocation.

Note: Scores for each LDA topic shown to four decimal points.

We may recall that the topic modelling process is based on an assumption that corpus documents exhibit relationships to *all* topics to varying degrees, and the figures in Table 14.3, displaying a random sample of texts, show those relationships in terms of a total score across all topics equal to 1. We may note the very marginal differences between topic allocations, and so corpus-level observations (for example, the differences between themes of *Emotion* and *Choice*, or the primacy of streaming and radio) need to be augmented by further, close readings before any claims can be reasonably made. The second observation relates to data collection methods outlined earlier in the chapter, and in particular that Harkive collects texts from numerous different channels across the course of a day, and has done so over a number of years. The 8773 separate texts processed by LDA in fact originate from only 2131 individuals because several respondents have provided multiple texts each year, across several years. Table 14.4 illustrates this by summarizing texts provided by a single user (n = 2097[4]), who has provided 150 texts via Twitter across the project's lifetime. Because LDA analyses the entire corpus to produce topic allocations, Figure 14.3 demonstrates how this respondent's texts have been allocated to multiple topics, and often in the same year.

Respondent	Method	Year	Number of texts
2097	Twitter	2013	73
2097	Twitter	2014	51
2097	Twitter	2015	5
2097	Twitter	2016	4
2097	Twitter	2017	16

TABLE 14.4: 150 texts supplied by respondent #2097, shown according to year and collection method.

Conversely, 1228 respondents (57 per cent of the total) provided only one text across the lifetime of the project. The manner in which LDA has allocated these to one of the eight topics is displayed in Figure 14.4, which also visualizes texts according to differing word counts. As such, although the corpus-wide LDA analysis provides overall themes that appear to have the potential to deliver insight into the music reception practices of Harkive respondents, those observations cannot be easily applied to either individuals or groups, but only to the corpus as a whole because of the differing levels of engagement amongst respondents.

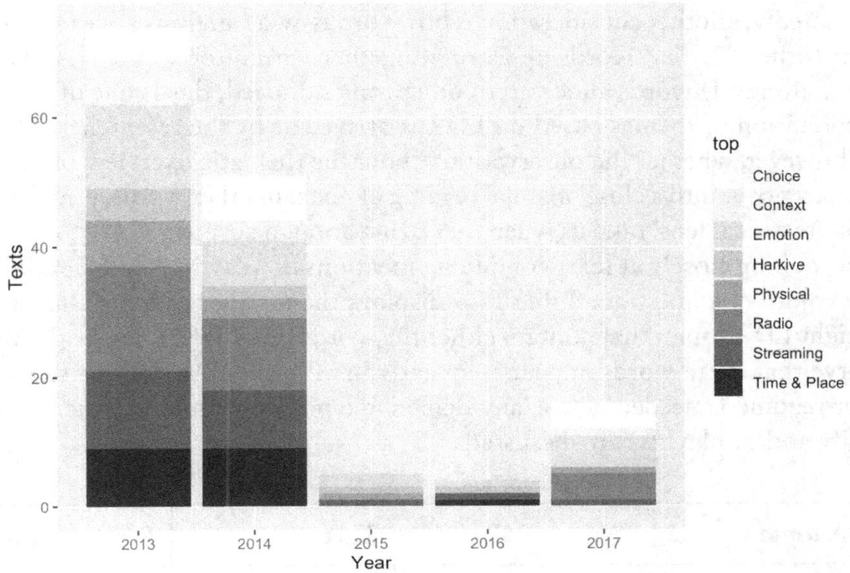

FIGURE 14.3: 150 texts supplied by respondent #2097, shown according to topic allocation and year.

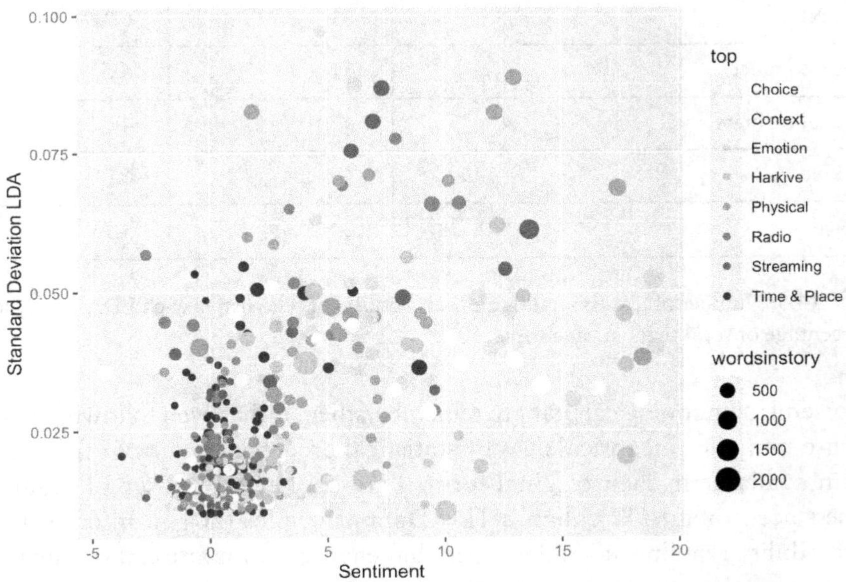

FIGURE 14.4: 1228 Harkive texts, each from an individual respondent, visualized according to sentiment analysis, topic, standard deviation in topic allocation scores and word count.

Relatedly, another consideration is how corpus-wide analysis appears to point towards the idea that words appearing together within topics are less likely to appear alongside words allocated to other topics. Indeed, this is one of the ways interpretation of themes based on LDA is arrived at by the researcher. We may ask, however, whether the observations about the thematic overview of Harkive texts carry over into a close, manual reading of texts. In other words, how far does Blei's 'statistical lens' take us when theorizing about a corpus?

By looking closely at texts containing mentions of 'playlists' and 'Spotify', we can explore this question. Table 14.5 displays the number of texts allocated to the eight LDA topics that contain either the words 'Spotify' or 'playlist'. We can observe that these words appear frequently in all topics. Again, this suggests a closer reading is needed before any defendable position could be taken on how Spotify and/or playlists are discussed.

LDA topic	Texts	Per cent of total
Streaming	244	18.96
Emotions and experience	75	4.17
Radio	68	4.46
Context	61	6.12
Time and place	61	6.53
Physical formats	47	4.72
Harkive	40	6.03
Choice	34	5.91

TABLE 14.5: Number of texts containing either 'Spotify' or 'Playlist' in each LDA Topic, shown as percentage of total texts in each topic.

A useful methodological point to remember, then, is that even following abstraction into numeric/categorical data by statistical processing, the texts nevertheless remain available in their original form. This is a key advantage of organizing datasets according to Wickham's Tidy Data principles (2014). In other words, the possibility remains of validating or challenging computational results via the sort of manual, close reading of texts more usually associated with humanities research. This provides an additional, practical means to interrogate the results and observations arrived at through computational processing and visualization.

In the case of Harkive data, but beyond the scope of this present chapter, by having a mechanism providing access to the original texts, we may find not only potentially interesting things about the music reception reflections of individuals or groups foregrounded by the visualizations and statistical clustering, but also an additional route towards exploring questions of how the process of computationally analysing data derived from complex social actions helps to produce forms of knowledge.

Reflection

With this work my aim has been to critically engage with the growing role of data technologies in music reception, whilst exploring computational techniques in popular music studies research. In short, Harkive has become a way of exploring Prey's negotiation alongside van Dijck's pitfalls. A key reflexive observation enabled by the analysis narrated in this chapter is that computational processes have both numerous benefits and limitations when used in humanities research by scholars such as myself who, returning to boyd and Crawford, lack the requisite skills, knowledge or resources to adequately address the complex socio-technical systems now so dominant in popular music. The responsibility for ascertaining the difference between the extremes of ability and ambition falls to the critical researcher, who is required to make careful decisions during the process. Just as music listeners and the various agencies involved with data collection and digital monitoring are involved in a co-production, a similar thing can be said of the researcher and their tools. The results and rationales of algorithmic processing being at various times complicated, maintained, challenged, replicated and dismantled by the epistemic position of the human researcher.

In the case of both understanding and using streaming services, and in the case of humanities researchers attempting to harness data technologies in their work, a fascinating area of interest is the location of the tensions that arise; in other words, in the unfolding detail of the negotiation process described by Prey. These tensions are particularly evident when the practices of people engaging with popular music meet with rationalized, empirical systems of data collection and analysis. How could an individual's specific experience with a song ever be adequately explained or understood by a data point? Conversely, to what extent could a data point be seen as significantly implicated or influential in an individualized action/reaction? These are the type of questions I suggest popular music scholars may wish to consider as starting points for future work.

To consider how we may undertake such work, I direct the reader to scholars such as Housley et al. (2014), who advocate the benefits of cross-disciplinary, collaborative work, or to Piper's (2016) argument that not only can computational techniques have a beneficial impact on cultural studies but equally importantly that cultural scholars can provide reciprocal benefits for computational practice. Readers may also wish to consider Sandvig and Hargittai's (2015) observations regarding the publication of 'benchwork' related to the kind of work described in this chapter. This is how 'researchers can reveal the messy details of what they are actually doing, aiming towards mutual reflection, creativity, and learning that advances the state of the art' (2015: 5). Towards that end, I submit to the reader the Harkive Data Explorer interface (www.harkive.org/data1317), which provides access to data and code employed in this chapter, alongside instructional materials and further reflection.

Conclusion

This chapter will, I hope, have raised new questions for the reader. My aim has been to sketch an argument for, and perhaps even a route towards, a critical engagement with data technologies through practice. My intention has been to provide a prompt for scholars to consider the efficacy of data systems within popular music culture, to challenge assumptions around what a data point can and does represent and to formulate new ways of working so that together we may critically engage with the digital, data and Internet technologies of popular music reception through work that attempts to understand their operations, affordances, benefits and consequences. Alongside this, and through the development of Harkive, the rich data it generates and the methods of analysis employed, my aim has also been to help build a better understanding of contemporary audience behaviour.

Based on the presentation of the analysis above we may wish to consider how Harkive respondents could, just like their texts, be clustered according to algorithmic processing. Such an outcome is redolent of issues discussed in this chapter regarding the occasionally problematic ways data processing can, in Prey's terms, 'construct' users according to ever-shifting statistical categorizations. I have also discussed how algorithmic processes can produce real-world consequences, and as such how they represent an intriguing new area of study. I discussed how numerous theorists have examined similar questions in terms of social media platforms, and in particular how automated recommendation suggests we consider changing our approaches and lines of questioning.

I conceive the activities related to music reception recorded through Harkive as both tactical expressions of cultural practice and manifestations of participation in wider, strategic systems of music commerce. The tensions between the two, and particularly in terms of how digital technologies and data collection relate to this, lie at the heart of what I am attempting to investigate and as such this is woven into the very conception of Harkive as a research process. Harkive is both a means through which those tensions can play out within a research environment, and simultaneously a method enabling investigation of those tensions, all contained within a process that seeks to foreground the roles of researcher, interface, tool, consumer and statistical/analytical method in the process of knowledge creation.

All of which is to say that statistical analyses can be used to tell many different stories, and it is through exploring how these stories are constructed that we can find routes to critical engagement with the socio-technical systems that are increasingly influential in our everyday experiences with popular music. I have demonstrated that arriving at an understanding of those systems is both a difficult but also hugely important task, and have suggested that a reflexive, experimental and exploratory methodological approach engaging both practically and critically with those technologies is a useful route forward. It is time, then, for popular music scholars to work collaboratively to explore data-derived knowledge within our field, and to forge new methods that may help us to better understand the contemporary conditions of popular music.

NOTES

1. For the purposes of this chapter, I am only using the data gathered between 2013 and 2017. A total of 8773 texts.
2. For a detailed breakdown of this process, see the instructional overview provided on the Harkive project website: http://harkive.org/datcolzap/.
3. Blei's article appears in the online *Journal of Digital Humanities*. As such no page numbers are attributed to his quotes.
4. Respondents are allocated a unique number during the analysis stage. Personal information, including social media usernames, is not made available in dissemination activities or via publicly available datasets. See http://harkive.org/research-ethics-informed-consent/.

REFERENCES

Amatriain, Xavier (2013), 'Mining large streams of user data for personalized recommendations', *ACM SIGKDD Explorations Newsletter*, 14:2, pp. 37–48.

Ananny, Mike (2016), 'Toward an ethics of algorithms: Convening, observation, probability, and timeliness', *Science, Technology, & Human Values*, 41:1, pp. 93–117.

Berry, David M. (2011), 'The computational turn: Thinking about the digital humanities', *Culture Machine*, 12, pp. 1–22.

Blei, David (2012), 'Topic modeling and digital humanities', *Journal of Digital Humanities*, 2, pp. 8–11.

Blei, David, Ng, Andrew Y. and Jordan, Michael I. (2003), 'Latent dirichlet allocation', *Journal of Machine Learning Research*, 3:Jan, pp. 993–1022.

boyd, danah and Crawford, Kate (2012), 'Critical questions for big data: Provocations for a cultural, technological, and scholarly phenomenon', *Information, Communication & Society,* 15:5, pp. 662–79.

Bucher, Tania (2016), 'The algorithmic imaginary: Exploring the ordinary affects of Facebook algorithms', *Information, Communication & Society*, 20:1, pp. 30–44.

Burkhart, Patrick (2014), 'Music in the cloud and the digital sublime', *Popular Music and Society*, 37:4, pp. 393–407.

Cheney-Lippold, John (2017), *We are Data: Algorithms and the Making of Our Digital Selves*, New York: NYU Press.

De Certeau, M. (1984), *The Practice of Everyday Life*, Berkeley: University of California Press.

Dredge, Stuart (2016), 'Matt Ogle talks Discover Weekly and Spotify evolution', Musically.com, http://musically.com/2016/03/21/matt-ogle-discover-weekly-spotify/. Accessed 14 September 2018.

Gandrud, Christopher (2016), *Reproducible Research with R and R Studio*, Boca Raton: Chapman and Hall/CRC.

Hagen, Anja N. (2015), 'The playlist experience: Personal playlists in music streaming services', *Popular Music and Society*, 38:5, pp. 625–45.

Hartmann, Philipp M., Zaki, Mohamed, Feldmann, Niels and Neely, Andy (2014), *Big Data for Big Business? A Taxonomy of Data-driven Business Models used by Start-up Firms,* Cambridge Service Alliance working paper, Cambridge: University of Cambridge, https://cambridgeservicealliance.eng.cam.ac.uk/resources/Downloads/Monthly%20Papers/2014_March_DataDrivenBusinessModels.pdf. Accessed 28 February 2019.

Hornik, Kurt and Grün, Bettina (2011), 'Topicmodels: An R Package for fitting topic models', *Journal of Statistical Software*, 40:13, pp. 1–30.

Housley, William, Procter, Rob, Edwards, Adam, Burnap, Peter, Williams, Matthew, Sloan, Luke, Rana, Omer, Morgan, Jeffrey, Voss, Alex and Greenhill, Anita (2014), 'Big and broad social data and the sociological imagination: A collaborative response', *Big Data & Society*, 1:2, pp. 1–15.

Jockers, Matthew (2015), 'Revealing sentiment and plot arcs with the Syuzhet Package', *Matthew L Jockers*, http://www.matthewjockers.net/2015/02/02/syuzhet/. Accessed 14 September 2018.

Kitchin, Rob (2014), 'Big data, new epistemologies and paradigm shifts', *Big Data & Society*, 1:1, pp. 1–12.

Kramer, Adam D., Guillory, Jamie E. and Hancock, Jeffrey T. (2014), 'Experimental evidence of massive-scale emotional contagion through social networks', *Proceedings of the National Academy of Sciences*, 111:24, pp. 8788–90.

Lefebvre, Henri (1991), *The Production of Space*, Oxford: Blackwell.

Leyshon, Andrew (2014), *Reformatted: Code, Networks, and the Transformation of the Music Industry*, New York: Oxford University Press.

Liu, Alan (2016), 'Drafts for *Against the Cultural Singularity* (book in progress)', *Alan Liu*, http://liu.english.ucsb.edu/drafts-for-against-the-cultural-singularity. Accessed 14 September 2018.

Lynch, Michael. P. (2016), *The Internet of Us: Knowing More and Understanding Less in the Age of Big Data,* New York: WW Norton & Company.

Mayer-Schönberger, Viktor and Cukier, Kenneth (2013), *Big Data: A Revolution That Will Transform How We Live, Work, and Think*, New York: Houghton Mifflin Harcourt.

Morris, Jeremy W. (2015), 'Curation by code: Infomediaries and the data mining of taste', *European Journal of Cultural Studies*, 18:4–5, pp. 446–63.

Morris, Jeremy W. and Powers, Devon (2015), 'Control, curation and musical experience in streaming music services', *Creative Industries Journal*, 8:2, pp. 106–22.

Negus, Keith (1997), *Popular Music in Theory: An Introduction*, Hanover: Wesleyan University Press.

Nowak, Raphaël (2016), 'When is a discovery? The affective dimensions of discovery in music consumption', *Popular Communication*, 14:3, pp. 137–45.

O'Neil, Cathy (2017), *Weapons of Math Destruction: How Big Data Increases Inequality and Threatens Democracy*, London: Penguin.

Pasnick, Adam (2015), 'The magic that makes Spotify's Discover Weekly playlists so damn good', *Quartz*, https://qz.com/571007/the-magic-that-makes-spotifys-discover-weekly-playlists-so-damn-good/. Accessed 14 September 2018.

Piper, Andrew (2016), 'There will be numbers', *CA: Journal of Cultural Analytics*, 1:1, https://culturalanalytics.org/article/11062. Accessed 14 March 2019.

Prey, Robert (2015), 'Henri Lefebvre and the production of music streaming spaces', *Sociologica*, 9:3, pp. 1–22.

——— (2019), 'Knowing me, knowing you: Datafication on music streaming platforms', in M. Ahlers, L. Grünewald-Schukalla, M. Lücke and R. Matthias (eds), *Big Data Und Musik*, Wiesbaden: Springer, pp. 9–21.

Puschmann, Cornelius and Burgess, Jean (2014), 'Big data, big questions: Metaphors of big data', *International Journal of Communication*, 8, p. 20.

Sandvig, Christian and Hargittai, Eszter (2015), 'How to think about digital research', *Digital Research Confidential: The Secrets of Studying Behavior Online,* Cambridge, MA: MIT Press.

Swant, Marty (2016), *'Even Spotify is surprised by the huge success of its Discover Weekly playlists', Adweek*, https://www.adweek.com/digital/even-spotify-surprised-huge-success-its-discover-weekly-playlists-173129/. Accessed 20 November 2018.

Thompson, Derek (2014), 'The Shazam effect', *The Atlantic*, https://www.theatlantic.com/magazine/archive/2014/12/the-shazam-effect/382237/. Accessed 14 September 2018.

Titlow, John P. (2015), 'Inside Spotify's plan to take on Apple Music', *Fast Company*, https://www.fastcompany.com/3049231/inside-spotifys-plan-to-take-on-apple-music. Accessed 20 November 2018.

Tufekci, Zeynep (2015), 'Algorithmic harms beyond Facebook and Google: Emergent challenges of computational agency', *Colorado Technology Law Journal*, 13, pp. 203–18.

Vanderbilt, Tom (2016), *You May Also Like: Taste in an Age of Endless Choice*, London: Simon and Schuster.

Van Dijck, Jose (2014), 'Datafication, dataism and dataveillance: Big data between scientific paradigm and ideology', *Surveillance & Society*, 12:2, pp. 197–209.

Webster, Jack, Gibbins, Nicholas, Halford, Susan and Hracs, Brian J. (2016), 'Towards a theoretical approach for analysing music recommender systems as sociotechnical cultural intermediaries', *Proceedings of the 8th ACM Conference on Web Science*, pp. 137–45.

Wickham, Hadley (2014), 'Tidy data', *Journal of Statistical Software*, 59:10, pp. 1–23.

Wikström, Patrick (2013), *The Music Industry: Music in the Cloud*, Cambridge, UK: Polity Press.

Zhu, Bin and Chen, Hsinchun (2008), 'Information visualization for decision support', in F. Bernstein and C. Holsaple (eds), *Handbook on Decision Support Systems 2*, Berlin: Springer, pp. 699–722.

Zimmer, Michael (2010), '"But the data is already public": On the ethics of research in Facebook', *Ethics and Information Technology*, 12:4, pp. 313–25.

——— (2015), 'The Twitter Archive at the Library of Congress: Challenges for information practice and information policy', *First Monday*, 20:7, https://journals.uic.edu/ojs/index.php/fm/article/view/5619/4653. Accessed 14 March 2019.

Notes on Contributors

David Arditi is associate professor of Sociology and director of the Center for Theory at the University of Texas at Arlington. His research addresses the impact of digital technology on society and culture with a specific focus on music. Arditi is author of *iTake-Over: The Recording Industry in the Digital Era* (Rowman & Littlefield, 2015) and his essays have appeared in *Critical Sociology*, *Popular Music & Society*, the *Journal of Popular Music Studies*, *Civilisations*, *Media Fields Journal* and several edited volumes. He also serves as editor of *Fast Capitalism*.

Vanessa Bastian has worked within the music industry for the last twenty years, inside EMI, Warner Music and Universal Music, and across academic research and journalism. She has had an interest in data from the earliest stage of her career, when she published and co-published reports and articles on the music industry and subsequently got involved in market and consumer research at first and increasingly in digital data and metadata projects on a global level. Her advisory role at Audiencenet led to a collaboration with the University of Hertfordshire to be the Consumer Research lead for the publication of the Intellectual Property Office commissioned research project *Measuring Infringement of Intellectual Property Rights* (2014).

Adam Behr is a lecturer in Contemporary and Popular Music at Newcastle University. He is a director of the knowledge exchange body Live Music Exchange. His interests include the intersection of music and politics, cultural policy and the music industries. His research has included live music censuses of Edinburgh and of the United Kingdom, and work on the cultural value of live music. He has also investigated digitization and copyright, the social dynamics of bands and the role of music tourism in the creative economy. He is currently developing work on the role of music in electoral campaigning.

Matt Brennan is reader in Popular Music at the University of Glasgow. He has served as chair of the UK and Ireland branch of the International Association for the Study of Popular Music (IASPM) and led the UK Live Music Census, the world's first national live music census. He has published several books in the field of popular music studies, including *Kick It: A Social History of the Drum Kit* (Oxford University Press, 2019) and *When Genres Collide* (Bloomsbury, 2017), the latter of which was named as one of Pitchfork's 'Favourite Music Books of 2017'.

Professor **Martin Cloonan** is the director of the Turku Institute for Advanced Studies (TIAS). His research interests focus on the political economy of the music industries. He is coordinating editor for the journal *Popular Music*. His latest book is *Players' Work Time: A History of the British Musicians' Union, 1893–2013* (Manchester University Press, 2016), which he co-wrote with John Williamson.

Dennis Collopy is senior research fellow at the University of Hertfordshire, specializing in music and intellectual property–related research, including various studies for UK Music and the Intellectual Property Office. In 2012 he co-founded the International Music Business Research Association (IMBRA) and its journal IJMBR. His other research interests encompass the changing value of music and the management of music rights. He has worked over four decades in music across artist management, record labels and music publishing at Chrysalis Music, RCA Records, Riva Music, BMG Music Publishing, EG Records and his own Menace Music Management. He is a former director of PRS for Music and and a board member of the Music Publishers Association.

Lola Costa Gálvez gained her Ph.D. in Research Content in the Digital Age (2015) at the Universitat Autònoma de Barcelona (UAB), with a thesis that focuses on music radio in Spain from the public service broadcasting perspective. Her research interests are in programming and digital policies concerning music in public radio, as well as its relationship to the music industry and local music scenes. She has published in *Radio Journal: International Studies in Broadcast&Audio, Westminster Papers in Communication and Culture, Trípodos, Observatorio (OBS*)* and *Derecom*.

Craig Hamilton is a research fellow in the School of Media at Birmingham City University. His research explores contemporary popular music reception practices and the role of digital, data and Internet technologies on the business and cultural environments of music consumption. This research is built around the development of The Harkive Project (www.harkive.org), an online, crowd-sourced method of generating data from music consumers about their everyday relationships with music and technology. He is also the co-managing editor of *Riffs: Experimental Writing on Popular Music* (www.riffsjournal.org).

Michael L. Jones is a senior lecturer in the Department of Music at the University of Liverpool and a member of the Institute of Popular Music. He is programme director for two MAs: MA in Music Industry Studies and MA Classical Music Industry. He was formerly a professional songwriter. In recent times he has written, directed and produced two musical biographies: *Where Light Falls* (a study of the career of Joni Mitchell) (a study of the career of Joni Mitchell, 2012) and *George Harrison's Journey into Indian Music* (2017).

Dave Laing's books include *The Sound of Our Time* (Sheed and Ward, 1969); *Buddy Holly* (MacMillan, 1971); *The Electric Muse: The Story of Folk into Rock*, co-authored with Karl Dallas, Robin Denselow and Robert Shelton (Eyre Methuen, 1975); *Encylopedia of Rock*, co-edited with Phil Hardy (HarperCollins, 1976) *The Marxist Theory of Art* (Prometheus, 1979); *One Chord Wonders* (Open University Press, 1985); *The Faber Companion to 20th Century Popular Music*, co-authored with Phil Hardy (Faber & Faber, 1990); *The Guerrilla Guide to the Music Business*, co-authored with Sarah Davies (Continuum, 2006); and *Popular Music Matters: Essays in Honour of Simon Frith*, co-edited with Lee Marshall (Ashgate, 2014).

Lucas Logan is assistant professor of Communication Studies at the University of Houston-Downtown. His research and teaching focuses on digital copyrights, privacy law, and Internet intermediary liability. He is the author of multiple journal articles and book chapters that have notably appeared in *Piracy: Leakages from Modernity*, *Oxford Research Encyclopedia of Communication* and *Communication Law Review*.

Marcus O'Dair is associate dean of Knowledge Exchange and Enterprise at University of the Arts London. He is the author of *Different Every Time: The Authorised Biography of Robert Wyatt* (Serpent's Tail, 2014) and *Distributed Creativity: How Blockchain Technology will Transform the Creative Economy* (Palgrave, 2018). He has also contributed to edited collections including *Business Transformation Through Blockchain* (Palgrave, 2019), *Jazz and Totalitarianism* (Routledge, 2017) and *Punk Pedagogies* (Routledge, 2018), as well as peer-reviewed journals including *Strategic Change, Popular Music, IASPM@ Journal, Life Writing* and the *International Journal of Entrepreneurship and Innovation*. He has a background as a music journalist and musician.

Richard Osborne is senior lecturer in Popular Music at Middlesex University. He is the author of *Vinyl: A History of the Analogue Record* (Ashgate, 2012) and co-editor with and Zuleika Beaven and Marcus O'Dair of *Mute Records: Artists,*

Business, History (Bloomsbury, 2018). Outside of academia, he has worked in record shops, held various posts at PRS for Music and co-managed a pub. He publishes widely in the field of popular music studies, including the blog 'Pop Bothering Me' (http://richardosbornevinyl.blogspot.co.uk/).

Shain Shapiro is the founder and president of Sound Diplomacy, the leading global advisor on growing music and night-time economies in cities and places. He is also the co-founder of Music Cities Convention, the world's largest event bringing together the music industry with city planners, developers, policy-makers and executives. Through Sound Diplomacy, he has consulted in over 60 cities and countries. He holds a Ph.D. from the University of London and was one of the top ten Creative Entrepreneurs in Britain in the British Council's 2013 h.Club100 list.

Emma Webster completed her Ph.D. entitled 'Promoting live music: A behind-the-scenes ethnography' in 2011 at the University of Glasgow. She has since held AHRC-funded post-doctoral positions at the Universities of Edinburgh and East Anglia for the UK Live Music Census and Impact of Festivals projects respectively, and a fellowship at Oxford Brookes University. She is co-author with Simon Frith, Martin Cloonan and Matt Brennan of *The History of Live Music in Britain* series and a founder and director of the research group Live Music Exchange. Before returning to academia, she worked in live music, specifically opera, festivals and club promotion.

Index

M

S

CPSIA information can be obtained
at www.ICGtesting.com
Printed in the USA
JSHW040024080123
35788JS00003B/1

9 781789 387520